WEST-E Social Studies

0081 Teacher Certification Exam

By: Sharon Wynne, M.S
Southern Connecticut State University

"And, while there's no reason yet to panic, I think it's only prudent that we make preparations to panic."

MANKOFF

XAMonline, INC.

Boston

To obtain permission(s) to use the material from this work for any purpose including workshops or seminars, please submit a written request to:

XAMonline, Inc.
21 Orient Ave.
Melrose, MA 02176
Toll Free 1-800-509-4128
Email: info@xamonline.com
Web www.xamonline.com
Fax: 1-781-662-9268

Library of Congress Cataloging-in-Publication Data
    Wynne, Sharon A.
Social Studies 10081 Teacher Certification / Sharon A. Wynne. -2nd ed. ISBN 978-1-58197-829-2
1. 1. Social Studies 10081 2. Study guides. 3. Praxis. 4. Teachers' Certification & Licensure.. 5. Careers

Managing Editor	Dr. Harte Weiner, Ph. D.
Senior Editor	Eleanor Binnings, MFA
Copy Editor	Sean Connell, M.A.
Assistant Editor	Kerrie Forbes, B.A.

Disclaimer:

The opinions expressed in this publication are the sole works of XAMonline and were created independently from the National Education Association, Educational Testing Service, or any state's Department of Education, National Evaluation Systems, or other testing affiliates. Between the time of publication and printing, state-specific standards as well as testing formats and website information may change that is not included in part or in whole within this product. Sample test questions are developed by XAMonline and reflect similar content as on real tests; however, they are not former tests. XAMonline assembles content that aligns with state standards but makes no claims nor guarantees teacher candidates a passing score. Numerical scores are determined by testing companies such as NES or ETS and then are compared with individual state standards. A passing score varies from state to state.

Printed in the United States of America   œ-1

PRAXIS: Social Studies 10081
ISBN: 978-1-58197-697-7

About the Subject Assessments

Praxis™: Subject Assessment in the Praxis I Social Studies 0081 examination

Purpose: The assessments are designed to test the knowledge and competencies of prospective secondary-level teachers. The question bank from which the assessment is drawn is undergoing constant revision. As a result, your test may include questions that will not count toward your score.

Test Version: The 130 equally weighted multiple-choice questions consist of no more than 60 percent knowledge, recall, and/or recognition questions and no less than 40 percent higher-order thinking questions. Some questions are based on interpreting material such as written passages, maps, charts, graphs, tables, cartoons, diagrams, and photographs. Between 10 and 15 percent of the questions contain content reflecting the diverse experiences of people in the United States as related to gender, culture, and/or race, and/or content relating to Latin America, Africa, Asia, or Oceania.

Note: This examination uses the chronological designations B.C.E. (before the common era) and C.E. (common era). These labels correspond to B.C. (before Christ) and A.D. (anno Domini), which are used in some world history textbooks.

Taking the Correct Version of the Subject Assessment: While some states offer just one test called a "social science secondary test," Praxis breaks out those topics into multiple tests. The (0089) is what you would take to become a middle school teacher and (0081) is what you would take if you plan on teaching at the high school level. However, as Praxis licensure requirements change, it is highly recommended that you consult your educational institution's teaching preparation counselor or your state's Board of Education teacher licensure division to verify which version of the assessment you should take. If you plan to apply for a position in another state, consider the licensure options for all social sciences disciplines. XAMonline.com web site can inform you of what you need to do to become certified in any particular state.

Time Allowance, Format, and Length: The time allowance is two hours to complete the test. The questions are presented in a 130-question, multiple-choice format. Praxis I 0081 does not test using constructed essays or other essay formats.

Content Areas: Both versions of the subject assessments share a degree of commonality in that the test content categories are divided into six broad areas that roughly overlap between test versions. However, version (1) has a narrower focus on specific disciplines than does version (2).

Test Taxonomy: Both versions of the subject assessments are constructed on the comprehension, synthesis and analysis levels of Bloom's Taxonomy. For many questions, the candidate must apply knowledge of more than one discipline in order to correctly answer the questions.

Additional Information about the Praxis Assessments: The Praxis™ series subject assessments are developed by the Educational Testing Service of Massachusetts. They provide additional information on the Praxis series assessments including registration, preparation and testing procedures, and study materials such as topical guides that are about 30 pages of information including approximately ten additional sample questions.

Topical guides versus study guides. The latest topical guide developed by the ETS is presented below. The topics are in bold. The numbers following the competencies represents the interpretation of the major topics by the Praxis test preparation staff.

Table of Contents

DOMAIN III: GOVERNMENT/CIVICS/POLITICAL SCIENCE

DOMAIN IV: GEOGRAPHY

DOMAIN V: ECONOMICS

Great Study and Testing Tips!

What to study in order to prepare for the subject assessments is the focus of this study guide, but equally important is *how* you study.

You can increase your chances of truly mastering the information by taking some simple but effective steps.

Study Tips:

1. Some foods aid the learning process. Foods such as milk, nuts, seeds, rice, and oats help your study efforts by releasing natural memory enhancers called CCKs (*cholecystokinin*) composed of *tryptophan*, *choline*, and *phenylalanine*. All of these chemicals enhance the neurotransmitters associated with memory. Before studying, eat a light, protein-rich meal of eggs, turkey, or fish. All of these foods release the memory-enhancing chemicals. The better the connections, the more you comprehend.

Likewise, before you take a test, stick to a light snack of energy-boosting and relaxing foods. A glass of milk, a piece of fruit, or some peanuts all release various memory-boosting chemicals and help you to relax and focus on the subject at hand.

2. Learn to take great notes. A by-product of our modern culture is that we have grown accustomed to getting our information in short doses (i.e., TV news sound-bytes or *USA Today*-style newspaper articles.)

Consequently, we've subconsciously trained ourselves to assimilate information better in neat little packages. But if you scrawl notes all over the paper, you fragment the flow of the information. Strive for clarity.

Newspapers use a standard format to achieve clarity. Your notes can be much clearer through use of proper formatting. A very effective format is called the **Cornell Method**.

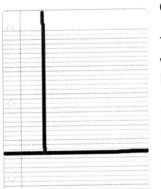

Take a sheet of lined, loose-leaf paper, and draw a line all the way down the paper about two and one-half inches from the left-hand edge.

Draw another line across the width of the paper about two inches up from the bottom.

Repeat this process on the reverse side of the page.

Look at the highly effective result. You have ample room for notes, a left-hand margin for special-emphasis items or for inserting supplementary data from the textbook, and an area at the bottom for a brief summary.

3. <u>Get the concept, and then the details</u>. Oftentimes, when we focus on details, we don't gain an understanding of the concept. Simply memorizing dates, places, or names may result in missing the whole point of the subject.

A key way to understand concepts is by using our own words. For example, if you are working from a textbook, automatically summarize each paragraph in your mind.

If you are outlining text, don't simply copy the author's words--but *rephrase* in your own words. We remember our own thoughts and words much better than someone else's thoughts and words, and then we subconsciously tend to associate those important details with the core concepts.

4. <u>Ask "Why?"</u> For example: If the heading is "Stream Erosion," flip it around to read "**Why** do streams erode?" Then answer the question.

If you train your mind to think in a series of questions and answers, not only will you learn more, but you will also lessen test anxiety because you are used to answering questions.

5. <u>Read for reinforcement and future needs</u>. Even if you only have ten minutes, put your notes or a book in your hand. Your mind is similar to a computer. You have to input data in order to have it processed. *By reading, you are creating the neural connections for future retrieval.* The more times you read something, the more you reinforce the learning of ideas.

Even if you don't fully understand something on the first pass, *your mind stores much of the material for later recall.*

6. <u>Relax to learn; go into exile</u>. Our bodies respond to an inner clock called biorhythms. "Burning the midnight oil" works well for some people who appreciate the quiet of the late hours--but not for everyone.

Either way, set aside a particular place to study that is free of distractions. Shut off the television, the cell phone, and the pager, and exile yourself from your friends and family during your study period.

♫ If you really are bothered by silence, try background music. Light classical music at a low volume has been shown to aid in concentration over other music. Music that evokes pleasant emotions without lyrics is highly suggested. Try just about anything by Mozart. It relaxes you.

7. Use arrows, not highlighters. ⟷ At best, it's difficult to read a page full of yellow, pink, blue, and green streaks.

Try staring at a neon sign for a while, and you'll soon see how the horde of colors obscures the message. A brief dash of color, an <u>underline</u>, or an arrow pointing to a particular passage is much clearer than a horde of highlighted words.

8. Budget your study time. Although you shouldn't ignore any of the material, *allocate your available study time in the same ratio that topics may appear on the test.*

Domain I: United States History

Skill 1.1a   Native American Peoples

Native American tribes lived throughout North America with a variety of different customs, different avenues of agriculture and food-gathering, and variations in weapons. Their cultures were established long before European explorers arrived.

One of the first to interact with newly arrived English settlers in Plymouth, Massachusetts were the **Algonquians**. The name now refers to the Algonquian-speaking people from Virginia north to Hudson Bay and west to the Rocky Mountains. The language is known as Anishinaabe or Ojibwe and became the language used for trade around the Great Lakes. The French were heavily involved in the fur trade with them.

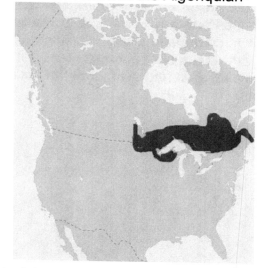

The Algonquians, in what is now Canada in the Upper St. Lawrence Valley, lived in wigwams and wore clothing made from animal skins. They were proficient hunters, gatherers, and trappers. They mostly lived too far north for agriculture although who lived south developed corn and other crops. Conflicts with the Iroquois had driven them out of the Adirondack Mountains and the upper Hudson Valley.

Squanto, an Algonquian who had been taken captive and sent to England, returned and shared his knowledge of agriculture with the English settlers, including how to plant and cultivate corn, pumpkins, and squash.

Other famous Algonquians included **Pocahontas** and her father, **Powhatan**, both of whom are immortalized in English literature, and **Tecumseh** and **Black Hawk**, known foremost for their fierce fighting ability. The French, Dutch, and British supplied the Algonquian with firearms.

Algonquins contributed wampum (made into belts to keep records) to the Native American culture, and they celebrated the first harvest with the Pilgrims, creating the first Thanksgiving.

Another group of tribes who lived in the Northeast were the **Iroquois**, who were fierce fighters and forward thinkers. They lived in longhouses and wore clothes made of buckskin. They, too, were expert farmers, growing

Long House of the Iroquois. (Bureau of Ethnology.)

the "**Three Sisters**" (corn, squash, and beans). Five of the Iroquois tribes formed a Confederacy which was a shared form of government. The False Face Society was composed of a group of medicine men who shared their medical knowledge with others but kept their identities secret while doing so. Their wooden masks are an enduring symbol of the Native American era.

Living in the Southeast were the **Seminoles** and **Creeks**, a huge collection of people who lived in chickees (open, bark-covered houses) and wore clothes made from plant fibers. They were expert planters and hunters and were proficient at paddling dugout canoes, which they made. The bead necklaces they created were some of the most beautiful on the continent. They are best known, however, for their struggle against Spanish and English settlers, especially led by the great **Osceola**.

The **Cherokee** also lived in the Southeast. One of the most advanced tribes, they lived in domed houses and wore deerskin and rabbit fur. Accomplished hunters, farmers, and fishermen, the Cherokee were known for their intricate and beautiful basketry and clay pottery. They also played a game called **lacrosse**, which survives to this day in countries around the world. After the Indian Removal Act was passed by Congress in 1830, the ultimate consequence was the **Trail of Tears** as the Cherokee were forced to march a thousand miles to Oklahoma Territory.

Between the Mississippi River to the Rocky Mountains, on the Great Plains lived the Plains tribes, including the **Sioux, Cheyenne, Blackfeet, Comanche, and Pawnee**. When traveling, they lived in east-facing teepees made of buffalo hides, but in their villages near the streams, their homes were earth lodges. Clothing was made from buffalo skins and deerskin. They hunted for elk, deer, and especially the buffalo. They were well known for many ceremonies including the Sun Dance, and for war pipes and peace pipes. Famous Plains people include **Crazy Horse** and **Sitting Bull**, authors of the Little Bighorn and the defeat of Custer; **Sacagawea**, guide for the Lewis and Clark expedition.

Dotting the deserts of the Southwest were (and still are) a handful of tribes, including the **Acoma, Hopi, Zuni**, and **Taos**, all of whom are **Pueblo**. Their homes were made of stone or adobe. Clothing was woven from wool and cotton. Agriculture included growing beans and domesticating turkeys—and, over time, other livestock.

 Kachina dolls are still given to children; the Kachina are spirits that bring rain and social good.

In 1680 a Pueblo revolt drove the Spanish out of their territories, but the Spanish re-conquered them several years later, and Mexican domination lasted until the close of the Mexican War, when the U.S. took over--and then created reservations. Pueblos are perhaps best known for the challenging vista-based villages constructed from the sheer faces of cliffs and rocks and for their **adobes**, mud-brick buildings that housed (and continue to house) living and meeting quarters.

Another well-known southwestern tribe was the **Apache**, with their famous leader **Geronimo**. The Apache lived in homes called wickiups, which were made of bark, grass, and branches. They wore cotton clothing and were excellent hunters and gatherers. Adept at basketry, the Apache believed that everything in Nature had special powers and that they were honored just to be part of it all.

The **Navajo**, also residents of the Southwest, lived (and continue to live) in hogans (round homes built with forked sticks) and wore clothes of rabbit skins. Their major contribution to the overall culture of the continent was in sand painting, weapon-making, silver-smithing, and weaving. Some of the most beautiful woven rugs ever were—and continue to be--crafted by Navajo hands.

The **Northwest Coastal** tribes lived in what is now Alaska, down the coast of the Pacific Ocean to Northern California. They lived in rectangular houses constructed of cedar planks, which would be home to 30 or more people. Clothing included rain capes made from cedar. Totem poles were a mode of communication. **Chief Joseph**, the famous Nez Perce leader, tried to lead his people to Canada when they'd been ordered to a reservation, and he is famous for his moving speech of surrender when the still-living among his people were trapped by the U.S. Army.

Alaska and Arctic Canada continue to be populated by the **Inuit.** Oftentimes, their homes were tents made from animal skins or igloos. Clothes were made of animal skins, usually seals or caribou. They were excellent fishermen and hunters, they crafted efficient kayaks and umiaks to take them through waterways, and they crafted harpoons with which to hunt animals. Inuit art includes carvings from stone, whalebone, and walrus tusk, a craft extended from the creation of tools, weapons, and utensils.

Skill 1.1b   European exploration and colonization

The Age of Exploration had its beginnings centuries before exploration actually took place. However, it is defined as beginning in the early fifteenth century and continuing into the seventeenth century. It is also known as the **Age of Discovery**, and it refers to European world exploration, derived from technologies for navigation, mapmaking, and advanced shipbuilding.

Prior to this period, the rise and spread of Islam in the seventh century and its subsequent control over Jerusalem led to Pope Urban II deciding upon the **First Crusade** in 1095 CE. The First Crusade resulted in Christian control of Jerusalem and other areas in the region for about two hundred years—the first western control of the region since the fall of the Roman Empire. The First Crusade marks the first organized violence against Jews. The Crusaders believed that Jews and Muslims ideally would be converted to Christianity. The Crusades, as they continued, were a political extension of Christendom.

The Byzantium Empire declined, and Italy's city-states of Florence, Genoa, and Venice became wealthy from trade with Asia—spices, salt, and other luxurious items. Merchant-bankers became a new rising social group who encouraged learning. A result of the decline of the Byzantium Empire was the immigration of merchants, scholars, and priests to western Europe—along with a good many of the Byzantium artistic and literary treasures. One consequence was intellectual stimulation that led to the Renaissance—which began in Italy about 1300 CE.

During the ninth century to the twelfth century CE, Venice was the naval and commercial power of Europe. By the late 1200s, Venice was the most prosperous city in Europe, and it held the most valuable trade with the Muslim world. The Genoese **Vivaldo brothers** and the Venetian **Marco Polo** wrote about their travels and experiences in the East. Survivors of the Crusades had made their way home from the Middle East bringing with them fascinating information about exotic lands, people, and customs, and desired foods and goods such as spices and silks.

Between sea voyages on the Indian Ocean and Mediterranean Sea and the camel caravans in central Asia and the Arabian Desert, the trade was controlled by the Italian merchants in **Genoa** and **Venice**. And--the trade routes between Europe and Asia were slow, difficult, dangerous, and very expensive.

In the mid-1300s, two-thirds of the nomad Mongol population along the western trade routes came down with the **black plague**. It spread eastward to China and killed two-thirds of the Chinese population. Merchants from Genoa travelled in 1346 to the Black Sea ports, caught the plague, and brought it home to Europe in 1347. Sixty percent of the population of Venice died. Approximately 25 million Europeans from a population of 40 million died. By 1349, one-third of the people of the Islamic world were also dead from the black plague.

The Mongol deaths contributed to the fall of the Mongol Empire. The Ottoman Turks, meanwhile, were not as affected by the plague, and so the Ottoman Empire began to grow while in Europe, government, trade, and commerce pretty much came to a stop.

While Jews were scapegoated for the plague, the Roman Catholic Church was also tested when people prayed in their churches and made donations, yet still lost their families to the plague. Thousands of priest and monks also died, and it seemed to many people that God was punishing the Church.

The literate survivors in Italy began to look backward to classic (and pagan) Rome and Greece, and there became a revival of interest in classical Greek art, architecture, literature, science, astronomy, and medicine. The chaos that resulted from the plague was a contributor to the beginning of the **Renaissance**.

Gutenberg's invention of the printing press in 1440 CE meant that by 1499, fifteen million books with thirty thousand different titles had been published. Among those books was Ptolemy's *Geography* which Ptolemy had first published in Egypt back in 2 CE. Now with the printing press, in 1477 numerous new maps were included in the book. Maps thus began to reach the populace.

Just as Ptolemy had been influenced by **Hipparchus** of Greece (120-190 BCE) who had invented latitude and longitude, geographers, astronomers and mapmakers of the Renaissance including the astronomer **Tycho Brahe** of Denmark and the Venetian mapmaker **Fra Mauro** studied and applied the works of **Hipparchus and Ptolem**y.

For many centuries, maps and charts had stimulated curiosity in the West. At the same time, the Chinese were using the magnetic compass in their ships; Pacific islanders were going from island to island covering thousands of miles in open canoes navigating by sun and stars; and Arab traders were sailing all over the Indian Ocean in their **dhows**.

Now it was time for the Age of Exploration to begin in earnest. By 1415, **Prince Henry of Portugal** (also called the Navigator) encouraged, supported, and financed the Portuguese seamen who led in the search for an all-water route to Asia. A shipyard was built along with a school for teaching navigation. New types of sailing ships were built which would carry the seamen safely through the ocean waters. Experiments were conducted with newer maps, newer navigational methods, and newer instruments. These included the **astrolabe** and the compass enabling sailors to determine direction, as well as latitude and longitude for exact location.

Although Prince Henry died in 1460, the Portuguese kept on sailing and exploring Africa's west coastline. In 1488, **Bartholomew Diaz** and his men sailed around Africa's southern tip and headed toward Asia. Diaz wanted to push on but turned back because his men were discouraged and weary from the long months at sea, extremely fearful of the unknown, they refused to travel any further. However, the Portuguese were finally successful ten years later in 1498 when **Vasco da Gama** and his men, continuing the route of Diaz, rounded Africa's Cape of Good Hope, sailing across the Indian Ocean, reaching India's port of Calicut (Calcutta).

Just six years after **Christopher Columbus** had sailed on his first transatlantic voyage to try to prove his theory that Asia could be reached by sailing west and had reached the New World and an entire hemisphere, da Gama proved Asia *could* be reached from Europe by sea and began the 450 years of Portuguese colonization in India, Asia, and Africa.

Long after Spain had dispatched explorers and her famed conquistadors to gather the wealth for the Spanish monarchs and their coffers, the British were searching valiantly for the "Northwest Passage," a land-sea route across North America and to the open sea that would lead to the wealth of Asia. It wasn't until after the Lewis and Clark Expedition when Captains Meriwether Lewis and William Clark proved conclusively that there simply was no Northwest Passage. It did not exist.

ROUTES OF THE ARMADA
X Fights in the channel
Wrecks

However, this did not deter exploration and settlement. Spain, France, and England, along with some participation by the Dutch, led the way in taking Western European civilization to the New World. These three nations had strong monarchial governments and were struggling for dominance and power in Europe. Between its privateers and its defeat of Spain's mighty **Armada** in 1588, England became the undisputed mistress of the seas. Spain lost its power and influence in Europe, and it was left to France and England to carry on their rivalry.

This search for passage to Asia led to eventual British control in Asia in what is now India, Pakistan, Kashmir, Sri Lanka and Myanmar (formerly called Burma), the southern part of Yemen (formerly called Aden), the Malay Peninsula, Singapore, Hong Kong, and Kuwait.

Columbus, a Genoan sailing for Spain, is credited with the discovery of America although he never set foot on its soil. **Magellan,** a Portuguese sailing for Spain, is credited with the first circumnavigation of the earth. **Amerigo Vespucci,** from Florence and sailing for Spain and Portugal, recognized, unlike Columbus, that he was not in Asia when he came upon Brazil, and the Americas were named after him. Other Spanish explorers made their marks in parts of what are now the United States, Mexico, and Central and South America including **Pizarro, Cortez, Ponce de Leon, Balboa, de Soto,** and **Coronado.**

For France, claims to various parts of North America were the result of the efforts of such men as **Champlain, Cartier, LaSalle, Father Marquette** and **Joliet.** Dutch claims were based on the work of **Henry Hudson. John Cabot** gave England its stake in North America along with **John Hawkins, Sir Francis Drake,** and the half-brothers **Sir Walter Raleigh and Sir Humphrey Gilbert.**

Colonists from England, France, Holland, Sweden, and Spain all settled in North America, on lands populated by Native Americans. Spanish colonies were mainly in the south; French colonies, in the extreme north and in the middle of the continent; and the rest of the European colonies, in the northeast and along the Atlantic coast.

The colonies were divided generally into three regions: New England, Middle Atlantic, and Southern. The culture of each was distinct and affected attitudes, ideas towards politics, religion, and economic activities. The geography of each region also contributed to its unique characteristics.

The **New England** colonies consisted of Massachusetts, Rhode Island, Connecticut, and New Hampshire. The vast majority of the settlers shared similar origins, coming from England and Scotland. Life in these colonies was centered on the towns because town boundaries would be drawn up as soon as some residents arranged to incorporate. The form of government was the town meeting where all adult males met to make the laws, and a board of selectmen had executive authority. The legislative body, the General Court, consisted of an upper and lower house.

The meadows where pilgrims first farmed in New England were actually the farms of Native Americans who died of smallpox and measles, introduced by the colonists. In addition to using these "meadows," the colonists had to cut down forest and clear the land for farming. Short summers made for short growing seasons. Additionally, the soil was generally not superior for farming, and an average farm had 20 acres, and corn was the leading crop. Fish was a dietary mainstay, and groundfishing became a New England industry. In addition, New Englanders exported furs and lumber, developed granite quarries, and ultimately developed a textile industry.

The **Middle or Middle Atlantic** colonies included New York, New Jersey, Pennsylvania, Delaware, and Maryland. New York and New Jersey were at one time the Dutch colony of New Netherland, and Delaware at one time was named New Sweden.

These five colonies, from their beginnings were "melting pots" with settlers from many different nations and backgrounds. The main economic activity was farming with the settlers scattered over the countryside cultivating rather large farms. The Indians did not threaten the colonists as much as in New England. The soil was very fertile, the land was gently rolling, and a milder climate provided a longer growing season. The farms produced a large surplus of food, not only for the colonists themselves but also for export. This colonial region became known as the "breadbasket" of the New World, and the New York and Philadelphia seaports were constantly filled with ships being loaded with dried meat, wheat, flour, corn, beans, butter, and sheep and hogs for the West Indies in particular. At least half of all ships sailed to the Indies to feed the population whose crop in many cases was solely sugar. The sugar was grown to make molasses, which was made into rum in the colonists' rum distilleries in Rhode Island and Massachusetts.

Other economic activities included shipbuilding, iron mines, and the production of items such as paper, glass, textiles, kettles, pots, pans, wrought iron, stove plates, nails, and wire so that these items did not need to be imported.

In all colonies, there was a standard government structure, including a royal governor, a governor's council, and a colonial legislature. The legislative body in Pennsylvania was unicameral, consisting of one house. In the other four colonies, the legislative body had two houses. Unlike the New England colonies, church and government were separate.

The **Southern** colonies were Virginia, North and South Carolina, and Georgia. Virginia was the first permanent successful English colony, and Georgia was the last. The year 1619 was a very important year in the history of Virginia and the United States with three significant events: 1) Sixty women were sent to Virginia to marry and establish families; 2) Twenty Africans, the first of thousands, arrived to be slaves; and 3) Virginia colonists were granted the right to self-government, and they began electing their own representatives to the House of Burgesses, their own legislative body.

Skill 1.1c American Revolution

The **American Revolution**, or War for Independence was largely due to economic and political changes.

After 1750 when England defeated its Armada, Spain was no longer the most powerful nation in Europe. The remaining rivalry was between Britain and France. They did not know how to co-exist peacefully together. War was their answer. For nearly 25 years, between 1689 and 1748, these two powers had engaged in a series of armed conflicts. Those conflicts ended up being fought in North America and are known here as **French and Indian Wars.**

- The War of the League of Augsburg in Europe, 1689 to 1697, also called King William's War and the Nine Years War, took place mostly in Flanders, but became the first French and Indian War.
- The War of the Spanish Succession, 1702 to 1713, also called Queen Anne's War, became the second French and Indian War.
- The War of the Austrian Succession, 1740 to 1748, also called King George's War, was the third French and Indian War.

Britain and France fought for possession of colonies--especially in Asia, the Caribbean, and North America--and for control of the seas. But none of these conflicts was decisive.

The final conflict, which decided once and for all who was the most powerful, was the fourth **French and Indian War.** In Europe where it began, it is known as the **Seven Years' War** and in Canada the **War of the Conquest**. No matter what name is used, this war caused over a million deaths, and in the twentieth century Winston Churchill called it a world war since it took place in Europe, Asia, and North America. The result was the end of France's being a major colonial power in North America--and Great Britain becoming the dominant power in the world.

In America, both sides had advantages and disadvantages. The British colonies were well-established and consolidated in a smaller area than the French settlements that were scattered over roughly half of the continent. Yet British colonists outnumbered French colonists 23 to 1. But the French settlements were united under one government and were quick to act and cooperate when necessary while the British colonies had separate, individual governments and seldom cooperated. In Europe, France was the more powerful of the two nations. In addition, the French had many more Indian allies than did the British.

Both sides had stunning victories and humiliating defeats. If there was one person who could be given the credit for British victory, it would have to be **William Pitt.** He was a strong leader, enormously energetic, supremely self-confident, and determined on complete British victory. Despite the advantages and military victories of the French, Pitt succeeded.

He got rid of the incompetents in the Army and replaced them with men who could do the job. He sent more troops to America, strengthened the British Navy, and gave the officers of the colonial militias equal rank to the British officers. In short, he saw to it that Britain took the offensive and kept it to victory.

Of all the British victories, perhaps the most crucial and important was winning Canada.

The French depended on the **St. Lawrence River** for transporting supplies, soldiers, and messages. The river was the link between New France and France. Tied into this waterway system were the connecting links of the Great Lakes and the Mississippi River and its tributaries. Along the waterway system were scattered French forts, trading posts, and small settlements.

William Pitt arranged for bombardment of Louisburg in 1758, and the British captured Louisburg on Cape Breton Island. New France was doomed. Louisburg gave the British Navy a base of operations that prevented French reinforcements and supplies from getting to their troops. Under Pitt's direction, other forts fell to the British: Frontenac, Duquesne, Crown Point, Ticonderoga, Niagara, forts in the Upper Ohio Valley, and, most importantly, Quebec--and finally Montreal. Spain entered the war in 1762 to aid France, but it was too late.

British victories occurred all around the world: in India, in the Mediterranean, and in Europe.

In 1763 in Paris, Spain, France, and Britain met to draw up the Treaty of 1763. Among Great Britain's prizes were most of India and all of North America east of the Mississippi River, excluding New Orleans. Britain also received from Spain control of Florida, but Britain returned Cuba and the islands of the Philippines to Spain. France lost nearly all of its possessions in America and India and was allowed to keep islands in the Caribbean: Guadeloupe, Martinique, Haiti on Hispaniola, plus Miquelon and St. Pierre, a group of small islands off Newfoundland. France gave Spain New Orleans as well as the vast territory of Louisiana west of the Mississippi River.

Britain was now the most powerful nation.

Where did this leave the British colonies? Colonial militias had fought with the British--and benefited as the militias and their officers gained much fighting experience. The thirteen colonies began to realize that cooperating with each other was the best way to defend themselves. That realization grew clearer with the war for independence and then setting up a national government. A start had been made.

By the end of the French and Indian War in 1763, Britain's American colonies were thirteen out of a total of thirty-three colonies scattered around the earth. Like all other countries, Britain strove for having a strong economy and a favorable balance of trade. That required wealth, self-sufficiency, and a powerful army and navy.

The English colonies, with only a few exceptions, were considered commercial ventures founded to make a profit for the Crown and for the financiers. The colonies would provide raw materials for the industries in England, and the colonies would be a market for finished products from England. England built a strong merchant fleet. The British desire to dominate the world in trade led to the **Navigation Acts**.

Between 1607 and 1763, the British Parliament enacted different laws to assist in getting and keeping a favorable trade balance. One series of laws required that most manufacturing be done only in England. Another law prohibited exporting any wool or woolen cloth from the colonies, and also prohibited manufacture of beaver hats or iron products. Other acts had greater impact upon the colonies.

The **Navigation Acts of 1651** put restrictions on shipping and trade within the British Empire, banning foreign ships from transporting goods to its colonies and banning foreign ships from transporting goods from elsewhere in Europe to England. These laws were directly focused upon the Dutch who were successful in international shipping.

British trade was required to utilize British ships. This increased the strength of the British merchant fleet and greatly benefited the American colonists. Since they were British citizens, they could have their own vessels, and build and operate them as well. By the end of the French and Indian War, the shipyards in the colonies were building one-third of the merchant ships under the British flag. There were quite a number of wealthy merchants among the colonists.

The **Navigation Act of 1660 and the Staple Act of 1663** required all European goods heading for the colonies to go through England or Wales first. A tax was charged that raised the prices and lengthened shipping times. Not only did Britain need to protect itself from competition from European rivals but also to protect its merchant ships from enemy ships and pirates.

The New England and Middle Atlantic colonies at first felt threatened by these laws since they had started producing many of the same products being produced in Britain. But they soon found new markets for their goods and began their own **"triangular trade**."

Colonial vessels started the first part of the triangle by sailing for Africa loaded with kegs of rum from colonial distilleries. On Africa's West Coast, the rum was traded for either gold or slaves. The second part of the triangle was from Africa to the West Indies where slaves were traded for molasses, sugar, or money. The third part of the triangle was home, bringing sugar or molasses to make rum--and also bringing gold and silver.

The major concern of the British government was that this triangular trade violated the 1733 **Molasses Act**. Planters in the British West Indies wanted the colonists to buy all of their molasses, but these islands could provide the traders with only about one-eighth of the amount of molasses needed for distilling the rum. The colonists had to buy the rest of what they needed from the French, Dutch, and Spanish islands, and they then evaded the law and did not pay the high duty to Britain on the molasses bought from these islands.

If Britain had enforced the Molasses Act, economic and financial chaos and ruin would likely have occurred. So for this Act and all the other mercantile laws, the British government followed the policy of **salutary neglect**, deliberately failing to enforce the laws.

In 1763, after the French and Indian War, Britain needed money for several reasons. Important needs were:

- To pay the British war debt
- For the defense of the empire
- To pay for the governing of thirty-three colonies scattered across the earth

It was decided to adopt a new colonial policy and pass laws to raise revenue. It was reasoned that the colonists were subjects of the king, and since the king and his ministers had spent a great deal of money defending and protecting them, it was only right and fair that the colonists should help pay the costs of defense--especially the American colonists. The earlier laws passed had been for the purposes of regulating production and trade and had generally put money into colonial pockets. These new laws would take some of that rather hard-earned money out of their pockets. This would be done, in colonial eyes, unjustly and illegally.

As the proportion of English-born colonists decreased and the diversity of settlers increased, fewer and fewer colonists felt a cultural tie to the country that held so much influence over the colonies' trade and government. Divisions between the colonies became more pronounced with settlers of differing religious and national groups establishing themselves.

Each colony had a lower legislative assembly that was elected and a higher council and governor that were elected or appointed in different ways depending on the how the colony was organized initially. In most colonies, the councils and governors were appointed by the King of England or by British property owners or agencies. In corporate colonies, the council and governors were elected by colonial property owners who maintained a close connection to England.

Thus, while the colonies were allowed to tax themselves and regulate much of their daily lives through representation in the colonial assemblies, Britain maintained control of international affairs and international trade by controlling the upper levels of colonial government. In practice, Britain allowed the colonies to go about their business without interference, largely because the colonies were providing important raw materials to the home country.

The first glimmers of dissent from the colonies came during the French and Indian War when **colonial militias** were raised to fight the French in America. Conflict arose with Britain over who should control these militias. The colonies wanted the assemblies to have authority. Although the British had had a victory over the French, Britain found itself in debt from the war--and looked to its colonies to provide revenue. Britain began enforcing the taxes on colonial trade that it had ignored prior to the war. And it began passing new regulations.

Residents of the thirteen colonies had begun to speak out about how cooperating with each other was important for defending themselves. Shortly after the start of the war in 1754, the French and their Indian allies had defeated Major George Washington and his militia at **Fort Necessity**. This left the entire northern frontier of the British colonies vulnerable and open to attack. In the wake of this, Benjamin Franklin proposed to the thirteen colonies that they unite permanently to be able to defend themselves.

Delegates from seven of the thirteen colonies met at Albany, New York, along with the representatives from the Iroquois Confederation and British officials. But Franklin's proposal, known as the Albany Plan of Union, was rejected by the colonists, along with a similar proposal from the British. Delegates simply did not want each of the colonies to lose its right to act independently. However, the seed was planted.

Before 1763, except for trade and supplying raw materials, the colonies had mostly been left to themselves. England looked on them merely as part of an economic or commercial empire. Little consideration was given as to how they were to conduct their daily affairs, so the colonists became independent, self-reliant, and extremely skillful at handling daily affairs. This, in turn, gave rise to leadership, initiative, achievement, and vast experience. In fact, there was a far greater degree of independence and self-government in America than could be found in Britain or the major countries on the Continent or any other colonies anywhere.

In America, as new towns and counties were formed, there began the practice of representation in government. Representatives to the colonial legislative assemblies were elected from the district in which they lived, chosen by qualified property-owning male voters, and representing the interests of the political district from which they were elected. Each of the thirteen colonies had a royal governor appointed by the king, representing his interests in the colonies. Nevertheless, the colonial legislative assemblies controlled the purse strings by having the power to vote on all issues involving money to be spent by the colonial governments.

Contrary to this was the established government in England. Members of Parliament were not elected to represent their own districts. They were considered representative of classes, not individuals. If some members of a professional or commercial class or some landed interests were able to elect representatives, then those classes or special interests were represented. It had nothing at all to do with numbers or territories. Some large population centers had no direct representation at all, yet the people there considered themselves represented by men elected from their particular class or interest somewhere else. Consequently, it was extremely difficult for the English to understand why the American merchants and landowners claimed they were not represented because they themselves did not vote for members of Parliament.

The colonists' protest of, "**No taxation without representation**" was meaningless to the English. Parliament represented the entire nation, was completely unlimited in legislation, and had become supreme. The colonists were incensed at this English attitude and considered their colonial legislative assemblies equal to Parliament, a position which was totally unacceptable in England.

There were now two different environments: the older, traditional British system and the American system with its new ideas and different ways of doing things.

In a new country, a new environment has little or no tradition, institutions, or vested interests. New ideas and traditions grew extremely fast in America, pushing aside what was left of the old ideas and old traditions. By 1763, Britain had changed its perception of its American colonies to their being a "territorial" empire. The stage was set. The conditions were right for a showdown.

In 1763, Parliament decided to have a standing army in North America to reinforce British control. In 1765, the **Quartering Act** was passed requiring the colonists to provide supplies and living quarters for the British troops. In addition, efforts by the British were made to keep the peace by establishing good relations with the Indians. Consequently, a proclamation was issued which prohibited any American colonists from making any settlements west of the Appalachians until provided for by treaties with the Indians.

The **Sugar Act of 1764** required efficient collection of taxes on any molasses that was brought into the colonies and gave British officials free license to conduct searches of the premises of anyone suspected of violating the law. The colonists were taxed on newspapers, legal documents, and other printed matter under the **Stamp Act of 1765**. Nine colonies assembled in New York to call for repeal of the Act.

At the same time, a group of New York City merchants organized a protest to stop the importation of British goods. Similar protests arose in Philadelphia and Boston and other merchant cities--often erupting in violence. Britain's representatives in the colonies--the governors and members of the cabinet and council--were sometimes the targets of these protests. Although a stamp tax was already in use in England, the colonists would have none of it, and after the ensuing uproar of rioting and mob violence, Parliament repealed the tax.

Of course, great exultation resulted when news of the repeal reached America. But attached to the repeal was the small, quiet Declaratory Act. This Act plainly, unequivocally stated that Parliament still had the right to make all laws for the colonies, and it denied their right to be taxed only by colonial legislatures.

Other acts leading up to armed conflict included the **Townshend Acts** passed in 1767, which taxed lead, paint, paper, and tea brought into the colonies. This also increased anger and tension, resulting in the British sending troops to New York City and Boston. In Boston, mob violence provoked retaliation by the troops. The result was the deaths of five people and the wounding of eight others. The so-called **Boston Massacre** shocked Americans and British alike.

Meanwhile, increased contact among the Americans enabled a growing patriot movement, and the issue of independence arose in thought and discussions.

When Britain proposed that the East India Company be allowed to import tea to the colonies without customs duty, the colonists were faced with a dilemma. They could purchase the tea at a much lower price than the smuggled Dutch tea they had been drinking. However, tea was still subject to the Townshend Act, and to purchase it would demonstrate acceptance of this Act. The **Boston Tea Party** was the result. A group of colonists seized a shipment of British tea in Boston Harbor and dumped it into the sea.

Britain responded with a series of even more restrictive acts, driving the colonies to come together in the **First Continental Congress** to make a unified demand that Britain remove these **Intolerable Acts**, as they were called by the colonists.

In 1774, the passage of the **Quebec Act** extended the limits of that Canadian colony's boundary southward to include territory located north of the Ohio River. However, the punishment for Boston's Tea Party came in the same year with the Intolerable Acts. Boston's port was closed; the royal governor of the colony of Massachusetts was given increased power, and the colonists were compelled to house and feed the British soldiers.

The patriot organization the underground **Sons of Liberty** undermined the Stamp Act, and the **Committee of Correspondence** communicated opposition and resistance to Acts throughout the colonies and arranged for written communications to be distributed to foreign governments.

Delegates from twelve colonies met in Philadelphia September 5, 1774, in the **First Continental Congress**. They opposed acts of lawlessness and wanted some form of peaceful settlement with Britain. They still maintained American loyalty to Britain, however, and affirmed Parliament's power over colonial foreign affairs. They did insist on repeal of the **Intolerable Acts** and demanded ending all trade with Britain until this took place. The reply from George III, the last king of America, was an insistence of colonial submission to British rule or be crushed.

Britain stood firm and sought to dissolve the colonial assemblies that were coming forth in opposition to British policies, and were stockpiling weapons and preparing militias. When the British military in America were ordered to break up the illegal meeting of the Massachusetts' assembly outside Boston, they were met with armed resistance at **Lexington and Concord** on April 19, 1775. The Revolutionary War was underway.

The Second Continental Congress met a month later in Philadelphia on May 10th to conduct the business of war and government for the next six years. Many of the delegates recommended a declaration of independence from Britain. The group established an army and commissioned George Washington as its commander.

The Declaration of Independence

The Declaration of Independence is an outgrowth of ancient Greek ideas of democracy and individual rights along with the ideas of the European Enlightenment and the Renaissance—and especially the ideology of the political thinker in England, **John Locke**. Thomas Jefferson (1743-1826), the principal author of the Declaration, borrowed much from Locke's theories and writings.

John Locke was one of the most influential political writers of the seventeenth century. He put great emphasis on human rights and put forth the belief that when governments violate those rights, people should rebel. His book *Two Treatises of Government* came out in 1690, and it had tremendous influence on political thought in the American colonies, helping to shape the Declaration of Independence and the U.S. Constitution.

Jefferson applied Locke's principles to the contemporary American situation. In the Declaration, Jefferson argues that the reigning King George III repeatedly violates the rights of the colonists as subjects of the British Crown.

The colonial petition for redress of grievances was a right guaranteed by the Declaration of Rights of 1689, the British Bill of Rights. According to the Declaration of Independence, King George was establishing "an absolute Tyranny over these States." The Declaration of Independence then states: "To prove this, let Facts be submitted to a candid world," and lists the King's violations, going on to say: "That these united Colonies are, and of Right ought to be Free and Independent States, that they are Absolved from all Allegiance to the British Crown, and that all political connection between them and the State of Great Britain, is and ought to be totally dissolved."

Jefferson's view of **natural rights** was much broader than Locke's and less tied to the idea of **property rights**. Jefferson's famous line in the Declaration about people's right to "life, liberty and the pursuit of happiness" was based upon Locke's idea of "life, liberty, and *private property*". Jefferson substituted the idea that human happiness is a fundamental right that is the duty of a government to protect.

Locke and Jefferson both stressed that individual citizen's rights are prior to and more important than any obligation to the state. Government is the *servant* of the people. The officials of government hold their positions to ensure that the rights of the people are preserved and protected by that government. The citizen comes first; the government comes second.

The Declaration of Independence turned out to be one of the most important historical documents because it expounds the inherent rights of all people. In June of 1775, British forces had attacked patriot strongholds at Breed's Hill and **Bunker Hill**. Although the colonists had withdrawn, the loss of life for the British was nearly fifty percent of the army. The next month King George III declared the American colonies to be in a state of rebellion. The war quickly began in earnest.

Although the colonial army was quite small in comparison to the British army, and although it was lacking in formal military training, the colonists had learned a new method of warfare from the Indians. To be sure, many battles were fought in the traditional style of two lines of soldiers facing off and firing weapons. But the advantage the patriots had was the understanding of guerilla warfare–fighting from behind trees and other defenses, and more importantly, fighting on the run.

By 1776, the colonists and their representatives in the Second Continental Congress realized that things were past the point of no return. On July 3, 1776, British General Howe arrived in New York harbor with 10,000 troops to prepare for an attack on the city. The next day, the **Declaration of Independence** was drafted and declared on July 4, 1776.

Revolutionary War

The first American victory of the Revolutionary War followed a surprise attack under the command of George Washington on British-Hessian troops at **Trenton**, New Jersey. Washington and his men crossed the icy **Delaware River** on Christmas Day, 1776, and attacked the next day, completely surprising the British. It helped to restore American morale.

Washington labored against tremendous odds to wage a victorious war. Although the suffering of troops during the winter of 177-1778 at **Valley Forge** is part of American folklore, other winter ordeals were probably worse. Valley Forge is well known because Washington stressed his army's suffering in order to gain political support. However, the army's discipline and efficiency improved during the winter, which marked a turning point in the war. Thus, the encampment became a symbol of endurance in adversity.

The turning point in the Americans' favor occurred in 1777 with the American victory at **Saratoga**. This victory led to the French to aligning themselves with the Americans against the British. With the aid of Admiral deGrasse and French warships blocking the entrance to Chesapeake Bay, British General Cornwallis was trapped at **Yorktown**, Virginia. He surrendered in 1781, and the war was over. The Treaty of Paris officially ending the war was signed in 1783.

Skill 1.1d   Establishing a New Nation

When the war began, the colonies began to establish state governments. To a significant extent, the government that was defined for the new nation was intentionally weak. The colonies/states feared centralized government. But the lack of continuity between the individual governments was confusing and economically damaging.

The **Articles of Confederation** was the first attempt of the newly independent states to reach an understanding. This was the first political system under which the newly independent colonies tried to organize themselves. It was drafted soon after the Declaration of Independence and was passed by the Continental Congress on November 15, 1777. After ratification by the thirteen states, it took effect on March 1, 1781.

The newly independent states were unwilling to give too much power to a national government. Fighting Great Britain, they certainly did not want to replace one harsh ruler with another. After many debates, the form of the Articles was accepted.

Each state agreed to send delegates to the Congress. Each state had one vote in the Congress. The Articles gave Congress the power to declare war, appoint military officers, and coin money. The Congress was also responsible for foreign affairs. The Articles of Confederation limited the powers of Congress by giving the states final authority. Although Congress could pass laws, at least nine of the thirteen states had to approve a law before it went into effect. Congress could not pass any laws regarding taxes. To get money, Congress had to ask each state for it; no state could be forced to pay.

Thus, the Articles created a loose alliance among the thirteen states. The national government was weak, in part, because it didn't have a strong chief executive to carry out laws passed by the legislature. This weak national government might have worked if the states were able to get along with each other. However, many different disputes arose, and there was no way of settling them.

The central government of the new United States of America consisted of a Congress of two to seven delegates from each state with each state having just one vote. The government under the Articles had solved some of the postwar problems but had serious weaknesses. Some of its powers included: borrowing and coining money, directing foreign affairs, declaring war and making peace, building and equipping a navy, regulating weights and measures, and asking the states to supply men and money for an army. But the delegates to Congress had no real authority as each state carefully and jealously guarded its own interests and limited powers under the Articles.

Also, the delegates to Congress were paid by their states and had to vote as directed by their state legislatures. The serious weaknesses were the lack of power to regulate finances, a lack of power over interstate trade and over foreign trade, lack of power to enforce treaties, and coordination of military power. Something better and more efficient was needed.

The Constitution

In May of 1787, delegates from all states (except Rhode Island) began meeting in Philadelphia. At first, they met to revise the Articles of Confederation but soon realized that much more was needed. So they set out to write a new Constitution, which became the foundation of all government in the United States and a model for representative government throughout the world.

The first order of business was the agreement among all the delegates that the convention would be kept secret. No discussion of the convention outside of the meeting room would be allowed. They wanted to be able to discuss, argue, and agree among themselves before presenting the completed document to the American people.

The delegates were afraid that if the people were aware of what was taking place before it was completed the entire country would be plunged into argument and dissension. It would be extremely difficult, if not impossible, to settle differences and come to an agreement. Between the official notes kept and the complete notes of future President James Madison, we have an accurate picture of the events of the Convention.

The delegates went to Philadelphia representing different areas and different interests. They all agreed on a strong central government but not one with unlimited powers. They also agreed that no one part of government could control the rest. It would be a republican form of government (sometimes referred to as representative democracy) in which the supreme power was in the hands of the voters who would elect the men who would govern for them.

Constitutional Compromises

One of the first serious controversies was over representation in Congress and involved the small states versus the large states. Virginia's Governor Edmund Randolph proposed the **Virginia Plan**, which said that state population would determine the number of representatives sent to Congress. New Jersey delegate William Paterson countered with the **New Jersey Plan**, with each state having equal representation.

After much debate, Roger Sherman proposed the **Great Compromise (or Connecticut Compromise)**. This resulted in the bicameral Congress. The Senate would have two Senators, giving equal powers in the Senate. The House of Representatives would have its members elected based on each state's population. And both houses could draft bills to debate and vote on--with the exception of bills pertaining to money, which must originate in the House of Representatives.

Another controversy involved economic differences between North and South. One concerned the counting of the African slaves for determining representation in the House of Representatives. The southern delegates wanted this counting but didn't want it to determine taxes to be paid. The northern delegates argued the opposite: count the slaves for taxes but not for representation. The resulting agreement was known as the **"three-fifths compromise."** Three-fifths of the slaves would be counted for both taxes and determining representation in the House.

The last major compromise, also between North and South, was the **Commerce Compromise**. The economic interests of the North were ones of industry and business whereas the South's economic interests were primarily in farming. The Northern merchants wanted the government to regulate and control commerce with foreign nations and with the states. Southern planters opposed this idea, concerned that any tariff laws passed would be unfavorable to them.

Congress was given the power to regulate commerce with other nations and the states, including levying tariffs on imports. However, Congress did not have the power to levy tariffs on any exports. This increased Southern concern about the effect it would have on the slave trade. The delegates finally agreed that the importation of slaves would continue for 20 more years with no interference from Congress. Any import tax could not exceed ten dollars per person. After 1808, Congress would be able to decide whether to prohibit or regulate any further importation of slaves.

Ratification of the Constitution

Once work was completed and the document presented, nine states needed to approve for it to go into effect. There was no little amount of discussion, arguing, debating, and haranguing. The opposition had three major objections:

- The states felt they were being asked to surrender too much power to the national government.
- The voters did not have enough control and influence over the men who would be elected by them to run the government.
- There was no "bill of rights" guaranteeing hard-won individual freedoms and liberties.

Great debate persisted between the **Federalists** and the **Anti-Federalists**. Ratification of the U.S. Constitution was by no means a foregone conclusion. The representative government had powerful enemies, especially those who had seen firsthand the failure of the Articles of Confederation. The strong central government had powerful enemies, including some of the guiding lights of the American Revolution.

Those who wanted to see a strong central government were called **Federalists**, because they wanted to see a federal government reign supreme. Among the leaders of the Federalists were Alexander Hamilton and John Jay. These two, along with James Madison, wrote a series of letters to New York newspapers, urging that that the states ratify the Constitution. These became known as the **Federalist Papers.**

In the **Anti-Federalist** camp were Thomas Jefferson and Patrick Henry. These men and many others like them were worried that a strong national government would descend into the kind of tyranny that they had just worked so hard to abolish. In the same way that they took their name from their foes, they wrote a series of arguments against the Constitution called the **Anti-Federalist Papers.**

In the end, both sides got most of what they wanted. The Federalists got their strong national government, which was held in place by the famous "checks and balances." The Anti-Federalists got the **Bill of Rights**, the first ten Amendments to the Constitution that protect some of the most basic of human rights. The states that were in doubt for ratification of the Constitution signed on when the Bill of Rights was promised. Eleven states finally ratified the document, and the new national government went into effect.

It was no small feat that the delegates were able to produce a workable document that satisfied all opinions, feelings, and viewpoints. The separation of powers of the three branches of government and the built-in system of checks and balances to keep power balanced were a stroke of genius. It provided for the individuals and the states as well as an organized central authority to keep a new, inexperienced nation on track.

They created a Constitution about which Ben Franklin said: "Because I expect no better, and because I am not sure, that it is not the best." The Constitution has lasted through civil war, foreign wars, the Depression, and social revolution for over 200 years. It is truly a living document because of its ability to remain strong while allowing itself to be changed with changing times.

Skill 1.1e Early Years of the New Nation.

In 1789 the Electoral College unanimously elected George Washington as the first President, and the new nation was on its way. The early presidential administrations established form and procedures still present today. For example, George Washington established the United States Cabinet when he appointed four people to act as his advisors and to oversee various functions of the executive branch.

Thomas Jefferson was Washington's Secretary of State, and Alexander Hamilton was his Secretary of the Treasury. Jefferson and Hamilton were different in many ways. Not the least was their views on what should be the proper form of government of the United States. This difference helped to shape the parties that formed around them. By the time Washington retired from office in 1796, the new political parties would come to play an important role in choosing his successor. Each party would put up its own candidates for office.

Because he'd come in second in the Electoral College when Washington was elected President, **John Adams** was the first Vice President. When it was time to elect the second President, the **Federalist Party** selected him as their first candidate for President. Thomas Jefferson (whose party was the Republican-Democratic) came in second behind Adams and so became Adams' Vice President.

Adams' administration was marked by the new nation's first entanglement in international affairs. Britain and France were at war, and Adams' Federalist Party supported the British while Vice President Thomas Jefferson's Republican Party supported the French. The United States was brought nearly to the brink of war with France, which had experienced the French Revolution, and now military battles were being led by Napoleon Bonaparte. Although the United States had several naval victories, enthusiasm for war was not widespread, never mind that Hamilton and other Federalists were strongly in favor of it.

Four laws were passed known as the **Alien and Sedition Acts.** These laws gave the president the authority to expel non-citizens he suspected of treason and made hostile words against the government illegal. The U.S. also began building warships and raising a provisional army. France decided against expanding New France and finally agreed to receive a diplomat to settle the controversies. Jefferson, who won the 1800 election, pardoned all of those that were convicted for crimes under the Alien and Sedition Acts.

Adams and Jefferson died on the same day, July 4, 1826.

Growth and Change of Political Parties

Political parties are never mentioned in the United States Constitution. In fact, Washington himself warned against the creation of "factions" in American politics that cause "jealousies and false alarms" and the damage they could cause to the body politic. Thomas Jefferson echoed this warning--yet he came to lead a party himself.

Americans had good reason to fear the emergence of political parties. They had witnessed how parties worked in Great Britain. Parties, called "factions" in Britain were made up of a few people who schemed to win favors from the government. They were more interested in their own personal profit and advantage than in the public good. Thus, new American leaders were interested in keeping factions from forming.

Ironically, the disagreements between Washington's chief advisors, Thomas Jefferson and Alexander Hamilton, had spurred formation of the first political parties. Hamilton wanted the federal government to be stronger than the state governments. Jefferson believed that the state governments should be stronger than the federal government. Hamilton supported the creation of the first Bank of the United States to pay off debt and enable creditors to have a vital interest in the success of the new country. Jefferson opposed it because he felt that it would take money from the poor and give too much power to wealthy investors.

Jefferson interpreted the Constitution strictly; he argued that nowhere did the Constitution give the federal government the power to create a national bank. He believed that the common people, especially the farmers, were the backbone of the nation. He thought that the rise of big cities and manufacturing would corrupt American life.

Hamilton interpreted the Constitution more loosely. He pointed out that the Constitution gave Congress the power to make all laws "necessary and proper" to carry out its duties. He reasoned that since Congress had the right to collect taxes, then Congress had the right to create the bank. Hamilton wanted the government to encourage economic growth. He favored the growth of trade, manufacturing, and the rise of cities as the necessary parts of economic growth. He favored the business leaders and mistrusted the common people.

At first Hamilton and Jefferson had their disagreements in private. But when Congress began to pass many of Hamilton's ideas and programs, Jefferson and James Madison, decided to organize support for their own views. They moved quietly and very cautiously in the beginning. In 1791, they went to New York and met with several important New York politicians including Governor George Clinton and Aaron Burr, a strong critic of Hamilton.

Before long, leaders in other states began to organize support for either Jefferson or Hamilton. Jefferson's supporters called themselves **Democratic-Republicans**. Hamilton and his supporters were known as **Federalists**, because they favored a strong federal government. The Federalists had the support of the merchants and ship owners in the Northeast and some planters in the South. Small farmers, craft workers, and some of the wealthier landowners supported Jefferson and the Democratic-Republicans.

In 1800 Thomas Jefferson was elected President. By the beginning of the 1800s, the Federalist Party, torn by internal divisions, had begun suffering a decline. Aaron Burr killed Alexander Hamilton in 1804 in a duel.

Jefferson was re-elected in 1804, and James Madison, another Democratic-Republican was elected in 1808. By 1816, after losing a string of important elections, the Federalist Party ceased to be an effective political force, and soon passed off the national stage.

By the late 1820s, new political parties had grown up. The **Democratic-Republican** Party was the major party for several years, but differences within it about the direction in which the country was headed caused a split after 1824.

Those who favored strong national growth took the name **Whigs** after a similar party in Great Britain and united around then-President John Quincy Adams who had been a Federalist and then had had set up a party called the National Republican Party. Many business people in the Northeast, as well as some wealthy planters in the South, supported the Whig Party.

Those who favored slower growth and were more oriented toward workers and small farmers went on to form the new Democratic Party, with Andrew Jackson being its first leader. Jackson defeated John Quincy Adams in 1828 and became the first president from this party. It is the forerunner of today's present party of the same name.

In the mid-1850s, the slavery issue was beginning to heat up. In 1854, the Whig Party, some Northern Democrats who opposed slavery, and other people opposed to slavery united to form the Republican Party. The Democratic Party was more heavily represented in the South and was, for the most part, pro-slavery.

Thus, by the time of the Civil War, the present form of the major political parties had been formed. Though there would sometimes be drastic changes in ideology and platforms over the years, no other political parties would manage to gain enough strength to seriously challenge the "Big Two" parties.

Power of the Supreme Court

Marbury v. Madison was the first case to establish what has become the Supreme Court's main duty, judicial review.

When Jefferson was elected in November 1800, he would not take office until the fourth of March, and President Adams, a Federalist, tried to get as many Federalist judges appointed as he could before Jefferson's inauguration. Adams appointed judges long into the night on the third of March. These appointments were known as the "**Midnight Judges**." One of these "Midnight Judges" was **William Marbury**, who was named to be Justice of the Peace for the District of Columbia.

The normal practice of making such appointments was to deliver a "**commission**," or notice, of appointment. This was done by the Secretary of State. Jefferson now was President, and his Secretary of State was **James Madison**. Jefferson told Madison not to deliver the commission for Marbury.

Chief Justice Marshall and the other Justices of the Supreme Court ruled that the power to deliver commissions to judges was not part of the Constitution. It was instead part of the Judiciary Act of 1789. And because the Judiciary Act conflicted with the Constitution, it was illegal since it gave the Judicial Branch powers not granted to it by the Constitution.

Thus Marbury did not become Justice of the Peace in the District of Columbia.

The ruling exemplifies the power of the Supreme Court to throw out unconstitutional laws of Congress. The Supreme Court always has the ultimate check on legislative and executive power.

McCulloch v. Maryland, which settled a dispute involving the Second Bank of the United States, ruled that any dispute between governments at the state and federal levels would be settled in favor of the federal government.

The State of Maryland voted to tax all bank business done with banks not chartered in Maryland. The law is viewed as particularly designed to target the Second Bank of the United States.

Andrew McCulloch, who worked in the Baltimore branch of the Second Bank of the United States, refused to pay the tax. The State of Maryland sued, and the Supreme Court accepted the case.

Supreme Court Chief Justice John Marshall wrote to uphold the right of Congress to charter a national bank. Further, he wrote that a state did not have the power to tax the federal government. "The right to tax is the right to destroy," he wrote. The ruling was that states should not have the power to tax the federal government. The Bank of the United States did not survive after 1841, but the judicial review of the Supreme Court did.

Effects on Native Americans

During the American Revolution many Native Americans sided with the British in hopes of stopping expansion of the American colonies into lands they occupied. The **Treaty of Paris** ceded a large amount of land occupied and claimed by American Indians to the United States, and the British did not inform them of the change.

The new U.S. government first tried to treat the tribes who had fought with the British as conquered people and claimed their land. This policy was later abandoned, however, because it could not be enforced.

The next phase of the government's policy toward the American Indians in order to continue national expansion was to purchase their land in treaties. This created tension. The expansion and settlement of new territory forced the Native Americans to move farther west. The Native Americans were gradually giving up their homelands, their sacred sites, and the burial grounds of their ancestors. Some of the American Indians chose to move west. Many, however, were relocated by force.

The Indian Removal Act of 1830 authorized the government to negotiate treaties with Native Americans to provide land west of the Mississippi River in exchange for lands east of

> http://www.pbs.org/wgbh/aia/part4/4p2959.html
> **Indian Removal**

the river. This policy resulted in the relocation of more than 100,000 Native Americans. Theoretically, the treaties were expected to result in voluntary relocation of the native people. In fact, however, many of the native chiefs were forced to sign the treaties.

One of the worst examples of "Removal" was the **Treaty of New Echota**. This treaty was signed by a

http://ngeorgia.com/history/nghisttt.html
The Trail of Tears

faction of the Cherokees in Georgia, but not by the actual leaders of the tribe. When the leaders attempted to remain on their ancestral lands, the treaty was enforced by President Martin Van Buren. The removal of the Cherokees came to be known as "**The Trail of Tears**" and resulted in the deaths of more than 4,000 Cherokees.

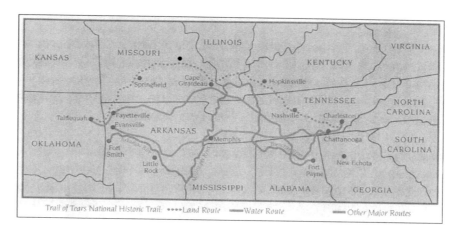

Skill 1.1f   Continued National Development.

When the United States declared independence from England, the founding fathers created a political point of view that created a national unity while respecting the uniqueness and individual rights of each of the thirteen colonies or states.

Some colonists had come to America in search of religious freedom, others for a fresh start, and others for economic opportunity. Each colony had a particular culture and identity.

As the young nation grew, new states were established. Religious interests, economic life, and geography defined particular regions. The Northeast tended toward industrial development. The South tended to rely upon agriculture. The West was an area of untamed open spaces where people settled and practiced agriculture. Each of these regions came to be defined, at least to some extent, on the basis of the way people made their living and the economic and social institutions that supported them.

In the industrialized North, the factory system tended to create a division between the tycoons of business and industry and the poor industrial workers. The conditions in which the labor force worked were far from ideal–long hours, bad conditions, and low pay. Of course, life in villages, in small towns, and on farms was also a major part of the life in the North.

In the South the cities were centers of social and commercial life. The agriculture that supported the South was practiced on "plantations" owned by the wealthy and worked by indentured servants and slaves.

The Northwest Territory located north of the Ohio River would become the states of Ohio (1803), Indiana (1816), Illinois (1818), Michigan (1837), Wisconsin 1848), and Minnesota (1858) where the Mississippi River begins. Land was inexpensive; fur, food, and freedom plentiful, and the challenges poignant because of harsh weather and a lack of Eastern goods.

The Southwest Territory south of the Ohio River and east of the Mississippi River became the states of Kentucky (1792), Tennessee (1796), Mississippi (1817) and Alabama (1819). Alabama and Mississippi were part of the Deep South where slavery was far more prevalent than it was in Tennessee and Kentucky.

The Louisiana Purchase

Because more war seemed inevitable between Britain and France, Napoleon Bonaparte decided to build barges to invade Britain and to sell Louisiana Territory to the United States. Jefferson had wanted to buy New Orleans because he was concerned that either Spain or France could block American trade at that portal city. To his surprise the entire territory was offered for only fifteen million dollars. The Louisiana Purchase more than doubled the size of the United States. No Native Americans were informed of the purchase although they were the occupiers of the land.

The Louisiana Purchase was comprised of what became 15 states: Louisiana, Arkansas, Missouri, Iowa, Oklahoma, Kansas, Nebraska, and part of Minnesota, most of North and South Dakota, part of New Mexico and Texas, and Colorado, Wyoming, and Montana east of the Continental Divide.

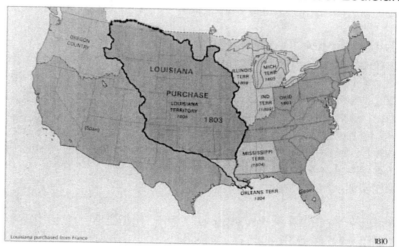

The Federalists were opposed to the Louisiana Purchase thinking it might extend slavery in the South as well as reduce political power in the North with growth in the West.

The Famous Duel

Federalist Alexander Hamilton's broke the tie between Democratic-Republicans Thomas Jefferson and Aaron Burr, making Jefferson President and Burr Vice

President. Election time came around again in 1804, and Hamilton thwarted Burr's attempt to be Vice President—and thwarted Burr's attempt become governor of New York. Burr challenged him to a duel. Hamilton died; Burr was charged with murder, but later acquitted.

In 1804 duels were a common method of men addressing conflict with each other. Later, even Abraham Lincoln was challenged to a duel, and he chose "cow pies" for weapons, but the weapon was changed to broadswords, and his opponent canceled as soon as he saw how proficient Lincoln would be. The last famous men involved in an American duel were Benjamin Brown and Thomas Reynolds who dueled in 1856 because Brown was an abolitionist editor of the newspaper in St. Louis, and Reynolds was a pro-slavery district attorney.

No Entangling Alliances

In the early years of the American nation, three primary ideas determined American foreign policy: **isolationism**, **no entangling alliances**, and **nationalism**.

Isolationism   Although many hoped the nation would grow, this expectation did not extend to efforts to plant colonies in other parts of the world.

"No Entangling Alliances" George Washington's farewell address espoused the intention of avoiding permanent alliances in any part of the world. This was echoed by Thomas Jefferson: "Equal and exact justice to all men, of whatever state or persuasion, religious or political; peace, commerce, and honest friendship with all nations–entangling alliances with none," said Jefferson. "We wish not to meddle with the internal affairs of any country, nor with the general affairs of Europe." And when James Madison led the nation into the War of 1812, he refrained from entering an alliance with France, which was also at war with England at the time.

Nationalism Following the **War of 1812**, nationalism in the United States grew as the "Era of Good Feelings" arose, with the winning of war against Great Britain.

War of 1812

The United States' unintentional and accidental involvement in what was known as the **War of 1812** came about due to the political and economic struggles between France and Great Britain. Napoleon's goal was complete conquest and control of Europe, including and especially Great Britain.

Although British troops were temporarily driven off the mainland of Europe, the navy still controlled the seas, the seas across which France had to bring the products needed. America traded with both nations, especially with France and its colonies.

The British decided to destroy American trade with France, mainly for two reasons:
- Products and goods from the U.S. gave Napoleon what he needed to keep up his struggle with Britain. Britain did want the Americans to aid their enemy.

- Britain felt threatened by the increasing strength and success of the U.S. merchant fleet. Americans were becoming major competitors with the ship owners and merchants in Britain.

The British issued the **Orders in Council,** a series of measures prohibiting American ships from entering any French ports--not only in Europe but also in India and the West Indies. At the same time, Napoleon began efforts for a coastal blockade of the British Isles.

Napoleon issued a series of Orders prohibiting all nations (including the United States) from trading with the British. He threatened seizure of every ship entering French ports after they had stopped at a British port or colony, and threatened to seize every ship that was inspected by British cruisers or that paid duties to the British.

The British were stopping American ships and impressing--that is conscripting--American seamen to serve on British ships. Americans were outraged.

In 1807, Congress passed the **Embargo Act,** a series of laws designed to use economic warfare instead of military warfare to protect American rights and to punish the British for forcing Americans to serve on their ships. But the Act led to an economic downturn in New England in particular, which led to spiraling unemployment, an antagonistic attitude toward the Democratic-Republicans, and smuggling. The Americans did not comply with the laws, and made fun of them calling them, among other things *O-grab-me* (embargo spelled backward).

The laws were withdrawn, but two additional acts were passed by Congress after James Madison became president. These laws attempted to regulate trade with other nations and to get Britain and France to remove the restrictions they had put on American shipping. The catch--despite America's intention to remain neutral—was that whichever nation removed restrictions, Americans would not trade with the other one.

Napoleon was first to remove restrictions, and this prompted Madison to issue orders prohibiting trade with Britain--ignoring warnings from the British not to do so. Although Britain eventually rescinded its Orders in Council, war came in June of 1812.

During the war, Americans were divided over not only whether or not it was necessary to even fight, but also over what territories should be fought for and taken. The nation was still young and just not prepared for war.

Two naval victories and one military victory stand out for the United States. Oliver Perry gained control of Lake Erie, and Thomas MacDonough fought on Lake Champlain. Both of these naval battles prevented British invasion of the United States from Canada. However, the primary American objective to conquer Canada was unsuccessful.

CAPTURE AND BURNING OF WASHINGTON BY THE BRITISH, IN 1814.

The Burning of Washington by Dolly Madison-**August 23, 1814** http://www.nationalcenter.org/Wash ingtonBurning1814.html

The British troops came down the Potomac River, then marched into Washington, DC, and burned the public buildings, including the White House, home to President James Madison and First Lady Dolly.

The war ended Christmas Eve, 1814, with the signing of the Treaty of Ghent, but that was not known yet in New Orleans on January 8th since communications were slow. Andrew Jackson's victory at New Orleans was a great morale booster to Americans.

The peace treaty established peace, released prisoners of war, restored all occupied territory, and set up a commission to settle boundary disputes with Canada. The War of 1812 proved to be a turning point in American history.

Monroe Doctrine

Previously, European events had profoundly shaped U.S. policies, especially foreign policies. In President Monroe's message to Congress on December 2, 1823, he delivered what is known as the **Monroe Doctrine**.

The United States was informing the powers of the Old World that the American continents were no longer open to European colonization, and that any effort to extend European political influence into the New World would be considered by the United States "as dangerous to our peace and safety." Nor would the United States interfere in European wars or internal affairs--and expected Europe to stay out of American affairs.

The American experience had created a profound wariness of any encroachment onto the continent by European countries. The Monroe Doctrine was a clear warning: no new colonies in the Americas.

Lewis and Clark Expedition

After the U.S. purchased the Louisiana Territory, Jefferson appointed Captains **Meriwether Lewis** and **William Clark** to explore it and to find out exactly what had been bought. The expedition went all the way to the Pacific Ocean, and the explorers returned two years later with maps, journals, and artifacts. This led the way for future explorers to make available more knowledge about the territory-- which resulted in westward movement.

Manifest Destiny

The nineteenth century was the age of "**Manifest Destiny**," the belief in the divinely given right of the nation to expand westward and incorporate more of the continent into the nation.

Westward expansion included the **Northwest Ordinance** (1787) and the **Louisiana Purchase** (1803).

John Gast 1872

Mass migration westward put the U.S. government on a collision course with the Indians, Great Britain, Spain, and Mexico.

Manifest Destiny was the justification of the **Mexican-American War** (1846-48) which resulted in the annexation of Texas and California, as well as much of the Southwest.

The last resolve between Great Britain and the U.S. was over the shared **Oregon** country in the Northwest. By the 1840s, with the conflict of free and slave states and the demand of the western settlers for government by the U.S., the conflict had to be resolved. In a treaty, signed in 1846, and just before the outbreak of the war with Mexico, President **James Polk** accepted a compromise with the U.S. boundary south of the **49th parallel.**

Mexican-American War

In the American Southwest, the results were exactly the opposite. Spain's claim to land in the region had begun in the 1540s. The claim had spread northward from Mexico City, and, in the 1700s, Spain had established missions, forts, villages, towns, and very large ranches. After the purchase of the Louisiana Territory in 1803, which included some of Texas, Americans began moving into Spanish territory. A few hundred American families were allowed to live there, but they had to agree to become loyal subjects to Spain.

In 1821, Mexico successfully revolted against Spanish rule, won independence, and was tolerant toward the American settlers and traders. The Mexican government encouraged and allowed extensive trade and settlement, especially in Texas. Many of the new settlers were southerners and brought with them their slaves. Slavery was outlawed in Mexico and, therefore, technically illegal in Texas, although the Mexican government looked the other way.

But friction increased with land-hungry Americans swarming into western lands. The clash was not only political but was also cultural and economic. Spanish influence permeated all parts of Southwestern life: law, language, architecture, and customs.

There came to be concern over the possible growth and development of an American state within Mexico. Settlement restrictions, cancellation of land grants, the forbidding of slavery, and increased military activity brought everything to a head. A clash was bound to occur.

The Mexican government owed debts to U.S. citizens whose property had been damaged or destroyed during the struggle for independence from Spain. Mexico became bitter over the American expansion into Texas and then by the Texas revolution in 1836--after which Texas considered itself an independent republic.

In the 1844 presidential election, the Democrats pushed for annexation of Texas (and Oregon also), which President Jackson had opposed. Now, under President Tyler, the procedure to admit Texas to the Union began. When statehood occurred in 1845 under President Polk, diplomatic relations between the U.S. and Mexico ended.

President Polk supported Manifest Destiny and wanted U.S. control of the entire southwest from Texas to the Pacific Ocean. The Whigs were largely opposed to the notion of Manifest Destiny and war with Mexico, while the Southern Democrats were in favor, especially with the idea that slave states could expand.

The Mexican government was weak, corrupt, and irresponsible. In poor financial shape, Mexico did not pay its war debts. President Polk sent a diplomatic mission with an offer to purchase New Mexico and Upper California and to forgive the $4.5 million it owed U.S. citizens, but the Mexican government—which was chaotic and in conflict--refused to receive the diplomats.

John Quincy Adams and Abraham Lincoln were two members of Congress who remained firm in their opposition to the war, but President Polk's declaration of war passed so that in 1846 the United States and Mexico were formally at war. Conflict over the **Wilmot Proviso,** an amendment to the war monies bill that stipulated none of the territory acquired in the Mexican War should be open to slavery revealed the continuing conflict over slavery in the nation.

Henry David Thoreau was jailed for refusing to pay taxes to support the war, and he wrote his famous essay entitled "Civil Disobedience."

Much of the war took place in Mexico and California.

The treaty signed in 1848 and a subsequent one in 1853 completed the southwestern boundary of the United States, and it extended to the Pacific Ocean, as President Polk had wished. Completed in 1854 for lands south of the Gila River and west of the Rio Grande, the **Gadsden Purchase**, added property for the purpose of building a transcontinental railroad. The outcome altogether included the land for the states of California, Nevada, and Utah as well as parts of Arizona, Colorado, New Mexico, and Wyoming.

The Era of Good Feelings

The "Era of Good Feelings" followed the War of 1812 and the decline of the Federalist Party. This period included:

- Henry Clay's Missouri Compromise
- Acquisition of Florida from Spain
- Monroe Doctrine
- Lack of partisan factions

The American System

After the War of 1812, Henry Clay and supporters favored economic measures that came to be known as the **American System**. This involved tariffs protecting American farmers and manufacturers from having to compete with foreign products, stimulating industrial growth and employment. With more people working:
- More farm products would be consumed
- Prosperous farmers would be able to buy more manufactured goods
- Additional monies from tariffs would make it possible for the government to make needed internal improvements.

In 1816, Congress not only passed a high tariff, but also chartered the Second Bank of the United States. One of the many duties of the Bank was to regulate the supply of money for the nation.

Jacksonian Democracy

The election of Andrew Jackson as President signaled a swing of the political pendulum from government influence of the wealthy, aristocratic Easterners to the interests of the Western farmers and pioneers and the era of the "common man." Jacksonian democracy was a policy of equal political power for all. In other words, every white man could vote, not just property owners as had been the case before.

Executive power and the **patronage system** were promoted along with strict constitutional interpretation. Removing Indians from the Southeast was also favored.

Laissez faire economics and the end of the Second United States Bank were supported. Upon becoming President, Jackson fought to get rid of the Bank because he believed it favored the wealthy. Congress voted in 1832 to renew the Bank's charter, but Jackson vetoed the bill, withdrew the government's money, and the bank finally collapsed.

Jackson also faced the "null and void," or nullification issue from South Carolina.

Congress passed a law in 1828, which in the South was called the "Tariff of Abominations." Signed by President John Quincy Adams, the law placed high tariffs on goods imported into the United States.

Southerners, led by Vice President John C. Calhoun (from South Carolina and Vice President under Adams and then Jackson), felt that the tariff favored the manufacturing interests of New England and the Northeast. The nullification theory claimed that any state could nullify any of the federal laws it considered unconstitutional. Calhoun resigned from office.

The tariff was lowered in 1832, but not low enough to satisfy South Carolina, which promptly threatened to secede from the Union. Although Jackson agreed with the rights of states, he also believed in preservation of the Union, so he signed the Force Bill which enabled him to send troops to South Carolina to force it to obey all federal laws.

The Compromise Tariff of 1833 designed by Henry Clay lowered the tariffs, and secession was averted for the time being, but tariff laws continued to pass, exemplifying another difference between the Southern Democrats and the Northern Whigs.

Slavery

Equality for everyone, as stated in the Declaration of Independence, did not yet apply to black Americans or American Indians. Voting rights and the right to hold public office were restricted in varying degrees in each state. All of these factors decidedly affected the political, economic, and social life of the country, and all three were focused in the attitudes of the three sections of the country on slavery.

Differences between North and South came to a head over the issue of slavery. The rise of the abolitionist movement in the North, the publication of **Uncle Tom's Cabin** by Harriet Beecher Stowe, and issues of trade and coalesced around the issue of slavery. As the South defended its lifestyle, its economy, and the right of the states to be self-determining, the North became stronger in its criticism of slavery.

Slavery in the English colonies had begun in 1619 when twenty Africans arrived in the colony of Virginia at Jamestown. From then on, slavery had a foothold, especially in the agricultural South, where a large amount of slave labor was needed for the extensive plantations. Nonetheless, the majority of farmers in the South were small family farms with few if any slaves.

In the West, pioneers moved into new frontiers seeking land, wealth, and opportunity. Free men refused to work for wages on the plantations when they could settle their own land on the frontier. Therefore, using indentured servants and slave labor was the only profitable course plantation owners saw.

The North, although it had many farms, was far more industrial than the South. Its economy was varied. While a variety of crops were grown in the North, the South had become increasingly dependent on one crop--cotton.
Cotton production rose from 150,000 pounds in the early 1800s to more than four million pounds in 1855, and slave population rose accordingly from about 900,000 in 1800 to over four million in 1860.

One of the slavery compromises at the Constitutional Convention had been the **"three-fifths compromise**," which determined that three-fifths of the slaves would be counted for both taxes and representation. Another compromise over slavery in those early days regarded disputes over how much regulation the central government would have over the slave trade. Southerners were worried about taxing slaves coming into the country and the possibility of Congress prohibiting slave trade altogether. The compromise allowed the states to continue importation of slaves for the next 20 years until 1808, at which time Congress would make the decision as to the future of the slave trade. During the 20-year period, no more than $10 per person could be levied on slaves coming into the country.

By 1808, cotton was becoming increasingly important in the primarily agricultural South, and the institution of slavery had become firmly entrenched in Southern culture. It is also evident that as early as the Constitutional Convention, active anti-slavery feelings and opinions were very strong, leading to extremely active groups and societies.

But the most intense and controversial was the abolitionists' efforts to end slavery, an effort alienating and splitting the country, hardening Southern defense of slavery, and leading to four years of bloody war. The abolitionist movement had political fallout, affecting admittance of states into the Union and the government's continued efforts to keep a balance between total numbers of free and slave states. Congressional legislation after 1820 reflected this.

Anti-slavery Organizations

- American Colonization Society - Created by the Protestant churches, with the goal of sending black people to Africa, the Society created the colony of Liberia. The former slaves sent there soon realized that the crops they had been growing in the South did not grow well in Liberia. Poverty was a fact.

- American Anti-Slavery Society - Quaker William Lloyd Garrison created a newspaper entitled *The Liberator*. The newspaper was highly supported by Abolitionists, and the State of Georgia offered a large reward for the capture of Garrison.

- Female Anti-Slavery Society - <u>Margaretta Forten</u> was one of the founders of Female Anti-Slavery Society, a group of black and white women which was formed because women were not allowed to be full members of the Anti-Slavery Society (that her father had helped form).

- Anti-Slavery Convention of American Women held its first meeting in 1838, Pennsylvania Hall, and this building they'd raised money for was burned down by a pro-slavery mob—while the meeting was in progress with Lucretia Mott as the speaker. That fire did not stop the women. They continued meeting at Sarah Pugh's schoolhouse.

- Female Vigilant Society - Many women were members of this group that raised money for refugee slaves and the Underground Railroad.

Life in America in the Nineteenth Century

During the nineteenth century, there arose a great spirit of reform. This spirit of reform found expression in the effort to protect the rights and opportunities of all.

> http://www.pbs.org/kcet/publicschool/index.
> html
> **History of Public Education from PBS.**

Education A new understanding of education led to major efforts for public education for all children. In Massachusetts, Horace Mann Mann published the *Common School Journal,* so the public could become more familiar with the importance of education. It was argued that common schooling could:

- Help to create good citizens
- Bring society together
- Prevent crime
- Prevent poverty.

As public schools were established, more people were literate, and so there was more participation in literature and the arts. The more literate society broadly appreciated newspapers and works of literature, art, and live entertainment. Education helped make people more informed about previously unknown areas, including the West.

At the conclusion of the nineteenth century, free, public, elementary school was available for all children in America.

Transportation Meanwhile, development continued for building roads, railroads, canals, and steamboats. The increased ease of travel facilitated westward movement. Increased ease of shipping boosted the economy because shipments were faster and cheaper over larger areas. One innovation was the **Erie Canal** completed in 1825 that connected the interior and Great Lakes with the Hudson River and the coastal port of New York. Many other natural waterways were connected by canals, and travel became far easier.

The invention of the steam engine resulted in many changes. John Fitch developed the steamboat, and Robert Fulton's *Clermont*, was the first commercially successful steamboat. Steam-powered railroads eventually became the most important transportation method and helped to open the West. Expansion into the interior of the country resulted in became America's becoming the leading agricultural nation in the world.

American farmers produced a vast surplus for export: cotton, grain, flour, and livestock. Implements such as the cotton gin and the reaper made production more efficient.

Travel and shipping were greatly assisted by the canals, the steamboat, the railroad, and improved roads such as the National Road in the East. New wagon trails also provided for the immigration westward and travel on these trails led to the invention of the **prairie schooner**.

- **Oregon Trail** from Missouri to Oregon
- **California Trail** that cut southward to California and was often used by gold seekers
- **Santa Fe Trail** from Missouri to Santa Fe

Industry Before 1800, most manufacturing activities were accomplished in small shops or in homes. However, starting in the early 1800s, the ability to build machines resulted in factories that made it easier to produce goods faster. More industries required more labor. Women, children, and, at times, entire families worked the long hours and days in mills and factories, and employers began hiring immigrants who were coming to America in huge numbers.

Early Labor Movemen. The first strike in America actually occurred in the eighteenth century in 1751 when bakers had withheld baking bread in a protest. By 1830, labor movements were underway. For example, Boston artisans including carpenters, masons and stonecutters led a movement to reduce workdays to ten hours in the 1830s to 1840s. In 1844 in Lowell, Massachusetts, female textile employees organized the Lowell Female Labor Reform Association for the same purpose. In fact, dozens of different trades during this time period struck in their effort for ten-hour workdays.

Great Awakening The **First Great Awakening** had taken place in the 1730s and 1740s under the preacher Jonathan Edwards, and the **Second Great Awakening** took place about sixty years later—between 1800 and 1830. The Second Great Awakening was an evangelical Protestant revival that preached personal responsibility for one's actions both individually and socially. Two dominant results:

- Personal behavior defined by strong work ethic, temperance, and avoidance of being wasteful
- Personal behavior moving from guilt for sins to facing injustice and helping to eliminate suffering in others

Interdenominational missionary groups began such as the **American Home Missionary Society** in 1826. Publishers of Christian literature included the **American Bible Society** and the **American Tract Society**.

Preachers traveled the country preaching the gospel of social responsibility. The point of view then extended to mainline Protestant denominations that the Christian faith should be expressed for the good of society. Preachers preached that people see God as one who looks after and cares for the individual and for society. Sin is selfishness; behavior should be benevolence; and people needed to purify for the coming arrival of the coming Kingdom when Jesus returns to Earth. Methodists and Baptists gained huge numbers. Some of the new denominations of the period were the Disciples of Christ, Latter Day Saints, and Seventh-Day Adventists.

Closely allied to the Second Great Awakening was the **temperance movement**. The Society for the Promotion of Temperance was organized in Boston in 1826. This movement to end the sale and consumption of alcohol arose from religious beliefs, the violence many women and children experienced from heavy drinkers, and from the effect of alcohol consumption on the work force.

Some Notable People Committed to Social Improvement

Horace Mann grew up a poor child with little opportunity for education except for his small community library. He took full advantage of it, however, and was admitted to Brown University, from which he graduated in 1819. Mann practiced law for several years and served in the Massachusetts House of Representatives. He served on the committee of the first school funded by public tax dollars in Dedham, Massachusetts, and in 1837 was appointed secretary to the newly formed State Board of Education. Mann became an outspoken proponent of educational reform, and fought for better resources for schools and teachers. Mann planned the Massachusetts Normal School system for training new teachers. The compulsory public education that is taken for granted today was a new idea in antebellum America, and Mann faced opposition to his ideas. Shortly after Massachusetts adopted this system, New York followed suit, laying the foundation for the present state-based educational system.

Dorothea Dix was an advocate for public treatment and care for the mentally ill. In the early 1840s, Dix called attention to the deplorable treatment and conditions to which the mentally ill in Massachusetts were subjected in a pamphlet entitled *Memorial.* Her efforts resulted in a bill that expanded the state hospital. Dix traveled to several other states, encouraging and overseeing the founding of state mental hospitals. Dix proposed federal legislation that would have sold public land with the proceeds being distributed to the states to fund care for the mentally ill. The legislation was approved by Congress, however, using public money for social welfare was a contentious issue, and President Franklin Pierce vetoed it on these grounds.

Other social issues were also addressed. It was during this period that efforts were made to transform the prison system and its emphasis on punishment into a penitentiary system that attempted rehabilitation.

The following is a partial list of well-known Americans who contributed their leadership and talents in various fields and reforms:

Emma Hart Willard, Catharine Esther Beecher, and Mary Lyon for **education for women**

Dr. Elizabeth Blackwell, the **first woman doctor**

Antoinette Louisa Blackwell, the **first female minister**

Elihu Burritt and William Ladd for **peace movements**

Horace Mann, Henry Barmard, Calvin E. Stowe, Caleb Mills, and John Swett for **public education**

Benjamin Lundy, David Walker, William Lloyd Garrison, Isaac Hooper, Arthur and Lewis Tappan, Theodore Weld, Frederick Douglass, Harriet Tubman, James G. Birney, Henry Highland Garnet, James Forten, Robert Purvis, Harriet Beecher Stowe, Wendell Phillips, and John Brown for **abolition of slavery and the Underground Railroad**

Louisa Mae Alcott, James Fenimore Cooper, Washington Irving, Walt Whitman, Henry David Thoreau, Ralph Waldo Emerson, Herman Melville, Richard Henry Dana, Nathaniel Hawthorne, Henry Wadsworth Longfellow, John Greenleaf Whittier, Edgar Allan Poe, Oliver Wendell Holmes, **famous writers**

John C. Fremont, Zebulon Pike, Kit Carson, **explorers**

Henry Clay, Daniel Webster, Stephen Douglas, John C. Calhoun, American **statesmen**

Robert Fulton, Cyrus McCormick, Eli Whitney, **inventors**

Noah Webster, American **dictionary**

The list goes on but the contributions of these and many, many others greatly enhanced the unique American culture.

Women's Rights

A group of women emerged in the 1840s that was the beginning of the first women's rights movement in the nation's history. Among the early leaders of the movement were **Elizabeth Cady Stanton, Lucretia Mott**, and **Ernestine Rose**. At this time very few states recognized women's rights to vote, own property, sue for divorce, or execute contracts. In 1869, **Susan B. Anthony**, Ernestine Rose and Elizabeth Cady Stanton founded the National Woman Suffrage Association.

The **Seneca Falls Convention** held in the New York mill town of Seneca Falls in 1848 was the first women's rights convention. Lucretia Mott had attended the World Anti-Slavery Society in Britain in 1840, but she was not allowed to speak from the floor nor to be seated as a delegate. This led to the discussion of how women could neither vote nor hold important positions in American government. Abigail Adams had addressed this subject with her husband John Adams many years before when the Constitution was being written.

Some 300 people attended the convention, which culminated in the publication of a "**Declaration of Sentiments**," largely written by Stanton and signed by 68 women and 32 men. Frederick Douglass described it as the

http://www.infoplease.com/spot/
womenstimeline1.html
Timeline of Women's Rights in the USA

"grand basis for attaining the civil, social, political, and religious rights of women." Others thoroughly objected. The structure of the document was based on the Declaration of Independence: "We hold these truths to be self-evident: that all men and women are created equal."

Skill 1.1g   Civil War Era

The first serious clash between the North and South occurred in 1819-20 during the presidency of James Monroe and concerned admitting Missouri as a state.

In 1819, the U.S. consisted of twenty-one states: eleven free states and ten slave states. Alabama had been admitted as a slave state and that had balanced the Senate with the North and South each having twenty-two senators. The Missouri Territory allowed slavery and, if admitted, would cause an imbalance in the number of U.S. Senators in states with and without slavery.

The first **Missouri Compromise** resolved the conflict by approving admission of the northern part of Massachusetts as the free state of Maine and Missouri as a slave state--thus continuing to keep a balance of power in the Senate with the same number of free and slave states.

An additional provision of this compromise was that with the admission of Missouri, slavery would not be allowed in the rest of the Louisiana Purchase territory north of latitude 36 degrees 30'. This was acceptable to the slave-state congressmen since it was not profitable to grow cotton on land north of this latitude line anyway.

It was thought that the crisis had been resolved, but in the next year, it was discovered that in its state constitution, Missouri discriminated against the free blacks by barring the immigration of free blacks to the state.

Anti-slavery supporters in Congress were determined to exclude Missouri from the Union. **Henry Clay**, known as the **Great Compromiser**, then proposed a second Missouri Compromise which was acceptable to everyone. His proposal stated that the Constitution of the United States guaranteed protections and privileges to citizens of states, and Missouri's proposed constitution could not deny these to any of its citizens. The acceptance in 1820 of this second compromise opened the way for Missouri's statehood.

However, this reprieve was only temporary.

The slavery issue flared again. In addition to the two factions of those who advocated prohibition of slavery and those who favored slavery, a third faction arose supporting the doctrine of "**popular sovereignty**" which stated that people living in territories and states should be allowed to decide for themselves whether or not slavery should be permitted. In 1849, California applied for admittance to the Union and the furor began.

The result was the **Compromise of 1850**, a series of laws designed as a final solution to the issue. Concessions included:

- Admission of California as a free state
- Abolition of slave trading in Washington, D.C.
- Creation of the New Mexico and Utah territories where residents would decide whether or not to permit slavery when becoming states
- Stricter measures to capture runaway slaves

A few years later, Congress took up consideration of new territories between Missouri and present-day Idaho. Again, heated debate over permitting slavery in these areas flared up.

Those opposed to slavery used the Missouri Compromise to prove their point, showing that the land being considered for territories was part of the area the Compromise had designated as banned to slavery. But on May 25, 1854, Congress passed the infamous **Kansas-Nebraska Act** which nullified this provision, created the territories of Kansas and Nebraska, and providing for the people of these two territories to decide for themselves whether or not to permit slavery to exist there.

Source: "Slavery in the Field" New York Tribune (Whig Newspaper). January 6, 1854

Feelings were so deep and divided that any further attempts to compromise would meet with little if any success. Political and social turmoil swirled everywhere. Kansas was called **"Bleeding Kansas"** because of extreme violence and bloodshed throughout the territory with two

http://www.pbs.org/wgbh/aia/part4/4p2952.html
PBS "Bleeding Kansas"

governments existing there--one pro-slavery and the other anti-slavery. Then the Supreme Court in 1857 handed down a decision guaranteed to cause explosions throughout the country.

Dred Scott Case. Dred Scott was a slave whose owner had taken him from slave state Missouri, to free state Illinois and into Minnesota Territory, which was free under the provisions of the Missouri Compromise--and then finally back to slave state Missouri. Abolitionists pursued the dilemma by presenting a court case, stating that since Scott, whose owner had died, had previously lived in free territory was in actuality a free man.

One lower court ruled in favor and one lower court against. The Supreme Court decided that residing in a free state and free territory did not make Scott a free man because Scott and all other slaves were not U.S. citizens or state citizens of Missouri. Therefore, he did not have the right to sue in state or federal courts.

The Court went a step further and ruled that the old Missouri Compromise was now unconstitutional because Congress did not have the power to prohibit slavery in the Territories.

http://www.us-civilwar.com/whig.htm
History of Whig Party

The **Compromise of 1850** along with the deaths of Daniel Webster and a division of pro- and anti-slavery members had put the Whig Party on its last legs. One of the platforms of the newly formed Republican Party was keeping slavery out of the Territories. Now, according to the decision in the Dred Scott case, this basic party principle was unconstitutional.

The only way to ban slavery in new areas was by a Constitutional Amendment, requiring ratification by three-fourths of all states. This was out of the question because of Southern opposition.

Lincoln-Douglas Debates

In 1858, former Whig **Abraham Lincoln** and Democrat Stephen A. Douglas were running against each other for the office of U.S. Senator from Illinois.

Lincoln viewed the Kansas-Nebraska Act that Douglas had sponsored as being immoral and disturbing. Lincoln, who had now become a Republican, was not an abolitionist, but he believed that slavery was morally wrong. Lincoln supported the Republican Party's principle that slavery must not be allowed to extend any further.

Douglas, on the other hand, originated the doctrine of "popular sovereignty" and was responsible for supporting and getting through Congress the inflammatory Kansas-Nebraska Act. Douglas, up for re-election, knew that if he won this race, he had a good chance of becoming president in 1860.

In the course of the debates, Lincoln challenged Douglas to show that popular sovereignty reconciled with the Dred Scott decision. Either way he answered Lincoln, Douglas would lose crucial support from one group or the other. If he supported the Dred Scott decision, Southerners would support him, but he would lose Northern support. If he stayed with popular sovereignty, Northern support would be his, but Southern support would be lost.

His reply to Lincoln stating that Territorial legislatures could exclude slavery by refusing to pass laws supporting it, gave him enough support and approval to be re-elected to the Senate. However, it cost him the Democratic nomination for president in 1860. Southern Democrats realized that Douglas was devoted to popular sovereignty but not necessarily to the expansion of slavery.

Lincoln received the nomination of the Republican Party for president.

Abolitionist John Brown

In 1859 in what is now West Virginia, abolitionist **John Brown** and his followers seized the federal arsenal at **Harper's Ferry**. His purpose was to take the guns stored in the arsenal, give them to slaves nearby, and lead them in a widespread rebellion. He and his men were captured by Colonel Robert E. Lee of the United States Army, and after a trial with a guilty verdict, he was hanged.

It wasn't the first illegal effort Brown had made. In Kansas Territory he and his sons had murdered five men who were pro-slavery in response to the sacking of Lawrence, Kansas, which was largely anti-slavery, an episode in Bleeding Kansas. Brown and his sons escaped, and he went on to solicit wealthy abolitionists to create a colony for runaway slaves

Most Southerners felt that the majority of Northerners approved of Brown's actions, and Southern newspapers frequently quoted the small, but well-known, minority of abolitionists who applauded Brown's actions. The execution of Brown and the survivors of the 22 involved in the Harper's Ferry takeover resulted in Northern abolitionists viewing the executions as an example of the government's support for slavery.

Yet, when economic issues and the issue of slavery came to a head, the North declared slavery illegal.

Nullification

The **doctrine of nullification** states that the states have the right to "nullify"–declare invalid–any act of Congress they believe to be unjust or unconstitutional. The doctrine of nullification was based on the assumption that the United States was a union of independent commonwealths and that the general government was merely their agent. Thus the South asserted that states could secede from the union and form their own government, just as Texas, for example, had seceded from Mexico.

The North saw the doctrine of nullification as the assumption that the United States was a league of states rather than a union the founders had intended when they had recognized that the Articles of Confederation did not work well. The North saw secession as a violation of the nation that could not be torn apart because of differences in component parts of it. Both Federalists and Anti-Federalists, North and South alike, had come to agreement on this in the constitutional period.

The nullification crisis of the mid-nineteenth century that had climaxed over the tariffs on manufactured goods led President Jackson, a Southern Democrat to say in his "Proclamation to the People of South Carolina" that the Constitution derives its authority from the *people*, not from the states. He said that "each State, having expressly parted with so many powers as to constitute, jointly with the other States, a single nation, cannot, from that period, possess any right to secede, because such secession does not break a league, but destroys the unity of a nation."

Presidential Election 1860

Candidates from four political parties:

- ○ Southern Democrats endorsed slavery - John Breckenridge
- ○ Republicans denounced slavery - Abraham Lincoln
- ○ Northern Democrats said democracy required the people themselves to decide on slavery locally - Stephen Douglas
- ○ Constitutional Union Party said the survival of the Union was at stake, and everything else should be compromised - John Bell

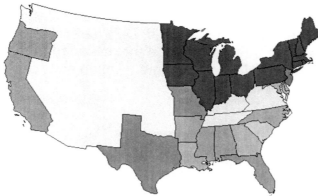

Republican
Southern Democrat
Constitutional Union
Northern Democrat

Note: Electors from South Carolina were appointed by the state legislature

- ○ Lincoln received 1,865,908 or 39.82 percent of the popular vote;
- ○ Stephen Douglas received 1,380,202 or 29.46 percent of the popular vote.

Lincoln received 59.4 percent of the electoral votes, making him the new president.

The Southern States Secede. The Southern states, one by one, voted to secede from the Union as they had promised they would do if Lincoln and the Republicans were victorious.

South Carolina was the first state to **secede** from the Union, and the first shots of the war were fired on **Fort Sumter** in Charleston Harbor.

Both sides quickly prepared for war.

Advantages of the North

The North had more in its favor: a larger population; superiority in finances and transportation facilities; manufacturing, agricultural, and natural resources. The North possessed most of the nation's gold, had about 92 percent of all industries, and had almost all known supplies of copper, coal, iron, and various other minerals. Since most of the nation's railroads were in the North and Midwest, men and supplies could more easily be moved wherever needed. Trade with nations overseas could continue due to control of the Navy and the merchant fleet.

The Northern states numbered twenty-four and included the western states of California and Oregon and the border states of Maryland, Delaware, Kentucky, Missouri, who did not secede and West Virginia, an area that seceded from Virginia after it seceded from the Union. (Nevada became a Union state during the Civil War also.)

Advantages of the South

The Southern states numbered making up the Confederacy numbered eleven: South Carolina, Georgia, Florida, Alabama, Mississippi, Louisiana, Texas, Virginia, North Carolina, Tennessee, and Arkansas.

Although outnumbered in population, the South was completely confident of victory. The rationale was that fighting a defensive war and protecting their own territory would lead to the North--who had to invade and defeat an area almost the size of Western Europe --tired of the struggle and gave up.

An advantage of the South was that a number of its best officers had graduated from the U.S. Military Academy at West Point and had had long years of Army experience, some even exercising varying degrees of command in the Indian wars and the war with Mexico.

Many men from the South were conditioned to living outdoors with a warmer climate and, because of lifestyle, were more familiar with horses and firearms than many men from northeastern cities. Since cotton was such an important crop, Southerners felt that British and French textile mills, dependent on raw cotton, would need to help the Confederacy in the war.

The South had specific reasons and goals for fighting the war. The major aim of the Confederacy never wavered: to win independence, to win the right to govern themselves as states as they wished, and to preserve slavery.

Strategies for the Civil War

The war strategies for both sides were relatively clear and simple.

The **South**:
- Planned a defensive war, wearing down the North until it agreed to peace on Southern terms.
- Gain control of Washington, D.C.
- Go north through the Shenandoah Valley into Maryland and Pennsylvania in order to drive a wedge between the Northeast and Midwest to interrupt the lines of communication

The theory was that this would end the war quickly.

The **North**:
- Blockading the Confederate coastline in order to cripple the South
- Seizing control of the Mississippi River
- Seizing control and interior railroad lines to split the Confederacy in two
- Seizing the Confederate capital of Richmond, Virginia, to head southward to join with Union forces coming east from the Mississippi Valley.

The **Emancipation Proclamation** that freed slaves was part of the Union's strategy. It resulted in aggressive recruitment of blacks, and more than 180,000 of them fought in the Union army and more than 10,000 in the navy.

Confederate Army in the North

The first **Battle of Bull Run** less than 40 miles from Washington was observed by the nearby populace who came out to picnic and cheer on, and this battle changed the general opinion of war being similar to a sporting event. In this first major battle, 2,900 of Northern General McDowell's troops were killed, wounded, captured, or missing and 2,000 of General Beauregard's met the same fate.

Union casualties
- 460 killed,
- 1,124 wounded
- 1,312 missing or captured

Confederate casualties
- 387 killed
- 1,582 wounded
- 13 missing

General Jackson was given the name "Stonewall Jackson" for his enduring, a waiting that enabled the South's victory when General Johnston arrived.

After success at **Chancellorsville**, General Robert E. Lee's Amy of North Virginia headed through the Shenandoah Valley, aiming toward Philadelphia. They met with the Union troops in Gettysburg, Pennsylvania, and the **Battle of Gettysburg** lasted from July 1 to July 3, 1863.

Four things worked against Lee at Gettysburg:

- The Union troops gained the best positions and the best ground first, making it easier to make a stand there.
- Lee's move into Northern territory put his army a long way from food and supply lines. They were more or less on their own.
- Lee thought that his Army of Northern Virginia was invincible and could fight and win under any conditions or circumstances.
- Stuart and his men did not arrive at Gettysburg until the end of the second day of fighting and by then, it was too little too late. He and the men had had to detour around Union soldiers, and he was delayed getting the information Lee needed.

The third and last day Lee launched a final attempt to break Union lines. **General George Pickett** sent his division of three brigades under Generals Garnet, Kemper, and Armistead against Union troops on Cemetery Ridge under command of General Winfield Scott Hancock. Union lines held, and Lee and the defeated Army of Northern Virginia made their way back to Virginia.

The Union had successfully turned back a Confederate charge, Lincoln's commander George Meade and troops did not pursue Lee and the Confederate soldiers. Casualties were more than 50,000.

This battle was the turning point for the North. After this, Lee never again had the troop strength to launch a major offensive.

The Confederacy won its last important victory at **Chickamauga** in September 1863.

Union Army in the South

General Ulysses Grant captured Fort Henry, Tennessee, on the Tennessee River, in February of 1862, the first major Union victory of the war.

The day after the Battle of Gettysburg ended, on July 4, Vicksburg, Mississippi, surrendered to Grant, thus severing the western Confederacy from the eastern part. In November, the Union victory at Chattanooga and Lookout Mountain and Missionary Ridge made it possible for Union troops to go into Alabama and Georgia, splitting the eastern Confederacy in two.

Lincoln gave Grant command of all Northern armies in March of 1864. The **Overland Campaign** began at the inconclusive battle at Wilderness of Spotsylvania where Lee eliminated the Union's artillery advantage. Casualties were high throughout the campaign, but the strategy of keeping Confederate forces engaged in battle, Grant forced Lee into the position that led to the end of the war.

Joining Grant, Sheridan smashed through the Confederate lines at **Five Forks** April 1, 1865, necessitating the evacuation of both Petersburg and Richmond, the Confederate capital. Confederate General Pickett's losses led to the retreat to Appomattox.

Meanwhile, the other armies under his direction tore the Confederacy apart. The Union won the Battle of Mobile Bay and in May 1864, **William Tecumseh Sherman** began his march to demolish Atlanta, then burn the way on to Savannah. Sherman and his troops turned northward through the Carolinas to meet with Grant in Virginia.

On April 9, 1865, Lee formally surrendered to Grant at the **Appamattox Courthouse** in Virginia.

Assassination of President Lincoln

Five days after the surrender, on April 14, 1865, Lincoln went to with wife Mary to the Ford Theater to attend the play *Our American Cousin*. During the third act of the play, **John Wilkes Booth** shot President Lincoln in the head. Doctors moved Lincoln from the theater to a house across the street, but he never regained consciousness and died at 7:22 the next morning.

Results of the War

The Civil War took more American lives than any other war in America's history for a total of more than 618,000, with the South losing one-third of its soldiers in battle compared to the North losing about one-sixth.

More than half of the total deaths were caused by disease and the horrendous conditions of field hospitals. Both sections paid a tremendous economic price, but the South suffered severely from direct damages.

The economic and social chaos in the South after the war was incredible. Starvation and disease ran rampant, especially in the cities. The U.S. Army provided some relief of food and clothing for both white and blacks, but the major responsibility fell to the Freedmen's Bureau. Though the Bureau agents helped southern whites, their main responsibility was to the freed slaves. They were to assist the freedmen in becoming self-sufficient and protect them from being taken advantage of by others. Northerners looked on it as a real, honest effort to help the South out of the chaos it was in. Most white Southerners charged the Bureau with deliberately encouraging the freedmen to consider former owners as enemies.

The Civil War changed methods of waging war. It introduced weapons and tactics that, when improved later, were used extensively in the wars that followed. Civil War soldiers were the first to:

- Fight in trenches
- Fight under a unified command
- Wage a defense called "major cordon defense," a strategy of advance on all fronts.
- Use repeating and breech-loading weapons.
- Utilize observation balloons during the war along with submarines, ironclad ships, and mines.
- Communicate by telegraph
- Travel by railroad

It was considered a modern war because of the vast destruction and was considered "total war" because it involved the use of all resources of the opposing sides.

The Union was now preserved, and reconstruction was the goal.

Reconstruction

Reconstruction refers to the period between 1865 and 1877 when the federal and state governments debated and implemented plans to provide civil rights to freed slaves and to set the terms under which the former Confederate states might once again join the Union.

Radical Republicans in Congress, such as **Charles Sumner** in the Senate viewed the Southern states as being in the same position as any unorganized Territory. House leader **Thaddeus Stevens** said: ""It would be best for the South to remain ten years longer under military rule, and that during this time we would have Territorial Governors, with Territorial Legislatures, and the government at Washington would pay our general expenses as territories, and educate our children, white and colored." President **Andrew Johnson** was conciliatory toward the South. He supported Black Codes, vetoed renewal of the Freedman Bureau, and vetoed the Civil Rights bill.

As a result, the Radical Republicans--who had been abolitionists before the war--gained control of both houses and came within one vote of convicting Johnson in when he was impeached.

Black Codes refused to let freedmen testify against whites, bear arms, or have large gatherings; mandated segregated schools; set rules that unemployed blacks would be arrested for vagrancy and then hired out as cheap labor; and prohibited freedmen from serving on juries.

The **Civil Rights bill** was submitted to counter the Black Codes.

The Republicans in Congress favored the extension of **voting rights** to black men but were divided as to how far to extend the right. Moderate Republicans wanted only literate blacks and those who had fought for the Union to be allowed to vote. Radical Republicans wanted to extend the vote to all black men. Conservative Democrats did not want to give black men the vote at all.

In the case of former Confederate soldiers, moderate Republicans wanted to allow all but former leaders to vote, while the Radical Republicans wanted to require an oath from all eligible voters stating they had never borne arms against the United States (which would have excluded all former rebels).

Lincoln's moderate plan for Reconstruction had been part of his effort to win the war. Lincoln and the moderates had thought that if it remained easy for states to return to the Union and if moderate proposals on black suffrage were made, that Confederate states involved in the hostilities might be swayed to re-join the Union rather than continue fighting the war.

The **Thirteenth Amendment** to the Constitution was passed on January 31, 1865, with the necessary two-thirds majority, and by December 18, 1865, three-quarters of the states ratified it, which ensured that "neither slavery nor involuntary servitude" would ever exist again in the United States.

Johnson's veto of the civil rights bills was overridden by Congress, and the bill became a law. In 1866, the Radical Republicans passed the **Reconstruction Acts** which placed the governments of the southern states under the control of the federal military.

The Radical Republicans began to implement policies such as granting all black men the vote and denying the vote to former confederate soldiers.

The **Fourteenth Amendment**, which overturned the Dred Scott case, was ratified on July 9, 1868. It defines American citizenship and requires equal protection under the law by all states to all persons within their jurisdiction, and guarantees the right to sue or serve on a jury.

The **Fifteenth Amendment**, ratified on February 3, 1870 guarantees that "the right of citizens of the United States to vote shall not be denied or abridged by the United States or by any State on account of race, color, or previous condition of servitude."

Ratification of these Amendments was a condition of readmission into the Union. Republicans found support in the South among **Scalawags**, southern whites who joined the Republican Party during Reconstruction and joined into a coalition with freedmen and newcomers from the North for control of the local and state governments. The newcomers from the North were called **Carpetbaggers** and arrived in the South for humanitarian reasons and/or to personally gain economically.

Scandals During Reconstruction

General **Ulysses Grant** was elected President in 1868 and served two scandal-ridden terms until 1877. He lacked Washington political experience, and his greatest weakness was a blind loyalty to his friends. One of result of the war was the rapid growth of business and industry with some large corporations being controlled by unscrupulous men. For example, on Wall Street **Jay Gould** and **James Fisk** attempted to corner the gold market; the **Whiskey Ring** was a conspiracy among government people and whiskey businessmen to steal tax revenues; bribes were used in exchange for the sale of **Native American trading posts**; and there was the graft scandal of **Crédit Mobilier**. Military control continued throughout Grant's administration, despite growing conflict both inside and outside the Republican Party.

End of Reconstruction

Reconstruction had three phases: Presidential Reconstruction; Congressional Reconstruction; and the Redemption. Reconstruction officially ended when the last Federal troops left the South in 1877 after the election of **Rutherford B. Hayes**.

Without the military support, the Republican governments were replaced by so-called **Redeemer** governments. The rise of the Redeemer governments marked the beginning of the **Jim Crow** laws and official segregation. Blacks were still allowed to vote, but ways were found to make it difficult for them to do so such as literacy tests and poll taxes.

Reconstruction did set up public school systems and expanded the legal rights of black Americans through amendments to the Constitution. However, in terms of its goals of reunification of the South with the North and the guaranteeing civil rights to freed slaves, Reconstruction was a limited success.

Skill 1.1h   Emergence of the Modern United States

The conclusion of the Civil War opened the floodgates for migration westward and settlement of new land. The availability of cheap land and the expectation of great opportunity, including the discovery of gold in California in 1849, had already prompted many to travel to the Great Plains and the West Coast. Now the numbers increased. In 1867, Russia ceded 557,390 square miles to the United States for $7,200,000. The **Alaska** land was more than twice the size of Texas.

Railroads

The first section of the **transcontinental railroad** from Omaha, Nebraska, to Sacramento, California, was completed in 1869 by the Union Pacific and Central

http://cprr.org/Museum/Chinese.html
Central Pacific Railroad Photographic History Museum

Pacific Railroads. Nine-tenths of the railroad workers in the West were Chinese, and much of the work was extremely dangerous.

Railroad development resulted in efficient transport of products across the nation. However, as the railroads developed, so did the effort to reward larger shippers with rebates and other incentives, oftentimes charging more for shipping products short distances. One result of this was hurting the family farmer.

Immigration

The **Naturalization Act of 1870** limited U.S. citizenship to "white persons and persons of African descent," and the **Chinese Exclusion Act of 1882** restricted immigration of Chinese immigrants into the U.S. One result of this Act was widening the ratio of Chinese men to Chinese women to 27:1.

Along with the arrival of the Chinese, between1820 to 1870, more than 7.5 million immigrants came from Northern Europe, especially from England, Ireland, and Germany. The Irish stayed on the East Coast; the Germans moved west. During the 1850s, the primary focus of the Know-Nothing Party had been demanding laws to reduce immigration.

During the 1870s, the U.S. suffered a recession, but immigration from northern Europe and China continued. Between 1881 and 1920, approximately 23.5 million immigrants arrived from all over the world--particularly from southern Europe. Prejudice increased against Roman Catholics, Jews, and Japanese.

The **Immigration Act of 1882** created a fifty-cent tax on immigrants when they arrived. The funds generated were used for regulating immigration, paying immigration agents, and caring for immigrants after landing, and it denied accepting immigrants who were convicts and "persons likely to become public charges."

In 1892 **Ellis Island** opened as the processing center for immigrants arriving in New York, and it served more than 12 million immigrants over the next 30 years.

In 1921, the first quota immigration act was passed, the **Emergency Quota Act** also known as the **Johnson Quota Act**. It limited the number of immigrant allowed to three percent of the foreign-born people of that nationality who lived in the United States in 1910.

Three main reasons for immigration are: economic opportunity; religious discrimination; and political unrest and war. Between 1870 and 1916, more than 25 million immigrants came into the United States.

Agriculture

Changes from hand-power to horses had been one of the first significant changes in agriculture. This revolution occurred between 1862 and 1875.

In 1862, the **Department of Agriculture** was created. The same year, the **Morrill Land-Grant Acts** that allowed for the creation of land-grant colleges were passed. The **Hatch Act of 1887** set up agricultural experiment stations in connection to the land grant colleges. The **Smith-Lever Act of 1914** set up a non-formal educational program or cooperative to help citizens become knowledgeable about agriculture, food, home economics, environment, and community development. Agricultural extension programs were funded to increase farm yields.

Benefits of irrigation were discovered, and during the mid-1800s new advances were introduced for cultivation, for breeding, for use of fertilizers, and for the rotation of crops. In 1892 the first successful gasoline-powered tractor was introduced in Iowa. (By the 1900s, one tractor could substitute for 17 men and 50 horses.) In 1893, 42 patented insecticides were sold to farmers. The steel plow made it possible for widespread cultivation on the dense soil of the Great Plains, the area that used to be called The **Great American Desert**. Ranches developed in the Southwest, primarily for raising cattle, including the longhorn, which can survive where no other breed can.

Other developments in farming and ranching were the silo, deep-well drilling, barbed wire, the combine, and cream-separators.

Then, during the late 1800s, prices for farm goods, especially for wheat and cotton, fell drastically. Family farms were facing the railroad strategies that including rebates to large customers. This was one factor that led to the formation of the **Populist Party**.

In the 1930s, drought affected nearly all the Great Plains for almost a decade The Soil Conservation Service was established in 1935.

While 90 percent of the people in the United States had been farmers in 1790, by 1890, those who worked on farms was 43 percent of the labor force. By 1930, it was 21 percent; by 1990, 2.5 percent.

Business and Industry

At the end of the Civil War, industry in America was small, but after the war, dramatic changes took place with the production of machines. A limited listing of some of the American inventers who helped bring America into the future:

Walter Hunt, Elias Howe, and Isaac Singer built America's first sewing machines; **Alexander Graham Bell** invented the telephone; **George Eastman,** the camera; **Thomas Edison,** the phonograph, the incandescent light bulb, and the motion picture; **Samuel Morse,** the telegraph; **Cyrus McCormick,** the reaper; **Charles Goodyear,** vulcanized rubber; **Nikola Tesla,** alternating current and the radio; **George Westinghouse,** the transformer and air brake; **Richard Gatling,** the machine gun; **Orville and Wilbur Wright,** the airplane.

Between 1860 and 1900, inventors registered almost 700,000 new patents.

The Gilded Age.

The popular name for the period from the end of the Civil War to the beginning of World War I is known as the **Gilded Age** or the **Second Industrial Revolution.** The new nation had the potential of enormous economic expansion as it moved from agriculture and mercantilism to industrialism, a system built on large industries instead of farming and craftsmanship.

Major industrialists and financiers:

- Philip Armour, Chicago - meatpacking
- John Jacob Astor IV, New York - inherited fortune, writer, businessman, hotelier; died at age 47 on the *Titanic*)
- Andrew Carnegie, Pittsburgh - railroads, steel; contributed libraries
- Jay Cooke, Philadelphia – finance
- Charles Crocker, Monterey – dry goods, railroads
- Daniel Drew, New York – cattle, finance, brokerage
- James Buchanan Duke, Durham, NC – tobacco
- James Fisk, New York – smuggler, stockbroker, railroads
- Henry Flagler, New York/Palm Beach – real estate, railroads, Standard Oil
- Henry Ford, Dearborn/Detroit – inventor, automobile, mass production
- Henry Clay Frick, Pittsburg /New York – steel
- John Warne Gates, Texas – wire, railroads, oil
- Jay Gould, New York – railroads, gold; involved in Tammany Hall and Boss Tweed
- E. H. Harriman, New York – railroads
- James J. Hill, St. Paul, MN – railroads, exports
- Mark Hopkins, San Francisco – railroads
- Collis P. Huntington, Sacramento, Richmond – railroads
- Andrew Mellon, Pittsburgh - oil, steel, ships, aluminum, banking
- J. Pierpont Morgan, New York - banking
- John D. Rockefeller and William Rockefeller, Cleveland – Standard Oil
- Jacob Schiff, New York – banker
- Leland Stanford, Sacramento/San Francisco – railroads
- Cornelius Vanderbilt, New York - railroads, shipping

While respected for business acumen and success, they were condemned for exploitation of workers and questionable business practices. They were also feared because of their power.

During the Gilded Age banks were established; department stores began; the chain store was born; and trusts developed.

Trusts

Government after the Civil War encouraged the growth of business. **Trusts** were developed when the stockholders of many competing companies would give the control of the stock to a group of trustees who would operate all the companies as if they were one company and pay the profits to the stockholders.

For example, more than seventy oil companies' stockholders gave control of the stock to the nine trustees of Standard Oil. Thus, nine men were in charge of 90 percent of all oil production in the U.S.

At the same time was a rise of monopolies. An owner of one successful company would buy all the other companies engaged in the same product(s). It was not uncommon either that the owners would drive other owners out of business. One method for doing this was to lower prices so the competition could not make a profit. After the monopolist is without competition, prices can skyrocket without competition. Plus, those companies with little or no competition would require their suppliers to supply goods at a low cost; and then, sell the finished products at high prices. Sometimes for higher profits, they would reduce the quality of the product to save money. And the consumer would have no choice because there would be competition.

Panic of 1873

The boom in the railroad industry had attracted speculators. Jay Cooke's and others' banks went bankrupt because they had invested so much in the railroads. Factories closed, and credit was gone. Workers suffered great cuts in pay. Part of the cause was the change in money—the **Coinage Act of 1873** changed to the gold standard and de-monetized silver.

The Populist Party

The Populist Party was officially formed out of an alliance between the **Farmers' Alliance** and the **Knights of Labor**.

The next economic recession hit the West and South before it did the cities in the 1890s. Drought struck; farm prices dropped, especially for cotton; and farmers found themselves deeply in debt. Tenant farmers had it the worst. All in all, the Farmers Alliance had the benefit of uniting rural poor people into a political force.

> http://www.nebraskastudies.org/0600/frameset_reset.html?http://www.nebraskastudies.org/0600/stories/0601_0302.html
> **Farmers' Alliance in Nebraska**

In the 1890s, the recession struck the industrial areas of the cities, and factory workers shared farmers' views against the industrialists. The Knights of Labor had been formed in 1869 under **Uriah Stephens**, and the goal remained to organize all workers--whether they were skilled or unskilled, black or white, male or female-- into one big union united for the rights of workers. Goals included the eight-hour workday, equal pay for women, the elimination of child labor, and cooperative ownership of factories and mines.

The platform of the Populist Party included:

- a national currency and unlimited coinage of silver and gold
- graduated income tax
- government ownership and operation of the railroads
- telegraph and telephone ownership and operation by the government
- secret ballot system
- liberal pensions to ex-Union soldiers and sailors
- restriction of immigration
- abolition of Pinkerton system
- limits to one term for President and Vice President
- direct vote for election of Senators
- abolition of subsidy to private corporations
- reclamation of railroad lands by government

Labor Movement

The labor movement began to grow. Numerous boycotts and strikes often became violent when the police or the militia were called in to stop the strikes.

The **Homestead Strike** in 1892 was perhaps the first well-organized strike. It took place between the Amalgamated Association of Iron and Steel Works (AA) and Carnegie Steel Company.

> http://www.pbs.org/wgbh/amex/carnegie/peopleevents/pande04.html
> **PBS-Homestead Strike**

There was gunfire between the strikers and the Pinkerton strikebreakers, and the Carnegie Steel Company eliminated a union at the plant.

The **Pullman Strike** in 1894 was in response to a 28 percent pay cut. George Pullman had built a company town, and while workers surely appreciated it for a time, it can be compared to a feudal society where everything is controlled and inspected by the feudal lord. The Pullman Strike was led by **Eugene Debs,** leader of the American Railway Union. Army troops were called in by President **Grover Cleveland** to break the strike, saying it interfered with the mail. Debs, who was represented by **Clarence Darrow**, ran for president of the U.S. five times.

Mother Jones.

Mary Harris Jones came to be known as **Mother Jones**. She was involved with the United Mine Workers of America (UMWA).

She organized a Children's Crusade in 1903, marching children to President Theodore Roosevelt's home in Oyster Bay, New York, protesting child labor. She was one of the founders of the Industrial Workers of the World (IWW).

The Panic of 1893

The Panic of 1893 was the role of the United States in a worldwide economic crisis. Railroads went bankrupt. Unemployment in factories was 20 to 25 percent. Industrial areas in cities, rural areas, and mill towns were hard hit. President Cleveland had repealed the **Sherman Silver Purchase Act** because he thought it caused the Panic. The Panic led to giving the Republican Party power. Americans began to view poverty as a broad economic failure rather than God's punishment of the individual.

Growth of Cities

The abundance of resources, together with growth of industry and the pace of capital investments led to the growth of cities. Populations were shifting from rural agricultural areas to urban industrial areas.

In 1871 in Chicago a fire killed hundreds. The wooden buildings, the ships on the Chicago River, the wood-plank sidewalks, and the lumber yards were destroyed when strong winds carried the fire. The next fire in 1903 at the Iroquois Theater killed 600. But between these events was the World Exposition in Chicago in 1893 that celebrated the 400th anniversary of Columbus' landing.

By the early 1900s a third of the nation's population lived in cities. As time went on, workers were being displaced by advances in machinery and automation.

Industrialization also brought an influx of immigrants from Asia (particularly Chinese and Japanese) and from Europe (particularly European Jews, Irish, and Russians). High rates of immigration led to the creation of communities in various cities such "Chinatown" or "little Russia" or "little Italy." Industrialization also led to overwhelming growth of cities with workers living close to their places of work. Increased urban populations, frequently packed into dense tenements, often without adequate sanitation or clean water, led to public health challenges that required cities to establish sanitation, and water and public health departments to cope with and prevent epidemics.

Political organizations also saw the advantage of mobilizing the new industrial working class and created vast patronage programs that sometimes became notorious for corruption in big-city machine politics such as **Tammany Hall** in New York led by William "Boss" Tweed, who stole hundreds of thousands of dollars from the taxpayers.

Skill 1.1i Progressive Era and the First World War through the New Deal

The **Progressive Era** began in the 1890s and lasted until the end of World War I. Progressives advocated against waste and corruption, and for workers' rights and safety. Progressives believed that science could resolve many issues, that government could help to endorse fairness and repair social problems, and that more people could be directly involved in the political process.

Disparity between rich and poor resulted in a public outcry for reform at the same time that there was an outcry for governmental reform that would end the political corruption and elitism of the day. Several political parties were formed out of this philosophy, including the Greenback Party, the Populist Party, the Farmer-Labor Party, the Progressive Party, and the Union Party. Additionally, there was the Single Tax movement that advocated to "abolish all taxation save that upon land values."

Fire was fueled by the writings of investigative journalists such as **Ida Tarbell, Jacob Riis,** and **Lincoln Steffens** and writers such as novelist **Upton Sinclair**–the **muckrakers**–who published scathing exposes of political and business wrongdoing and corruption. As a result, many issues were addressed such as child labor laws, workmen's compensation, and trust-busting.

Although Progressive leaders came from many different backgrounds and were driven by different ideologies, they shared a common fundamental belief that government should work toward eradicating social ills and promoting the common good. Among reforms were:

- Seventeenth Amendment – Popular election of U.S. Senators
- Eighteenth Amendment – Prohibition of alcohol
- Nineteenth Amendment – Right of women to vote.
- Sherman Antitrust Act – Opened the door for breaking up trusts and monopolies
- Elkins Act and Hepburn Act – Regulating railroads
- Initiative and referendum laws at a state level - Enable citizens to put propositions before the public to vote on
- Recall laws- Enable the recall of elected officials
- Food and Drugs Act – Require accurate labeling and prohibit poisonous additives
- Meat Inspection Act - Regulated the meat industry to protect the public against tainted meat.
- Department of Commerce and Labor - Created

Responding to concern over the environmental effects of the timber, ranching, and mining industries, **Theodore Roosevelt** set aside 238 million acres of federal lands to protect them from development. Wildlife preserves were established, the national park system was expanded, and the National Conservation Commission was created. The Newlands Reclamation Act also provided federal funding for the construction of irrigation projects and dams in semi-arid areas of the country.

The Wilson Administration carried out additional reforms. The **Federal Reserve Act** created a national banking system, providing a stable money supply. The Sherman Act and the Clayton Antitrust Act defined unfair competition, made corporate officers liable for the illegal actions of employees, and exempted labor unions from antitrust lawsuits. The **Federal Trade Commission** was established to enforce these measures. Finally, the Sixteenth Amendment was ratified, establishing a graduated income tax. This measure was designed to relieve the poor of a disproportionate burden in funding the federal government and make the wealthy pay a greater share of the nation's tax burden.

Among Progressives were:

Jane Addams - Chicago social reformer and first woman to win Nobel Peace Prize
Robert La Follette – Against corruption and entry into World War I
W.E.B. duBois – Civil rights activist and leader -- worldwide
John R. Mott – YMCA leader and Nobel Prize winner
Booker T. Washington – Educator who began life as a slave
Margaret Sanger – Birth control activist
William Jennings Bryan – Supporter of Prohibition and opponent of Darwinism
Thorstein Veblen – Sociologist and economist
Walter Lippman – Investigative journalist
Ida B. Wells – Civil rights and women's rights advocate

The Native Americans

Indians of the Great Plains were Cheyenne, Arapaho, Comanche, Kiowa and Plains Apache, Crow, Blackfoot, Assiniboine, Lakota, Liban, Plains Cree, Sarsi, Tonkaw, and Shosone. Others for whom the buffalo was important were the Arikara, Hidatsa, Iowa, Kansa, Mandan, Omaha, Osage, Otoe, Pawnee, Ponca, and Wichita. Buffalo or the American bison were vital to these tribes. The white settlers killed this animal for the hides or just shooting as many as possible from the trains. Both types of shooters left the carcasses on the prairie to decay.

Numerous conflicts, often called the "**Indian Wars**," broke out between the U.S. army and many different native tribes. Many treaties were signed with the various tribes, but most were broken by the government. One of the most known battles was the **Battle of Little Bighorn** also known as **Battle of the Greasy Grass and Custer's Last Stand** in 1876, in which native people defeated General Custer and his forces.

Chief Sitting Bull's Hunkpapas in 1871 learned that the Northern Pacific Railway was intending to make a railway route directly through their lands. The Panic of 1873 when Jay Cooke's bank went under eliminated this plan. But then General Custer came to the Black Hills to seek gold--as well as to select a site for a fort. The finding of gold led to the government insisting that all Sioux move to the Sioux reservation. When they refused, the government termed them "hostile." More than 3,000 Native Americans left their reservations to follow Sitting Bull. The result was the death of General Custer, but that led to the government's pressing harder on the tribes. Chief Sitting Bull moved to Saskatchewan, then came back to surrender, spent some time in jail, and then joined Buffalo Bill Cody's *Wild West Show*.

In 1876, the U.S. government ordered all surviving Native Americans to move to reservations. Continued conflict led to passage of the **Dawes Act of 1887**. This was in

> http://etext.virginia.edu/railton/roughingit/map/bufmaypenny.html
> "Our Indian Wards"

response to the recognition that confinement to reservations was not working. The law intended to break up the Indian communities and bring about assimilation into white culture by deeding portions of the reservation lands to individual Indians who were expected to farm their land. The policy continued until 1934.

> http://www.kporterfield.com/aicttw/articles/boardingschool.html#section2
> **Indian Boarding School**
>
> http://www.english.uiuc.edu/maps/poets/a_f/erdrich/boarding/index.htm
> **About Indian Boarding Schools**

In addition, during the late nineteenth century, the avid reformers of the day instituted a practice of trying to "civilize" Indian children by educating them in **Indian Boarding Schools**. The children were forbidden to speak their native languages, they were forced to convert to Christianity, and generally the children were forced to give up all aspects of their native culture and identity. There are numerous reports of abuse of the Indian children at these schools

Armed resistance essentially came to an end in 1890 as a result of the well-known massacre of Native Americans at **Wounded Knee**. The surrender of **Geronimo** and the massacre at Wounded Knee led to a change of strategy by the Indians. Thereafter, the resistance strategy was to preserve their culture and traditions.

Some Native Americans served with the **Rough Riders** in the Spanish-American War in 1898-1902, and in 1916, General John J. Pershing took Apache scouts on American invasion into Mexico in search of **Pancho Villa**. During World War I, although Native Americans were rarely defined as citizens, more than 17,000 were drafted into military service. A growing desire to see the native people effectively merged into mainstream society led to the enactment of the **Indian Citizenship Act of 1924**, by which Native Americans were granted U.S. citizenship.

Nonetheless federal policies have continued to marginalize Native Americans. The first reservations were set up under President Grant, and life on the reservations ever since has been difficult for many Native Americans. The policies of extermination and relocation have significantly decimated their numbers. There exist about 300 Indian reservations.

Expanding America

Captain Brooks of the Hawaiian Bark Gambia discovered **Midway Island** and named the islands "Middlebrook." Then Captain **William Reynolds** of the **USS Lackawanna** took possession of the islands in 1867, marking the first acquisition of an island by the United States. Elsewhere in the Pacific, the United States lent its support to American sugar planters and assisted in overthrowing the **Kingdom of Hawaii**, an act that many scholars have been considered imperialistic

By the 1880s Secretary of State **James G. Blaine** favored a **Pan-American Congress,** which refers to economic, commercial, social, military, and political cooperation throughout the Americas. In the 1890s, President **Grover Cleveland** interpreted the **Monroe Doctrine** to mean there were an American interests everywhere in the Western Hemisphere. The U.S. became involved in a border dispute between Great Britain and Venezuela, taking Venezuela's side for a good relationship between the U.S. and Venezuela.

The Spanish-American War

During the 1890s, Spain still controlled overseas possessions including Puerto Rico, the Philippines, and Cuba.

Spain had taken over the island of Cuba after Columbus's discovery of it, then decimated the population, making them work in gold mines. When the people became too feeble, the Spanish imported slaves from Africa. Slaves had revolted several times, but the Spanish had put down the revolts and continued to use them, and demand from them cheap products. Slavery ended in 1886, and the Cubans were once again ready to revolt.

In 1853, when **Franklin Pierce** was President, the United States had offered Spain $130 million for Cuba. The offer was not accepted.

Americans were still interested.

The 'first media war" was underway. **William Randolph Hearst** and **Joseph Pulitzer** were selling newspapers. **Yellow journalism** was a method for pleasing the customer with melodrama. The reports of gross atrocities were reported in the newspapers, and what was happening in Cuba was not melodrama but real. That influenced Progressives to favor helping the Cubans. At the same time, industrialists had an economic interest. Others could see that strategically, Cuba was important since the British had used the Caribbean waters during the Revolution and the War of 1812. **Jose Julian Marti y Perez wrote** the "Proclamation of Montercristi" --,an outline of the goals for Cuba's revolt—a war for independence.

THE EVIL SPIRITS OF THE MODERN DAILY PRESS.

Marti had said that "the white man's fear of the Negro would impede Cuba's independence." Marti was killed in the first battle against the Spanish.

President William McKinley, who had won the presidency against William Jennings Bryan, initially refused to recognize the Cubans' rebellion, but affirmed the possibility of American intervention. There could be a good base in Cuba for coaling U.S. Navy ships. At first President McKinley wanted Cuba to be free and would rather negotiate than become involved in a war. Then the U.S. battleship *The Maine* was blown up in Havana Harbor with a loss of 260 lives.

The argument still goes on whether Spain caused it or if it happened by another cause. Evidence at the time indicated that Spain had caused the explosion. Two months later Congress declared war on Spain—and less than four months later in August of 1898, the war was over. In the Philippines, Commodore Dewey had sunk every Spanish ship in Manila Bay. Theodore Roosevelt and the Rough Riders took possession of San Juan Hill near Santiago de Cuba, and the Spanish surrendered. The United States had defeated Spain and instantly became a world power.

Victory over Spain proved fruitful for American territorial ambitions. Although in response to McKinley's war message, Congress had passed the **Teller Amendment** that stated that the United States could not annex Cuba but leave "control of the island to its people," the United States gained control **Philippines** and various other Pacific islands formerly possessed by Spain.

The decision to occupy the **Philippines**, rather than grant it independence led immediately to a guerrilla war. It was a three-year struggle with the Filipinos who wanted independence from the Americans. Emilio Aguinaldo, the leader, was finally captured. He freed himself by taking an oath of allegiance to the United States, which continued to rule the Philippines until 1942, benignly.

The peace treaty signed in Paris in December 1898 had also given the U.S. possession of **Puerto Rico, Guam, and Hawaii**. The **Platt Amendment** to the Army Appropriations Act in 1901 ceded Cuba's Guantanamo Bay to the U.S. Under **President Theodore Roosevelt**, the **Cuban-American Treaty** provided that Guantanamo Bay be perpetually leased to the U.S. for coaling and naval stations.

Panama Canal

Although the idea of a canal in Panama goes back to the early sixteenth century, work did not begin until 1880 by the French who had built the Suez Canal to join the Mediterranean and Red Seas. The Panama effort collapsed, and the U.S. completed the task, opening the **Panama Canal** in 1914.

Construction was an enormous task of complex engineering. Because the area is mountainous, it was built as a lock-and-lake canal, meaning that ships are lifted on the locks to travel across a man-made lake. The forty-mile long Panama

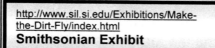
http://www.sil.si.edu/Exhibitions/Make-the-Dirt-Fly/index.html
Smithsonian Exhibit

Canal was built by cutting through the isthmus that joins North and South America in order to connect the Atlantic and Pacific Oceans. This eliminated the trip around Cape Horn, a savings of 8,000 nautical miles for ships. The Canal was completed in 1914.

The U.S. helped Panama win independence from Colombia in exchange for control of the Panama Canal Zone.

The Open Door Policy

The **Open Door Policy** was developed after the United States won the Philippines because that created a foothold in Eastern Asia. Japan and the European powers had created **spheres of influence** throughout China as they had defeated Chinese armies—and the United States sent 2,500 sailors and marines to China to assert U.S. power in China. Secretary of State **John Hay** under President Theodore Roosevelt wanted to guarantee equal trading rights for all engaged in China and announced the Open Door Policy. He also recommended protecting the integrity of the Chinese empire.

Big Stick Diplomacy was a term Theodore Roosevelt attributed to an African proverb: "Speak softly and carry a big stick." The **Roosevelt Corollary** rose from this statement of the United States' police power. The intention was to safeguard American economic interests in Latin America—and to prevent European interests from dominating.

The policy led to the expansion of the U.S. Navy and to greater involvement in world affairs. Should any nation in the Western Hemisphere become vulnerable to European control because of political or economic instability, the U.S. had both the right and the obligation to intervene. As a result, the U.S. intervened in Cuba, Nicaragua, Haiti, and the Dominican Republic in the years before World War II.

Dollar Diplomacy describes the U.S. efforts under **President William Howard Taft** to extend its foreign policy goals in Latin America and East Asia through economic power. The designation derives from Taft's claim that U.S. interests in Latin America had changed from "warlike and political" to "peaceful and economic." Taft justified this policy in terms of protecting the Panama Canal. The practice of dollar diplomacy was from time to time anything but peaceful, particularly in Nicaragua. When revolts or revolutions occurred, the U.S. sent troops to resolve the situation. Immediately upon resolution, bankers were sent in to loan money to the new regimes. The policy persisted until the election of **Woodrow Wilson** to the Presidency in 1913.

Wilson repudiated the dollar diplomacy approach to foreign policy within weeks of his inauguration. Wilson's "**moral diplomacy**" became the model for American foreign policy to this day.

Wilson envisioned a federation of democratic nations, believing that democracy and representative government were the foundation stones of world stability. Specifically, he saw Great Britain and the United States as the champions of self-government and the promoters of world peace. Wilson's beliefs and actions set in motion an American foreign policy that was dedicated to the interests of all humanity rather than merely American national interests. Wilson promoted the power of free trade and international commerce as the key to acquiring a voice in world events.

Wilson believed that democratic states would be less inclined to threaten U.S. interests, and he advocated 1) maintaining a combat-ready military to meet the needs of the nation; 2) promoting democracy abroad; and 3), improving the U.S. economy through international trade.

The First World War

The **First World War** (WWI) was a global military conflict fought mostly in Europe between the years 1914 and 1918. When the war began in 1914, triggered by the assassination of Austrian Archduke Francis Ferdinand and his wife in Sarajevo, **President Woodrow Wilson** declared that the U.S. was neutral. Most Americans were opposed to involvement and wanted to stay out of the war.

In 1915, a German U-boat sunk the British luxury passenger liner RMS **Lusitania**, killing more than 1,000 civilians including more than 100 Americans. This attack outraged the American public and turned public opinion against Germany. The attack on the Lusitania became a rallying point for those advocating US involvement in the European conflict.

In 1916, Wilson's campaign was based on the slogan "He Kept Us out of War," and he was reelected. He continued efforts to end the war, but German submarines began unlimited warfare against American merchant shipping. The development of the German *unterseeboat* or **U-boat** allowed Germans to efficiently attack merchant ships from Canada and the US. that were supplying Germany's European enemies. Then the British intercepted a telegram Germany had sent to the Mexican government proposing that Germany would help Mexico to invade the United States.

The telegram know as the **Zimmerman Note,** along with continued German destruction of American ships, resulted in the U.S. entering into the war.

The economy was directed to the war effort, and more than four million Americans served in the military with over two million of them serving overseas. Nearly 50,000 Americans were killed in battle and an additional 221,000 were wounded. More than nine million soldiers were killed on the various battlefields, and millions of civilians died in the fighting.

Central Powers Germany, Austria-Hungary, Bulgaria, and the Ottoman Empire.

TELEGRAM RECEIVED.

FROM 2nd from London # 5747.

"We intend to begin on the first of February unrestricted submarine warfare. We shall endeavor in spite of this to keep the United States of America neutral. In the event of this not succeeding, we make Mexico a proposal of alliance on the following basis: make war together, make peace together, generous financial support and an understanding on our part that Mexico is to reconquer the lost territory in Texas, New Mexico, and Arizona. The settlement in detail is left to you. You will inform the President of the above most secretly as soon as the outbreak of war with the United States of America is certain and add the suggestion that he should, on his own initiative, invite Japan to immediate adherence and at the same time mediate between Japan and ourselves. Please call the President's attention to the fact that the ruthless employment of our submarines now offers the prospect of compelling England in a few months to make peace." Signed, ZIMMERMANN.

Allied Powers – France, United Kingdom . Russia (until 1917 when the Russian Revolution took place); United States (from April 6, 1917)

Minor allies – Australia, Belgium, Canada, Japan, Greece. Italy (from May 23, 1915), Montenegro, Newfoundland. New Zealand, Romania, Serbia, South Africa

The War Effort at Home

Railroads In December of 1917, the government assumed control of all of the railroads in the nation and consolidated them into a single system with regional directors. The goal was to increase efficiency and enable the rail system to meet the needs of both commerce and military transportation. The understanding was that private ownership would be restored after the war. The restoration occurred in 1920. In 1918 telegraph, telephone and cable services were also taken over by the federal government; they were returned to original management and ownership in 1919.

The **American Red Cross** and the volunteers who supported their effort knitted garments for both the Army and the Navy. In addition, they prepared surgical dressings, hospital garments and refugee garments. More than eight million people participated.

Liberty Bonds To secure the huge sums of money needed to finance the war, the government sold **Liberty Bonds**. Nearly $25 billion worth of bonds were sold in four issues of bonds.

The first Liberty bond was issued at 3.5 percent; the second, at 4 percent; the remaining ones at 4.25 percent. More than one-fifth of U.S. residents bought bonds. For the first time in their lives, millions of people had begun saving money. After the war "**Victory Bonds**" were sold.

War Production The war effort required massive production of weapons, ammunition, radios, and other equipment of war. For example, at the beginning of the war, the U.S. had little overseas shipping. Attacks by German submarines soon resulted in existing ships being destroyed faster than new ships could be built. Scores of shipyards were quickly constructed to build both wooden and steel ships. At the end of the war the United States had more than 2,000 ships. The cost of the war on April 30, 1919, was over 22.5 billion dollars.

President Wilson proposed his **Fourteen Points** to Congress in January 1918. The hope was bringing the war to an end with an equitable peace settlement. Five points set out general ideals; eight points pertained to immediately resolving territorial and political problems; and the fourteenth point counseled establishing an organization of nations to help keep world peace.

When Germany agreed in November of 1918 to an armistice, it assumed that the peace settlement would be drawn up on the basis of the Fourteen Points. However, the peace conference in Paris in 1919, but there were many contradictory agreements and disagreements that ignored these points. Wilson insisted upon the **League of Nations** being included in the Treaty of Versailles.

Italy, France, and Great Britain wanted retribution, and so peace treaties punished the Central Powers, taking away arms and territories and requiring payment of reparations. Germany was punished more than the others and, according to one clause in the treaty, was forced to assume the responsibility for causing the war.

Senator Henry Cabot Lodge of Massachusetts in 1918 became became both majority leader and Foreign Relations Committee chairman, and he wanted unconditional surrender of Germany. Wilson ignored Lodge and took no senators along to the peace proceedings in Paris. In November, Lodge sent to the treaty to the Senate floor with 14 reservations, but Wilson was unwilling to negotiate, and on November 19, 1919, The Senate rejected the peace treaty. The United States did not become a part of the League of Nations.

The 1920s

During wartime, work hours were shortened, wages were increased, and working conditions improved. The decade of the 1920s saw tremendous changes. One change was a shift from farm life to city life for many. While many Americans experienced prosperity, there were, however, also millions living below the poverty line of $2,000 per year.

The automobile and entertainment industry resulted in the fast-paced **Roaring Twenties**, also known as the **Jazz Age**. Movie stars, sports figures and national heroes such as aviator **Charles Lindbergh**, influenced Americans to admire, emulate, and support individual accomplishments. Professional boxing provided new entertainment for the public

Laissez faire economics, mass production, electrification, the building of highways, and the invention of the radio were great influencers. Telephone lines and indoor plumbing for many homes became common luxuries. The first skyscrapers were built, and mass transit systems were developed.

The **Harlem Renaissance** literary and artistic movement began. African Americans left the rural South and migrated to the North in search of opportunity, and many settled in Harlem in New York City. By the 1920s Harlem had become a center of life and activity. The artistic expressions that emerged from this community in the 1920s and 1930s celebrated black experience, black traditions, and the voices of black America. Major writers and works of this movement included Langston Hughes (*The Weary Blues*), Nella Larsen (*Passing*), Zora Neale Hurston (*Their Eyes Were Watching God*), Claude McKay, Countee Cullen, and Jean Toomer.

The **Eighteenth Amendment**, known as the **Prohibition Amendment,** which had been ratified in 1917 and prohibited selling alcoholic beverages throughout the U.S. led to a rise in

> http://www.pbs.org/jazz/exchange/exchange_speakeasies.htm
> PBS Speakeasies

bootlegging, organized gangster crime, and the creation of **speakeasies**. The Charleston dance and the "flapper look" were popular.

The decade was a time of optimism and exploration of new boundaries. It was a clear movement in many ways away from conventionalism. The jazz musical style perfectly typified the mood of society. Jazz is essentially free-flowing improvisation on a simple theme with a four-beat rhythm. Jazz originated in the poor districts of New Orleans as an outgrowth of the Blues. The leading jazz musicians of the time included: Buddy Bolden, Joseph "King" Oliver, Duke Ellington, Louis Armstrong, and Jelly Roll Morton.

The era of the **Big Band** appeared by the mid-1920s and developed into **Swing Jazz** by the early 1930s. Some notable musicians were Bing Crosby, Frank Sinatra, Don Redman, Fletcher Henderson, Count Basie, Benny Goodman, Billie Holiday, Ella Fitzgerald, and The Dorsey Brothers.

In painting and sculpture, the new direction of the decade was **realism**. In the early years of the twentieth century, American artists had developed several realist styles.

The Eight or **The Ashcan School** developed around the work and style of Robert Henri. Their subjects were everyday urban life that was presented without adornment or glamour. **The American Scene painters** produced a tight, detailed style of painting that focused on images of American life that were understandable to all. In the Midwest, a school within this group was called **regionalism**. One of the leading artists of regionalism was **Grant Wood**, best known for *American Gothic.* Other important realists of the day were **Edward Hopper** and **Georgia O'Keeffe**.

Many Americans favored isolating the country from world affairs, and in 1920, the **Nineteenth Amendment** guaranteeing women the right to vote was ratified. Roles and opportunities for women grew, and more of them sought careers outside the home. **Amelia Earhart** flew solo across the Atlantic; **Greta Garbo** was a favorite movie star; Jeanette Rankin was a pacifist, politician, and social activist who helped make sure the Nineteenth Amendment passed.

In Tennessee, William Jennings Bryan, three-time presidential candidate for the Southern Democrats, led the Fundamentalist position for banishing Darwin's theory of evolution. **H. L.**

http://www.npr.org/templates/story/story.php?storyId=4723956 NPR Scopes Monkey Trial

Mencken, editor of the *American Mercury* and reporter for *The Baltimore Sun*, covered the story of the "**Monkey Trial**" in which young biology teacher **John Scopes** was defended by **Clarence Darrow**, and then fined $100 for teaching evolution in a Tennessee science class.

The **National Origins Act of 1924** also known as **Johnson-Reed Act** limited immigration to two percent of the number of foreign-born persons of any nationality that had been in the United States in 1890. Asians were prohibited, and there were far fewer Italians admitted than Germans. Following the war and the Bolshevik Revolution in Russia, there was fear of anarchists, communists and immigrants

The decade witnessed an increase in a religious tradition known as "revivalism" or emotional preaching.

Although law and order were demanded by many Americans, the administration of **President Warren G. Harding** was marked by widespread corruption and scandal. President Harding promised a return to "normalcy" following World War I. But under his administration was the **Teapot Dome** scandal when his Secretary of the Interior Albert Fall made a secret deal with two oilmen to pump oil out of the fields and sell it for themselves and reward him. Others in Harding's "Ohio Gang" accepted bribes. The stress of learning about his friends may have been the cause for his heart attack that took Harding's life and put his Vice President **Calvin Coolidge** into the presidency.

During the war, about nine million people in the nation were employed in war-related industries. An additional four million were serving in the military. When the war ended, most of these people were without jobs. There was a small depression in 1920-21. Two groups were highly visible at the time: the **International Workers of the World** (IWW) and the **Socialist Party** led by **Eugene Debs**.

A huge wave of labor strikes sought a return to wartime working conditions when the workday was shorter, wages were higher, and conditions were better. Many labor strikes were violent. Many viewed the early strikes as the work of radicals, who were labeled "reds" (communists). As the news spread and other strikes occurred, the **Red Scare** swept the country. Some Americans feared a Bolshevik-type revolution in America. As a result, people were jailed for expressing views that were considered anarchist, communist or socialist. In an attempt to control the potential for revolution, civil liberties were ignored and thousands deported. The Socialist party came to be viewed as a group of anarchist radicals.

Several state and local governments passed a variety of laws designed to reduce radical speech and activity. Congress considered more than 70 anti-sedition bills, though none was passed. Within a year, the Red Scare had essentially run its course.

Marcus Garvey, an English-educated Jamaican, established an organization to build black nationalism and independence

http://www.pbs.org/wgbh/amex/garvey/
PBS Marcus Garvey

called the **Universal Negro Improvement Association** (**UNIA**). By 1920 followers numbered about four million, and by the early 1920s, there were 700 branches established in 38 states.

The **Ku Klux Klan** (KKK) was formed in 1866 by veterans of the Confederate Army seeking to resist Reconstruction. Beliefs encompassed white supremacy, anti-Semitism, racism, anti-Catholicism and nativism. Typical methods of intimidation have included terrorism, violence, and cross-burning. The Klan enjoyed a renaissance beginning in 1915. Using the new film medium, they spread its message with **D.W. Griffith's *The Birth of a Nation***. Klan members published a number of anti-Semitic newspaper articles. Its membership did not begin to decline until the Great Depression. Although the KKK began in the South, its membership at its peak extended into the Midwest, the Northern states, and even into Canada. Membership during the 1920s reached approximately four million—20 percent of the adult white male population in many regions and as high as 40 percent in some areas. The political influence of the group was significant since members essentially controlled the governments of Tennessee, Indiana, Oklahoma, and Oregon as well as some southern legislatures.

The **National Association for the Advancement of Colored People (NAACP)** was incorporated in 1911. One struggle was to eliminate **Jim Crow** laws, and members protested **The Birth of a Nation.** The NAACP helped **to** enable black men to become officers in the military during WWI. The group organized voters to oppose Woodrow Wilson's efforts to weave racial segregation into federal government policy. During the 1920s the NAACP was led by **James Weldon Johnson** to combat lynchings, and in the 1930s it led support for the **Scottsboro Boys**, accused of rapes they did not commit.

The **American Civil Liberties Union** was formed in 1920. It was an outgrowth of the American Union Against Militarism which had opposed American involvement in WWI and provided legal advice and assistance for conscientious objectors and those who were being prosecuted under the Espionage Act of 1917 and the Sedition Act of 1918. The agency attempted to:

- Protect immigrants threatened with deportation and citizens threatened with prosecution for communist activities
- Oppose efforts to repress the Industrial Workers of the World and other labor unions

The Anti-Defamation League was created in 1913 to stop discrimination against Jewish people. Its charter states: "Its ultimate purpose is to secure justice and fair treatment to all citizens alike and to put an end forever to unjust and unfair discrimination against ridicule of any sect or body of citizens." The organization has historically opposed all groups considered anti-Semitic or racist, including the Ku Klux Klan.

The Great Depression

The **1929 Stock Market Crash** was the powerful event that generally marks the beginning of the **Great Depression** in America. Although the crash of the Stock Market was unexpected, it was not without identifiable causes. The 1920s had been a decade of social and economic growth. But the attitudes and actions of the 1920s regarding wealth, production, and investment created several trends that quietly set the stage for the 1929 disaster.

The stock market crash of 1929 meant financial ruin for many investors, a weakening of the nation's economy, and fuel for the Great Depression of the 1930s. The Depression resulted in bank failures, loss of jobs due to cutbacks in production, and a lack of money leading to a sharp decline in spending. This affected businesses, factories, and stores. Farm products were no longer affordable, and so farmers suffered. Foreign trade sharply decreased, and in the early 1930s, the U.S. and European economies were effectively paralyzed.

Uneven distribution of wealth:

In the 1920s, the distribution of wealth between the rich and the middle-class was grossly disproportionate. In 1929, the combined income of the top 0.1 percent of the population was equal to the combined income of the bottom 42 percent. The top 0.1 percent of the population controlled 34 percent of all savings, while 80 percent of American had no savings.

Between 1920 and 1929, the top 0.1 percent of the population enjoyed an increase in disposable income of 75 percent; for the rest of the population, the increase was 9 percent. Average worker productivity in manufacturing increased 32 percent during this period, yet wages in manufacturing increased only 8 percent. As production costs fell and prices remained constant, profits soared. Many believed that capitalism was enriching the wealthy at the expense of the workers.

The legislative and executive branches during Coolidge's presidency tended to favor business and the wealthy. The **Revenue Act of 1926** significantly reduced income taxes for the wealthy. For example, a person with a million-dollar income would have seen taxes reduced from $600,000 to $200,000.

Despite the rise in members of labor unions, even the Supreme Court ruled in ways that further widened the gap between the rich and the middle class. In the case of **Adkins v. Children's Hospital** (1923), the Court ruled that minimum wage legislation was unconstitutional.

The distribution of wealth between the rich and the middle-class mirrors the uneven distribution of wealth between industries. In 1929, half of all corporate wealth was controlled by just 200 companies. The automotive industry was growing exceptionally quickly, but agriculture was steadily declining. In fact, in 1921 food prices dropped about 70 percent due to surplus. The average income in agriculture was only about one-third of the national average across all industries.

Disparity in distribution of wealth weakened the economy. The concept of buying on **credit** caught on quickly. Buying on credit, however, created artificial demand for products people would not have ordinarily afforded. This has three effects in time:

- Less need to purchase products because they have already been bought;
- Paying for previous purchases on credit makes it impossible to purchase new products.
- This results in a surplus of goods.

The economy also relied on investment and **luxury spending** by the rich in the 1920s. Luxury spending, however, only occurs when people are confident with regard to the economy and the future. Should these people lose confidence, that luxury spending would come to an abrupt halt. This is precisely what happened when the stock market crashed in 1929.

Investing in business produces returns for the investor, and during the 1920s, investing was very healthy. Investors, however, began to expect greater returns on their investments. This led many to make speculative investments in risky opportunities.

Two industries, **automotive** and **radio**, drove the economy in the 1920s. The government tended to support new industries rather than support agriculture.

During WWI, the government had subsidized farms and paid high prices for grains. Farmers had been encouraged to buy and farm more land and to use new technology to increase production to feed much of Europe during and in the aftermath of the war. When the war ended, these farm policies were cut off. Prices plummeted, farmers fell into debt, and farm prices declined. The agriculture industry was on the brink of ruin before the stock market crash.

The concentration of production and economic stability in the automotive industry and the production and sale of radios was expected to last forever. But there came a point when the growth of an industry slowed due to market saturation. When these two industries declined, due to decreased demand, they caused the collapse of other industries upon which they were dependent (e.g., rubber tires, glass, fuel).

Risky speculative investments in the stock market contributed to the stock market crash of 1929. Stock market speculation was spectacular throughout the 1920s. In 1929, shares traded on the New York Stock Exchange reached 1,124,800,410. In 1928 and 1929, stock prices doubled and tripled. For example, RCA stock prices rose from 85 to 420 within one year. The opportunity to achieve such profits was irresistible.

In much the same way that buying goods on credit became popular, **buying stock on margin** allowed people to invest a very small amount of money in the hope of receiving exceptional profit. This created an investing craze that drove the market higher and higher. But brokers also charged higher interest rates on margin loans (nearly 20 percent). If the price of the stock dropped, the investor owed the broker the amount borrowed plus interest. Another factor contributing to the Great Depression was that in 1929, the Federal Reserve increased interest rate.

In September 1929, stock prices began to slip somewhat, yet people remained optimistic. On Monday, October 21, prices began to fall quickly. The volume traded was so high that the tickers were unable to keep up. Investors started selling quickly. This caused further collapse. But for the next two days, prices stabilized somewhat.

On **Black Thursday**, October 24, prices plummeted again, and on Monday the 28th, prices declined by 13 percent in one day. The next day, **Black Tuesday, October 29**, saw 16.4 million shares traded. Stock prices fell so far that many were unwilling to buy at any price.

When the stock market crashed, banks and other businesses collapsed. Without demand for products, other businesses and industries collapsed. This set in motion a domino effect, bringing down the businesses and industries that provided raw materials or components to these industries. Unemployment quickly reached 25 percent nationwide. Hundreds of thousands became jobless. The jobless often became homeless. Desperation prevailed.

People thrown out of their homes created makeshift domiciles of cardboard, scraps of wood and tents. With unmasked reference to President Hoover, who was quite obviously overwhelmed by the situation and incompetent to deal with it, these communities were called "**Hoovervilles.**"

Families stood in bread lines, rural workers left the plains to search for work in California, and banks failed. More than 100,000 businesses failed between 1929 and 1932.

Economic disaster was furthered by **natural disaster**. The Florida Keys were hit by the **Labor Day Hurricane** in 1935. This was one of only three hurricanes in history to make landfall as a Category 5 storm. More than 400 died in the storm, including 200 WWI veterans who were building bridges for a public works project. In the Northeast, the **Great Hurricane of 1938** struck Long Island, causing more than 600 fatalities, demolishing much of Long Island, and resulting in millions of dollars in damage to the coast from New York City to Boston.

By far the worst natural disaster of the decade came to be known as the **Dust Bowl.** The severe and prolonged drought in the Great Plains and inappropriate farming techniques led to a series of dust storms in the 1930s. Plowing the plains removed the grass and exposed the soil. When the drought occurred, the soil dried out and became dust. Crops were ruined, the land was destroyed, and people either lost or abandoned homes and farms. Between 1934 and 1939 winds blew the soil to the east, all the way to the Atlantic Ocean. The dust storms, called "black blizzards" created huge clouds of dust that were visible all the way to Chicago.

In Texas, Arkansas, Oklahoma, New Mexico, Kansas and Colorado over half a million people were homeless. Fifteen percent of Oklahoma's population left. Estimates of the number of people displaced by this disaster range from 300,000 or 400,000 to 2.5 million. The migrants came to be called "**Okies**" no matter where they came from. Many of these people journeyed west in the hope of making a new life in California.

President Herbert Hoover was urged to provide government relief. He responded by urging the nation to be patient. By the time he signed relief bills in 1932, it was too late.

The New Deal

During President Hoover's first campaign, Prohibition and religion had been the primary concerns. Hoover had run against **Al Smith**, a Catholic, on the slogan "A chicken in every pot and a car in every garage," and he'd favored continuing Prohibition.

Hoover's bid for re-election in 1932 failed. **Franklin D. Roosevelt** won the White House on his promise to the American people of a "new deal."

One aim of Roosevelt's "**New Deal**" programs was to provide relief to hard-hit workers by providing government-sponsored work programs such as the Civilian Conservation Corps. This contrasted with Hoover, who believed that the government should neither provide direct aid to citizens nor be directly involved in the economy.

Upon assuming the office, Roosevelt and his advisers immediately launched a massive program of innovation and experimentation to bring the Depression to an end. Congress gave the President unprecedented power to act. During the next eight years, the most extensive and broadly-based legislation in the nation's history was enacted. The legislation was intended to accomplish three goals: **relief, recovery, and reform.**

The first step in the "**New Deal**" was to relieve suffering. This was accomplished through a number of job-creation projects. The second step, the recovery aspect, was to stimulate the economy. The third step was to create social and economic change through innovative legislation. **The National Recovery Administration** attempted to accomplish several goals:

- Restore employment
- Increase general purchasing power
- Provide character-building activity for unemployed youth
- Encourage decentralization of industry and thus divert population from crowded cities to rural or semi-rural communities
- Develop river resources in the interest of navigation and cheap power
- Complete flood control on a permanent basis
- Enlarge the national program of forest protection and to develop forest resources
- Control farm production and improve farm prices
- Assist home builders and home owners
- Restore public faith in banking and trust operations
- Recapture the value of physical assets, whether in real property, securities, or other investments.

Among the "**alphabet organizations**" set up to work out the details of the recovery plan:

- **Agricultural Adjustment Administration (AAA)** designed to readjust agricultural production and prices, thereby boosting farm income
- **Civilian Conservation Corps (CCC)** designed to provide wholesome, useful activity in the forestry service to unemployed young men
- **Works Progress Administration (WPA)** designed to move individuals from relief rolls to work projects or private employment
- **Tennessee Valley Authority (TVA)** designed to improve the navigability of the Tennessee River and increase productivity of the timber and farm lands in its valley; built 16 dams that provided water control and hydroelectric generation
- **Public Works Administration (PWA)** along with the **Civil Works Administration (CWA)**, employed Americans on over 34,000 public works projects at a cost of more than $4 billion. Among these projects was the construction of a highway that linked the Florida Keys and Miami, the Boulder Dam (now the **Hoover Dam**) and numerous highway projects.

To provide economic stability and prevent another crash, Congress passed the **Glass-Steagall Act**, which separated banking and investing. The **Securities and Exchange Commission** (SEC) was created to regulate dangerous speculative practices on Wall Street. The **Wagner Act** guaranteed a number of rights to workers and unions in an effort to improve worker-employer relations. The **Social Security Act of 1935** established pensions as well as a system of unemployment insurance.

Regulating business operations, from activities of corporations to labor problems, included:

- Protecting bank depositors and the credit system of the country
- Employing gold resources and currency adjustments to aid permanent restoration of normal living
- Establishing a line of subsistence below which no useful citizen would be permitted to sink

During the first 100 days in office, the Roosevelt Administration responded to this crisis with programs designed to restore ecological balance. One action was the formation of the **Soil Conservation Service** (now the Natural Resources Conservation Service).

The story of this natural disaster and its toll in human suffering is poignantly preserved in the photographs of **Dorothea Lange**.

The deaths of the WWI veterans in the Labor Day Hurricane resulted in a Congressional investigation into possible negligence. The Central Valley Project upset farmers who lost tillable land and some water supply because of the construction of the Hoover Dam. Tennesseans were concerned with the changes in river flow and navigation when the Tennessee Valley Authority began its construction of dams and the directing of water to form reservoirs and to power hydroelectric plants. Some businesses and business leaders did not appreciate minimum wage laws; restrictions and controls on working conditions; and limitation of work hours. The numerous import/export tariffs of the period were also controversial.

In the long view, however, much that was accomplished under the New Deal had positive long-term effects on economic, ecological, social and political issues for the next several decades. The Tennessee Valley Authority and the Central Valley Project in California provided a reliable source and supply of water to major cities, as well as electrical power to meet the needs of an increasingly electricity-dependent society. For the middle class and the poor, the labor regulations, the establishment of the **Social Security Administration**, and the separation of investment and banking have served the nation for more than six decades.

Organized Labor

Because the **National Recovery Administration** lacked clarity regarding unions, Congress passed the **Wagner Act** (The National Labor Relations Act), which established:

- a legal basis for unions
- set collective bargaining as a matter of national policy required by the law
- provided for secret ballot elections for choosing unions
- protected union members from employer intimidation and coercion

This law was later amended by the **Taft-Hartley Act** (1947), which listed unfair labor practices on the part of unions, and by the **Landrum Griffin Act** (1959) which contains a bill of rights for union members. The Wagner Act was upheld by the Supreme Court in 1937, but the National Recovery Act was declared unconstitutional in 1935.

One of the most common tactics of the union was the **strike**. Half a million Southern mill workers walked off the job in the Great Uprising of 1934, establishing the precedent that without workers, industry could not move forward. Then, in 1936, the United Rubber Workers staged the first **sit-down strike** where instead of walking off the job, they stayed at their posts but refused to work. The **United Auto Workers** used the sit-down strike against General Motors in 1936.

Strikes were met with varying degrees of resistance by the companies. Sometimes, "**scabs**" were brought in to replace the striking workers. In 1936, the **Anti-Strikebreaker Act** (the Byrnes Act) made it illegal to transport or aid strikebreakers in interstate or foreign trade. In part this was an attempt to stem the violence often associated with management's attempts to bully the workers back into their jobs.

As the leaders of industry were often powerful community figures, they sometimes employed law enforcement to disrupt the strikes. During a strike in 1937 of the Steel Workers Organizing Committee against Republic Steel, police attacked a crowd gathered in support of the strike, killing ten and injuring eighty. This came to be called **The Memorial Day Massacre**.

A number of acts were designed to provide fair compensation and other benefits to workers. The **Davis-Bacon Act**, passed in 1931 provided that employers of contractors and subcontractors on public construction should be paid the prevailing wages. States also provided measures. Wisconsin created the first unemployment insurance act in the country in 1932.

The Public Contracts Act or **Walsh-Healey Act** of 1936 established labor standards, including minimum wages, overtime pay, child and convict labor provisions, and safety standards on federal contracts.

The **Fair Labor Standards** Act created a $0.25 minimum wage, stipulated time-and-a-half pay for hours over 40 per week. The Social Security Act was approved in 1935.

The Supreme Court upheld the **Railway Labor Act** in 1930, including its prohibition of employer interference or coercion in the choice of bargaining representatives.

The **Guffey Act** stabilized the coal industry and improved labor conditions in 1935, but a year later it was declared unconstitutional because it enabled the federal government to control prices.

General Motors recognized the **United Auto Workers** and US Steel recognized the **Steel Workers Organizing Committee**, both in 1937. Then in 1938 Merchant Marine Act created a **Federal Maritime Labor Board**.

One of labor's biggest unions was formed in 1935. The **Committee for Industrial Organization (CIO)** was formed within the **American Federated Labor Union (AFL)** to carry unionism to the industrial sector. By 1937, however, the CIO had been expelled from the AFL over charges of dual unionism or competition. It then became known as the **Congress of Industrial Organizations**.

Federal labor efforts included:

- The Anti-Injunction Act of 1932 which prohibited federal injunctions in most labor disputes.
- The Wagner-Peyser Act which created the United States Employment Service within the Department of Labor in 1933.
- The Secretary of Labor in 1934 calling for the first National Labor Legislation Conference to get better cooperation between the federal government and the states in defining a national labor legislation program.
- The U.S. joining the International Labor Organization (also in 1934).
- National Apprenticeship Act establishing the Bureau of Apprenticeship within the Department of Labor in 1937.

Many of the steps taken by the Roosevelt administration alleviated the economic disaster of the Great Depression, enacted controls to mitigate the risk of another stock market crash, and provided greater security for workers. The nation's economy, however, did not fully recover until America entered World War II.

Skill 1.1j   Second World War

World War II: 1939 to 1945

After the war began in Europe, U.S. President Franklin D. Roosevelt announced that the United States would remain neutral. Most Americans, although hoping for an Allied victory, wanted the U.S. to stay out of the war.

President Roosevelt and his supporters were called "**interventionists**" because they favored all aid--except outright war--to the Allied nations fighting Axis aggression. Interventionists were concerned that an Axis victory would seriously endanger all democracies. Roosevelt's plan was to defeat the Axis nations by sending the Allied nations the equipment needed to fight--ships, aircraft, tanks, and other war materials.

The American Neutrality Act was amended In November of 1939 to permit the Allies to have "cash and carry" purchases.

Between 1941 and 1945, under the **Land Lease** project, more than $50 billion worth of supplies were shipped to the allies.

The "**isolationists**" were against any U.S. aid being given to the warring nations and accused President Roosevelt of leading an unprepared United States into a war. America First Committee with spokesman Charles A. Lindbergh said that it was best to stay out of the war in Europe, and that:

- The United States must build an invulnerable national defense
- No foreign power, nor group of powers, can successfully attack an America that is prepared
- American democracy can be preserved only by keeping out of the war in Europe
- "Aid short of war" weakens national defense at home and threatens to involve America in war abroad.

When Japan invaded China in 1937, the United States stopped exports to Japan. Japan's industry depended on importing petroleum, scrap metal, and other raw materials. Then Roosevelt refused the Japanese request to withdraw its funds from American banks.

General Tojo became Japanese Premier in October 1941. The U.S. Navy was powerful enough to block Japanese expansion into Asia, and on December 7, 1941, the Japanese bombed the U. S. Pacific Fleet, at anchor in **Pearl Harbor** in Hawaii, destroying many aircraft and disabling much of the U.S. Pacific Fleet.

Germany and Japan had created the **Tipartite Pact** which formalized the Axis Powers. The Pact said that except for the USSR, any country that attacked an Axis Power would be at war with all three. The day after the attack at Pearl Harbor, the United States declared war on Japan. On the 11th, Germany and Italy declared war on the United States, and then on the 13th, Hungary and Bulgaria declared war, also.

Before the war, Hitler and Stalin had signed a **non-aggression pact** in 1939—that indicated Germany and the USSR would split up Poland and eastern Europe between them. Hitler violated the agreement in 1941 by invading the Soviet Union.

Military strategy in the European theater of war as developed by Roosevelt, **Winston Churchill**, and **Josef Stalin** was to concentrate on Germany's defeat first, then Japan's.

Beginning in the summer of 1942, an Allied push began in **North Africa** to drive the Axis forces off the continent, ending successfully in May of 1943. While the Allies drove them out of Africa, the German army suffered a major defeat at **Stalingrad.** German troops died by starvation and freezing trapped in winter conditions. It marked a turning point in the war.

The liberation of Italy began in July 1943 and ended on May 2, 1945. The third part of the strategy was **D-Day, June 6, 1944**, with the Allied invasion of France at Normandy. At the same time, starting in January 1943, the Soviets began pushing the German troops back into Europe. By April 1945, Allies occupied positions beyond the Rhine, and the Soviets moved on to Berlin, surrounding it by April 25th. Germany surrendered on May 7th, and the war in Europe was finally over.

http://library.thinkquest.org/10826/yalta.htm
Yalta Conference -ThinkQuest

The **Yalta Conference** took place in Yalta in February 1945, between the Allied leaders Winston Churchill, Franklin Roosevelt and Joseph Stalin. With the defeat of Nazi Germany within sight, the three allies met to determine the shape of post-war Europe. Germany was to be divided into **four zones of occupation**, as was the capital city of **Berlin**. Germany was also to undergo demilitarization and to make reparations for the war. Poland was to remain under control of Soviet Russia. Roosevelt also received a promise from Stalin that the Soviet Union would join the new **United Nations**.

Following the surrender of Germany in May, 1945, the Allies called the **Potsdam Conference** in July, between

http://www.trumanlibrary.org/teacher/potsdam.htm
Truman Library - Potsdam

Clement Attlee, Harry Truman and Stalin. Goals were to finalize the administration of post-war Germany. The **Security Council** of the United Nations was determined to be the United States, United Kingdom, U.S.S.R., China, and France. Germany was demilitarized, and Japan was asked to surrender. "The alternative for Japan is prompt and utter destruction."

In the six months after it attacked Pearl Harbor, Japanese forces had moved across Southeast Asia and the western Pacific Ocean. By August 1942, the Japanese Empire stretched northeast to Alaska's Aleutian Islands, west to Burma, and south to what is now Indonesia. Invaded and controlled areas included Hong Kong, Guam, Wake Island, Thailand, part of Malaysia, Singapore, and the Philippines.

The raid of **General Doolittle**'s bombers on Japanese cities, the American naval victory at **Midway**, and the fighting in **the Battle of the Coral Sea** helped turn the tide against Japan. Island-hopping by the U.S. Seabees and Marines resulted in pushing the Japanese back.

The United States dropped two atomic bombs on the cities of **Hiroshima** and **Nagasaki** to finally end the war in the Pacific. Japan formally surrendered on September 2, 1945, aboard the U.S. battleship *Missouri*, anchored in Tokyo Bay.

The war was finally ended.

Allies agreed:

- Germany's armed forces would be abolished
- The Nazi Party outlawed
- Territory east of the Oder and Neisse Rivers taken away.
- Nazi leaders accused of war crimes would be brought to trial.
- Many Germans were relocated from areas of Germany and from territories that Germany had claimed in the war. Others in various Central and Eastern European countries were also relocated. The United States and U.K. viewed that as necessary to create ethnic homogeneity and prevent violence.

After Japan's defeat, the Allies began a military occupation directed by American **General Douglas MacArthur** who introduced a number of reforms:

- Ridding Japan of its military institutions
- Transforming it into a democracy.

A constitution was drawn up in 1947 that transferred all political rights from the emperor to the people. The constitution also granted women the right to vote, and denied Japan the right to declare war. War crimes trials of twenty-five war leaders and government officials were also conducted. The U.S. did not sign a peace treaty until 1951. The treaty permitted Japan to rearm in self-defense but took away its overseas empire.

The **United Nations** that was to work to promote peace around the earth was set up, and the charter was drawn up and signed by the four Allied powers in October 1945.

America and Minorities

The **Alien Registration Act** of 1940, also known as the **Smith Act**, required the fingerprinting and registration of all aliens over the age of 14. Aliens were also required to report any change of address within five days. Almost five million aliens registered under the provisions of this Act.

From the turn of the twentieth century, there was tension between Caucasians and Japanese in California. A series of laws were passed discouraging Japanese immigration and prohibiting land ownership by Japanese.

The Japanese attack on Pearl Harbor (December 7, 1941) raised suspicion that Japan was planning a full-scale attack on the West Coast. Many believed that American citizenship did not necessarily imply loyalty. Some authorities feared sabotage of both civilian and military facilities within the country.

By February 1942, presidential executive orders had authorized the arrest of all aliens suspected of subversive activities and the creation of exclusion zones where people could be isolated and held. Here, they could not damage national infrastructure. These **War Relocation Camps** were used to isolate about 120,000 Japanese and Japanese Americans (62 percent were citizens) during World War II.

The 442nd Regimental Combat Team was a unit composed of Japanese Americans who fought in Europe. This unit was the most highly decorated unit of its size in the history of the U.S. Army. This self-sufficient force served with great distinction in North Africa, Italy, southern France, and Germany. The medals earned by the group include 21 Congressional Medals of Honor (the highest award given). The unit was awarded 9,486 purple hearts for being wounded in battle. The casualty rate, combining those killed in action, missing in action, and wounded and removed from action, was 93 percent.

The Tuskegee Airmen were a group of African American aviators who made a major contribution to the war effort. Although they were not considered eligible for the gold wings of a Navy Pilot until 1948, these men completed standard Army flight classroom instruction and the required flying time. These fliers were the first blacks permitted to fly for the military. They flew more than 15,000 missions, destroyed over 1,000 German aircraft, and earned more than 150 Distinguished Flying Crosses and hundreds of Air Medals.

The Navajo Code Talkers have been credited with saving countless lives and accelerating the end of the war. There were over 400 Navajo Indians who served in all six Marine divisions from 1942 to 1945. At the time of WWII, fewer than 30 non-Navajos understood the Navajo language. Because it was a very complex language and because it was not a code, it was unbreakable by the Germans and the Japanese. The job of these men was to talk and transmit information on tactics, troop movements, orders and other vital military information. Not only was the enemy unable to understand the language, but it was far faster than translating messages into Morse Code. It is generally accepted that without the Navajo Code Talkers, Iwo Jima could not have been taken.

Some statistics on minority representation in the military during WWII:

African Americans	1,056,841
Chinese	13,311
Japanese	20,080
Hawaiians	1,320
Native Americans	19,567
Filipinos	11,506
Puerto Ricans	51,438

Statistics were not kept on how many Hispanics served in the war.

Advancements during WWII

Women served in the military as drivers, nurses, communications operators, clerks, soldiers, and pilots. The **Flight Nurses Corps** was created at the beginning of the war. War required people to build planes, tanks, ships, bombs, torpedoes, and other items. A vast campaign combining patriotism and emotions was launched to recruit women to these tasks. One of the most famous recruiting campaigns featured "**Rosie the Riveter**."

By the middle of 1944, more than 19 million women had entered the work force. Women built planes and tanks. Some operated large cranes to move heavy equipment; some loaded and fired machine guns and other weapons to ensure that they were in working order; some operated hydraulic presses; some were volunteer fire fighters; some were welders, riveters, drill press operators, and cab drivers. Women worked all manufacturing shifts making everything from clothing to fighter jets. Most women and their families tended "**Victory Gardens**" to produce food items that were in short supply.

The years between WWI and WWII produced significant advancement in aircraft technology, but the pace of aircraft development and production was dramatically increased during WWII. Major developments included:

- Flight-based weapon delivery systems such as the long-range bomber
- First jet fighter,
- First cruise missile
- First ballistic missile (although the cruise and ballistic missiles were not widely used during the war)
- Glider planes (heavily used in WWII because they were silent upon approach)
- Broad use of paratrooper units
- Hospital planes to extract the seriously wounded from the Front to hospitals for treatment.

Weapons and technology in other areas also improved rapidly during the war. These advances were critical in determining the outcome of the war. Used for the first time were:

- Radar
- Electronic computers
- New tank designs
- Nuclear weapons

More new inventions were registered for patents than ever before. Most of these new ideas were aimed to either kill or prevent being killed.

The war began with essentially the same weaponry that had been used in WWI. The aircraft carrier joined the battleship; the primary landing craft was invented; light tanks were developed to meet the needs of a changing battlefield; and other armored vehicles were developed. Submarines were also perfected during this period.

Numerous other weapons were also developed or invented to meet the needs of battle during WWII:

bazooka
rocket-propelled grenade
anti-tank weapons
assault rifles
the tank destroyer
mine-clearing Flail tanks
flame tanks
submersible tanks
cruise missiles
rocket artillery
air-launched rockets;
guided weapons
torpedoes
self-guiding weapons
napalm

The **atomic bomb** was surely the most profound military development of the war years. This invention made it possible for a single plane to carry a single bomb that was sufficiently powerful to destroy an entire city.

It was believed that the bomb would serve as a deterrent to any nation because then aggression against a nation with a bomb would be a decision for mass suicide. Developing and using nuclear weapons marked the beginning of a new age in warfare that created greater distance from the act of killing and eliminated the ability to minimize the effect of war on non-combatants.

The two nuclear bombs dropped in 1945 on Nagasaki and Hiroshima caused the immediate deaths of 100,000 to 200,000 people, and far more deaths over time. This has been a controversial decision. Those who opposed the use of the atom bomb argued that was an unnecessary act of mass killing, particularly of non-combatants. Proponents argued that it ended the war sooner, thus resulting in fewer casualties on both sides.

Regardless of the arguments, the U.S. nuclear weapons quickly led to the development of similar weapons by other nations. Fear of the effects of the use of these weapons included the fear of **radiation poisoning** and **nuclear winter**.

Skill 1.1k   Post-Second World War Period

Declaring itself "the arsenal of democracy", the U.S. entered the Second World War and emerged not only victorious, but also as the *strongest power* on the Earth. It would now have a permanent and leading place in world affairs.

After the war, the United States perceived its greatest threat to be the expansion of Communism in the world. To that end, it has devoted a larger and larger share of its foreign policy, diplomacy, and both economic and military might to combating it.

During World War II, the federal government had greater control over the economy and key institutions and services to ensure security. This led to a significant growth in both the reach and the size of the federal government.

The nation had faced two major crises: The Great Depression and World War. The government had assumed greater responsibility for ensuring the basic needs of its citizen[1]s, promoting economic opportunity for all, and managing economic growth. The government had also taken on the role of ensuring security of the nation against foreign enemies.

This marked the culmination of a major change in the role of the federal government that many have called "**the rise of the welfare state**". Since the First World War, regulatory agencies had been created to control the actions of big business, to protect labor, and to protect the rights and privileges of minorities. In addition, a truly national culture had emerged from the shared hardships, the growth of the railroad and the radio, the introduction of the automobile, and the war effort itself. These factors had smoothed out many of the regional differences that previously divided the social and cultural interests of the American people.

The attempts to bring the nation through both the Depression and the war had utilized much experimentation. Franklin Roosevelt and his administration drew upon past experience and experimentation to bring the nation through crisis. Roosevelt's use of the radio to speak to the American people in his "**fireside chats**" permitted him to rally the populace and persuade the public to consider new ideas and new approaches to the problems of the day. Essentially, Roosevelt convinced the nation that a more active role for the federal government both internationally and at home would prevent another depression and another world war.

This transition was important in American history and in the national ethos. Americans had traditionally distrusted a centralization of authority in the federal government. They had also traditionally repudiated international alliances and commitments. Yet both of these changes came about in the years following WWII.

In many ways, the period from 1945 to 1972 was a time of unprecedented prosperity for everyone in the nation. Wages increased, car and home ownership increased, and average educational levels increased when the veterans of the war took full advantage of the opportunity to receive a college education paid for by their **G.I benefits**. People were willing to give the government this major role in perpetuating this prosperous society.

Just as WWII had united the people in a common commitment to the purpose of supporting the troops and winning the war, they again rallied together to support the government in the Cold War.

Presidents of the 1950s and 1960s

Harry S. Truman. Truman became president near the end of WWII. He is credited with some of the most important decisions in history. When Japan refused to surrender, Truman authorized the dropping of atomic bombs on Japanese cities dedicated to war support: Hiroshima and Nagasaki.

Truman took to the Congress a 21-point plan that came to be known as the **Fair Deal**. It included:

- expansion of Social Security
- a full-employment program
- public housing
- slum clearance
- permanent Fair Employment Practices Act.

The Truman Doctrine provided support for Greece and Turkey when they were threatened by the Soviet Union. The **Marshall Plan** named for Secretary of State George Marshall, stimulated economic recovery for Western Europe. Truman participated in the negotiations that resulted in the formation of the **North Atlantic Treaty Organization (NATO)**. He and his administration believed it necessary to support South Korea when it was threatened by the communist government of North Korea. But he contained American involvement in Korea so as not to risk conflict with China or Russia.

Dwight David Eisenhower succeeded Truman. Eisenhower obtained a truce in Korea and worked during his two terms to mitigate the tension of the Cold War. When Stalin died, he was able to negotiate a peace treaty with Russia that neutralized Austria. His domestic policy was a middle road. He continued most of the programs introduced under both the New Deal and the Fair Deal. When desegregation of schools began, he sent troops to **Little Rock, Arkansas** to enforce desegregation of the schools. He ordered the complete **desegregation of the military**. During his administration, the Departments of Health, Education and Welfare were established and the **National Aeronautics and Space Administration** was formed.

John F. Kennedy is widely remembered for his Inaugural Address in which the statement was made, "Ask not what your country can do for you—ask what you can do for your country." His campaign pledge was to get America moving again. During his brief presidency, his economic programs created the longest period of continuous expansion in the country since WWII. He wanted the U.S. to again take up the mission as the first country committed to the evolution of human rights. Through the **Alliance for Progress** and the **Peace Corps**, the hopes and idealism of the nation reached out to assist developing nations. He was deeply involved in the cause of equal rights for all Americans, and he drafted new civil rights legislation. He also drafted plans for a broad attack on the systemic problems of poverty. He believed the arts were critical to a society and instituted programs to support the arts.

Lyndon B. Johnson assumed the presidency after the assassination of Kennedy in 1963. His vision for America was called "**A Great Society**." He won support in Congress for the largest group of legislative programs in the history of the nation. These included programs Kennedy had been working on at the time of his death, including a new civil rights bill and a tax cut. He defined the "**great society**" as "a place where the meaning of man's life matches the marvels of man's labor." The legislation enacted during his administration included an attack on disease, **urban renewal**, **Medicare**, aid to education, conservation and beautification, development of economically depressed areas, the **War on Poverty**, voting rights for all, and control of crime and delinquency. Johnson managed an unpopular military action in **Vietnam** and encouraged the exploration of space. During his administration, the Department of Transportation was formed and the first African-American, **Thurgood Marshall**, was nominated and confirmed to the Supreme Court.

Korean War

The first "hot war" in the post-World War II era was the Korean War, begun June 25, 1950 and ending July 27, 1953. It was the first war in which a world organization played a major military role and it presented quite a challenge to the UN, which had only been in existence five years.

Troops from Communist North Korea invaded democratic South Korea in an effort to unite both sections under Communist control. The United Nations asked member nations to furnish troops to help restore peace. Many nations responded and President Truman sent American troops to help the South Koreans. The war dragged on for three years and ended with a truce, not a peace treaty. Korea remains divided to this day.

Korea was under control of Japan from 1895 to the end of the Second World War in 1945. At war's end, the Soviet and U.S. military troops moved into Korea with the U.S. troops in the southern half and the Soviet troops in the northern half with the **38 degree North Latitude** line as the boundary.

The **General Assembly** of the UN in 1947 ordered elections throughout all of Korea to select one government for the entire country. The Soviet Union would not allow the North Koreans to vote, so they set up a Communist government. The South Koreans set up a democratic government, but both claimed the entire country. At times, there were clashes between Korean troops from 1948 to 1950. After the U.S. removed its remaining troops in 1949 and announced in early 1950 that Korea was not part of its defense line in Asia, the Communists decided to act and invaded South Korea.

Participants in Korea were: North and South Korea, United States of America, Australia, New Zealand, China, Canada, France, Great Britain, Turkey, Belgium, Ethiopia, Colombia, Greece, South Africa, Luxembourg, Thailand, the Netherlands, and the Philippines.

http://www.koreanwar-educator.org/home.htm   Korean War Educator

The war began June 25, 1950 and ended July 27, 1953.

A truce was drawn up and an armistice agreement was signed ending the fighting. A permanent treaty of peace has never been signed, and the country remains divided between the Communist North and the democratic South, and the war destroyed villages and homes, displacing and/or killing millions of people.

Cuban Missile Crisis

In 1962, during the administration of President **John F. Kennedy**, Premier **Nikita Khrushchev** and the Soviets decided to install nuclear missiles on the island as a protective measure for Cuba against an American invasion. In October, American U-2 spy planes photographed over Cuba what were identified as missile bases under construction, touching off the **Cuban Missile Crisis**.

Because both the U.S. and U.S.S.R. had nuclear weapons, a week of tension and anxiety gripped the entire world.

The Soviets were concerned about American missiles installed in Turkey and aimed at the Soviet Union. They were also concerned about an invasion of Cuba which had just experienced a change in its power structure. If successful, Khrushchev would demonstrate to the Russian and Chinese critics of his policy of peaceful coexistence that he was tough and not to be intimidated.

At the same time, the Americans feared that if Russian missiles were put in place and launched from Cuba to the U.S., the short distance of 90 miles would not allow enough time for adequate warning. Furthermore, it would originate from a direction that radar systems could not detect. If America allowed Soviet presence, American security was endangered.

President Kennedy had not attempted to prevent the erection of the **Berlin Wall** and was reluctant to commit American troops to invade Cuba. The Soviets assumed this was a weakness and decided they could install the missiles without any interference.

The only recourse was removal of the missile sites and preventing more being set up. Kennedy announced that the U.S. had set up a "quarantine" of Soviet ships heading to Cuba. It was in reality a blockade, but the word itself could not be used publicly as a blockade was actually considered an act of war. Soviet ships carrying missiles for the Cuban bases turned back, and the crisis eased.

The missiles in Turkey were removed. A telephone "**hot line**" was set up between Moscow and Washington to make it possible for the two heads of government to have instant contact with each other. The U.S. agreed to sell its surplus wheat to the Soviets.

The Civil Rights Movement

The economic boom following the war led to prosperity for many Americans in the 1950s. However, this prosperity did not extend to the poor blacks of the South. Efforts began to end discrimination in education, housing, and jobs, and to end widespread poverty.

Taking inspiration from similar struggles in India at the time led by **Mahatma Ghandi**, the Civil Rights movement began to gain momentum.

Key people in the Civil Rights movement are:

Rosa Parks - A black seamstress from Montgomery Alabama who, in 1955, refused to give up her seat on the bus to a white man. This event is generally understood as the spark that lit the fire of the Civil Rights Movement. She has been generally regarded as the "mother of the Civil Rights Movement."

Martin Luther King, Jr. - The most prominent member of the Civil Rights movement. King promoted **nonviolent** methods of opposition to segregation. His "**Letter from Birmingham Jail**" explains nonviolent action and injustice to the clergy of Birmingham, Alabama.

King led the march on Washington in 1963, at which he delivered his "**I Have a Dream**" speech.

He received the 1968 Nobel Prize for Peace.

He was assassinated in 1968 in Memphis, Tennessee.

James Meredith – The first African American to enroll at the University of Mississippi.

Emmett Till – A teenage boy who was murdered in Mississippi while visiting from Chicago. The crime of which he was accused was "whistling at a white woman in a store." He was beaten and murdered, and his body was dumped in a river. His two white abductors were apprehended and tried. They were acquitted by an all-white jury. After the acquittal, they admitted their guilt, but remained free because of double jeopardy laws. His death became one of the key events in the movement.

Ralph Abernathy – A major figure in the Civil Rights Movement who succeeded Martin Luther King, Jr. as head of the Southern Christian Leadership Conference

Malcolm X – On February 27,1946, Malcolm began serving his sentence at the Massachusetts State Prison for theft. His family had been the target of Black Legion, a white supremacist group who he believed killed his father, Earl Little.
Malcolm X was a black nationalist, and became a prominent Black Muslim.

Stokely Carmichael – A leader who called for independent development of political and social institutions for blacks, Carmichael called for black pride and maintenance of black culture. He was head of the Student Nonviolent Coordinating Committee, participated in the Freedom Rides, and coined the term "Black Power."

Adam Clayton Powell – A leader in the Harlem civil rights movement who led efforts for jobs and housing and was chairman of the **Coordinating Committee for Employment.** Powell's rent strikes and campaigns increased the hiring of black workers. Among other events, Powell organized a bus boycott in 1940 that led to more hiring, and he fought also to have black hired in Harlem pharmacies.

Jesse Jackson – A young man when King selected him as head of the Chicago Operation Breadbasket in 1966, Jackson went on to organize boycotts to pressure businesses to hire blacks for jobs and to work with black contractors.

Key events of the Civil Rights movement include:

Brown vs. Board of Education, 1954

Rosa Parks and the Montgomery Bus Boycott, 1955-56 – After refusing to give up her seat on a bus in Montgomery, Alabama, Parks was arrested, tried, and convicted of disorderly conduct and violating a local ordinance. When word reached the black community a bus boycott was organized to protest the segregation of blacks and whites on public buses. The boycott lasted 381 days, until the ordinance was lifted.

Strategy shift to "direct action" – nonviolent resistance and civil disobedience, 1955 – 1965. This action consisted of bus boycotts, sit-ins, **freedom rides**. **Formation of the Southern Christian Leadership Conference, 1957.** This group was formed by Martin Luther King, Jr.; John Duffy; Rev. C. D. Steele; Rev. T. J. Jemison; Rev. Fred Shuttlesworth; Ella Baker; A. Philip Randolph; Bayard Rustin; and Stanley Levison. The group provided training and assistance to local efforts to fight segregation. Non-violence was its central doctrine and its major method of fighting segregation and racism.

The Desegregation of Little Rock, 1957

Following the decision of the Supreme Court in *Brown vs. Board of Education*, the Arkansas school board voted to integrate the school system. The NAACP chose Arkansas as the place to push integration because it was considered a relatively progressive Southern state. Governor Orval Faubus called up the National Guard to prevent nine black students from attending Little Rock's Central High School.

President Eisenhower then federalized the Arkansas National Guard, who were then ordered back to their armories.

Sit-ins – In 1960, students began to stage "sit-ins" at local lunch counters and stores as a means of protesting the refusal of those businesses to desegregate. The first was in Greensboro, North Carolina. This led to similar campaigns throughout the South. Demonstrators began to protest segregation of parks, beaches, theaters, museums, and libraries. When arrested, the protesters made "jail-no-bail" pledges. This put the financial burden of providing jail space and food on the cities.

Freedom Rides – Activists traveled by bus throughout the South to desegregate bus terminals. These protesters undertook dangerous protests. Many buses were firebombed, and protestors were attacked by the KKK and beaten. They were crammed into small, airless jail cells and mistreated in many ways. Key figures in this effort included John Lewis, James Lawson, Diane Nash, Bob Moses, James Bevel, Charles McDew, Bernard Lafayette, Charles Jones, Lonnie King, Julian Bond, Hosea Williams, and Stokely Carmichael.

The Birmingham Campaign, 1963-64. A campaign was planned to use sit-ins, kneel-ins in churches, and a march to the county building to launch a voter registration campaign. The City obtained an injunction forbidding all such protests. The protesters, including Martin Luther King, Jr., believed the injunction was unconstitutional, and defied it. They were arrested. While in jail, King wrote his famous "Letter from Birmingham Jail."

Students left school to protest Reverend King's being jailed. This was called the **"Children's Crusade."** More than 600 students skipped school and were jailed. The next day a thousand students joined the protest, and police dogs were brought out, and fire hoses were used to knock them down.

The media broadcast vivid pictures to the nation. While this resulted in the Kennedy administration's intervention, the motel where the members of the SCLC were staying was burned, and four months later, the Ku Klux Klan bombed a black church **Sixteenth Street Baptist Church**, killing four girls who were attending Sunday School that morning. Two years later, J. Edgar Hoover, Director of the FBI, closed the case, saying that conviction would be "remote."

The March on Washington, 1963. This was a march on Washington for jobs and freedom. It was a combined effort of all major civil rights organizations. The goals of the march were:

- meaningful civil rights laws
- a massive federal works program
- full and fair employment
- decent housing
- the right to vote
- adequate integrated education

It was at this march that Martin Luther King, Jr. made the famous "I Have a Dream" speech.

Mississippi Freedom Summer, 1964. Students came from other states to Mississippi to assist local activists in registering voters, teach in "Freedom Schools" and form the Mississippi Freedom Democratic Party. Three workers disappeared--murdered by the KKK. It took six weeks to find their bodies.

The national uproar forced President Johnson to send in the FBI. Congress passed the **Civil Rights Act of 1964**.

Edgar Ray "Preacher" Killen was convicted of three cases of manslaughter on June 21, 2005. None of the other men found guilty served more than six years for the murders.

Selma to Montgomery marches, 1965. Attempts to obtain voter registration in Selma, Alabama, had been largely unsuccessful due to opposition from the city's sheriff. Reverend King came to the city to lead a series of marches. He and over 200 demonstrators were arrested and jailed. Each successive march was met with violent resistance by police.

In March, a group of over 600 intended to walk 54 miles from Selma to Montgomery. Six blocks into the march, state and local law enforcement officials attacked the marchers with billy clubs, tear gas, rubber tubes wrapped in barbed wire, and bull whips. The marchers were driven back to Selma. National broadcast of the footage provoked a nationwide response. The **Voting Rights Act of 1965** was signed into law on August 6, 1965.

http://www.jimcrowhistory.org/ Jim Crow History

Key policies, legislation and court cases included the following:

Brown v. Board of Education, 1954 – The Supreme Court declared that *Plessy v. Ferguson* was unconstitutional. This was the ruling that had established "Separate but Equal" as the basis for segregation. With this decision, the Court ordered immediate desegregation.

Civil Rights Act of 1964 bars discrimination in public accommodations, employment and education

Voting Rights Act of 1965 suspended poll taxes, literacy tests, and other voter tests for voter registration. This law irrevocably changed the political landscape of the South.

The assassination of Martin Luther King in Memphis, Tennessee, on April 4, 1968, sparked racial riots in many American cities.

Senator **Robert F. Kennedy** is remembered for the speech he gave after the assassination to try to bring calm to the black community. Kennedy was assassinated in Los Angeles on June 6, 1968, after winning the California Democratic Primary. It was likely that he would have won the Democratic Party's nomination--running on an anti-war platform.

Vietnam

Vietnam prior to 1946 was part of the French colony of Indochina since 1861--along with Laos and Kampuchea (Cambodia). When France fell to Hitler in 1940, the Japanese seized Vietnamese rice so that millions starved to death. Vietnamese continued to fight French troops for control of the country.

The **Geneva Conference of 1954** granted Vietnam independence from France and divided the country into northern and southern zones. The United States did not participate in the Conference. The Vietnamese believed that unification was to follow. They considered the war one of national liberation, a struggle to avoid continual dominance and influence of a foreign power.

The United States' aid and influence continued as part of the **Cold War** foreign policy to help any nation threatened by Communism. The U.S. was particularly concerned about communism in China, and thus had been aiding the French there. About a half-million Catholic Vietnamese moved south when the CIA used messages such as the slogan: "The Virgin Mary is moving South."

The Vietnam War divided the American public. Many saw as it the first war fought on foreign soil, in which U.S. combat forces were unable to achieve objectives.

The **1968 Democratic National Convention** in Chicago was contentious, both on the floor of the convention and outside, where thousands had gathered to protest the Vietnam War. Vice President **Hubert H. Humphrey** became the party's nominee, but he led a divided party.

The turning point became the **Tet Offensive** that went on in 1968 between January and September. The communist North struck over 100 cities, which resulted in thousands of deaths and destruction of homes. In the U.S. the advisers to President Johnson concluded that the war would go on as an endless violent stalemate.

President Richard Nixon who took office in 1969 began the offensive in Cambodia with secret campaigns for bombings and then in Laos. The escalation of the war in Vietnam led to antiwar demonstrations, and following the invasion of Cambodia was the killing of peaceful students at the college of **Kent State** in Ohio by the National Guard. Student protests grew. Protest of the military draft led to the end of the draft in 1973.
The escalation of drug abuse, the weakening of the family unit, homelessness, poverty, mental illness experienced by the Vietnam veterans contributed to a country divided and tom apart. Returning veterans faced not only readjustment to normal civilian life, but also bitterness, anger, rejection, and no heroes' welcomes.

A cease-fire was arranged in January 1973 and a few months later, U.S. troops left for good. The final phase consisted of fighting between the Vietnamese but ended April 30, 1975. With the surrender of South Vietnam, the entire country became united under the Communist ruler.

The Cold War

U.S. foreign policy from the end of World War II to 1990 was the post-war struggle between non-Communist nations led by the United States and the Soviet Union and other Communist nations. It was referred to as a "**Cold War**" because its conflicts did not lead to a major war of fighting, or a "hot war." It was a "cold" war because no large-scale fighting took place directly between the two big protagonists. Form of government and economics were the main concerns.

Both the Soviet Union and the United States embarked on an arsenal buildup of **atomic and hydrogen bombs**. Both nations had the capability of destroying each other, but because of the continuous threat of nuclear war and accidents, extreme caution was practiced on both sides.

Following the end of the war in 1945, social and economic chaos continued in Western Europe. The **Marshall Plan** sent economic aid to Europe in the aftermath of the Second World War aimed at preventing the spread of communism.

In 1946, Josef Stalin stated that capitalism and its development of the world's economy made international peace impossible. In response, **George F. Kennan**, an American diplomat in Moscow, proposed a statement of U.S. foreign policy that would come to be known as "**Containment**." The goal of the U.S. was to contain the expansion of Soviet communist policies and activities.

After Soviet efforts in Iran, Greece, and Turkey, U.S. President Harry Truman stated what is known as the **Truman Doctrine**. Truman said that the U.S. would support other nations with a policy of economic and military aid in order to contain the Soviet sphere of communist power.

http://www.intelligence.go v/0-natsecact_1947.shtml National Security Act

The **National Security Act of 1947** established the **Department of Defense**, the **National Security Council**, and the **Central Intelligence Agency (CIA)**.

With respect to the division into zones of Germany, in February 1948, Britain and the U.S. combined their two zones; France joined in June.

The Soviets were opposed to German unification. In April 1948, the Soviets blocked all road traffic access to West Berlin from West Germany.

To avoid armed conflict, from June 1948 to mid-May 1949 during the **Berlin Airlift**, Allied air forces flew in food and supplies for the West Berliners. As a result of the airlift, the Soviets lifted their blockade and permitted vehicles access to the city.

The **Cold War** had begun.

The **North Atlantic Treaty Organization (NATO)** was formed in 1949. The United States and several Western European nations, for the purpose of opposing communist aggression, stated: "The Parties of NATO agreed that an armed attack against one or more of them in Europe or North America shall be considered an attack against them all."

In response the **Warsaw Pact** was signed in 1955 by Albania, Bulgaria, Czechoslovakia, East Germany, Hungary, Poland, Romania, and the Soviet Union, and stated they would come to aid of each other if attacked.

The **Berlin Wall** was built in 1961. The "**Iron Curtain**" referred to the ideological, symbolic and physical separation of Europe between East and West.

In Asia, the Soviet Union's allies were China, North Korea, and North Vietnam, and U.S. allies were Japan, South Korea, Taiwan, and South Vietnam.

The main symbol of the Cold War was the **arms race**, a continual buildup of missiles, tanks, and other weapons that became ever more technologically advanced and increasingly more deadly. Spending on weapons and defensive systems eventually occupied great percentages of the budgets of the U.S. and the USSR. Some historians argue that this high level of spending played a large part in the end of the Soviet Union.

The Cold War drew to a close in the late 1980s with the introduction of **Mikhail Gorbachev**'s reform programs and the fall of the Berlin Wall. The Soviet Union its ceded power over Eastern Europe and was dissolved in 1991, and this marks the end of the Cold War.

The 15 republics of the former USSR became independent nations with varying degrees of freedom and democracy in government and together formed the Commonwealth of Independent States (CIS). The former communist nations of Eastern Europe also emphasized their independence with democratic forms of government.

Technology

Discoveries and innovations in science and technology throughout history are directed to enhancing life and building up military. In the United States following World War II, there were significant advances in preventing and curing disease.

Life expectancy rose, and with it, the desire to develop new enhancements for living. In 1900, life expectancy for males was age 47 in the United States; in 1950 it was age 64 for men and 67 for women; in 2001, age 75 for men and 80 for women.

Returning veterans from World War II, Korea, and Vietnam took advantage of the **G.I. Bill** and obtained more education, which resulted in expansion of college facilities.

The Soviet Union was first to begin a program of space flight and exploration, launching **Sputnik** in 1957 and putting the first man in space, Yuri Gagarin, in 1961. In 1969 the United States landed space crews on the moon.

Major technological developments since 1945:

- Penicillin (1945)
- Detonation of the first atomic bombs (1945)
- Xerography process invented (1946)
- Exploration of the South Pole
- Studies of X-ray radiation
- U.S. airplane first flies at supersonic speed (1947)
- Invention of the transistor (1947)
- Long-playing record invented (1948)
- Chemo-genetics (1948)
- Mount Palomar reflecting telescope (1948)
- Idlewild Airport (JFK) - New York City first commercial flight (1948)
- Cortisone (1949)
- USSR tests its first atomic bomb (1949)
- U.S.-guided missile launched; traveled 250 miles (1949)
- Plutonium separated (1950)
- Tranquilizer meprobamate (Miltown ®) (1950)
- Antihistamines (1950)
- Electric power produced from atomic energy (nuclear power) (1951)
- First heart-lung machine (1951)
- First solo flight over the North Pole (1951)
- Yellow fever vaccine (1951)
- Isotopes in medicine and industry (1952)

- Contraceptive pill (1952)
- First hydrogen bomb exploded (1952)
- Nobel Prize in medicine for discovery of streptomycin (1952)
- Cave Cougnac discovered with prehistoric paintings (1953)
- USSR explodes hydrogen bomb (1953)
- Hillary and Tenzing reach summit of Mount Everest (1953)
- Lung cancer connected to cigarette smoking (1953)
- First U.S. submarine converted to nuclear power (1954)
- Polio vaccine (1954)
- Discovery of Vitamin B12 (1955)
- Discovery of the molecular structure of insulin (1955)
- Development of "visual telephone" (1956)
- Transatlantic cable telephone service (1956)
- USSR launches first earth satellites (Sputnik I and II) (1957)
- Mackinac Straits Bridge in Michigan - longest suspension bridge (1957)
- Stereo recordings (1958)
- NASA created (1958)
- USSR launches rocket with two monkeys aboard (1959)
- Nobel Prize for Medicine for synthesis of RNA and DNA (1959)

Immigration

After WWII the U.S. and Canada began to distinguish between economically- motivated immigrants and **political refugees**. The United Nations created the **International Refugee Organization** in 1946. Over the

> http://www.digitalhistory.uh.edu/historyonline/immigration_chron.cfm
> Landmarks in Immigration – Digital History

next three years this organization relocated over a million European refugees who'd been made homeless by the war. Fear of persecution caused massive migrations, and immigration policy in the U.S. was carefully aligned with foreign policy.

President Truman proposed the **Displaced Persons Act,** Congress passed it in 1948. The Act facilitated the admission of more than 400,000 displaced persons from Europe who were survivors of concentration camps and refugees of the Soviet-occupied regions of Europe.

The **Internal Security Act of 1950**, also known as the **McCarran-Wood Act**, set up required registration with the Attorney General's office for anyone who was a member of the American Communist Party and made it illegal if a member of that Party concealed it if seeking a job with the government, and they were prohibited from using a U.S. passport. Communists could be deported. Truman vetoed that Act and also the **McCarran-Walter Act Immigration Nationality Act of 1952**, but Congress overrode his vetoes. The 1952 Act maintained the quota system at the rate of one-sixth of one percent of each nationality's population in the United States in 1920. It set up a *racial* quota for Asians, not one of nationality.

Refugees from Communist Europe were admitted under the **President's Escapee Program** of 1952 and the **Refugee Relief Act** of 1953. 200,000 non-quota visas were granted for Europeans, many of whom were Hungarians.

Many immigrants were highly trained and skilled scientists, teachers, inventors, and executives. This migration added to the American "**melting pot**" experience. The immigrants provided new sources of labor for a booming economy and the introduction of new cultural ideas and contributions to science and technology.

Migration and Refugee Assistance Act of 1962 provided for refugee assistance, and the **Immigration Act of 1965** abolished the national-origin quotas. A consequence has been a decline of the relative proportion of the white population.

Immigration Reform and Control Act (IRCA) 1986. Signed by President Reagan, the Act granted amnesty to about three million illegal immigrants and made it illegal to knowingly hire illegal immigrants.

Skill 1.1I   Recent Developments

Oil Crisis

The decision of the **Organization of Petroleum Exporting Countries (OPEC)** ministers to cut back on oil production, thus raising the price of a barrel of oil, created a fuel shortage. Energy and fuel conservation became necessary as Americans experienced shortages of fuel oil for heating and gasoline for cars and other vehicles.

Presidents of the 1970s

Richard Nixon inherited racial unrest and the Vietnam War. His administration is probably best known for:

- End of the Vietnam War
- Improved relations with both China and the USSR.
- Appointment of conservative justices to the Supreme Court
- New anti-crime legislation
- Approved the **National Environmental Policy Act** and legislation on clean air, national parks, endangered species, pesticides, coastal protection, and ocean dumping restrictions
- Revenue sharing legislation, that is, block grants that permitted state and local government to receive financial assistance
- End of the draft
- Watergate scandal

After withdrawal of troops from Vietnam, Nixon first sent his Secretary of State **Henry Kissinger** on a secret trip to Peking, China. The U.S. had not recognized Communist China and claimed Chiang Kai-shek who was exiled on the island of **Taiwan** to be the legitimate leader. In 1972 President Nixon and the First Lady traveled to Communist China and met with the leaders. Agreements were made for re-unification of China, and in 1979, the U.S. formally recognized Communist China.

A landmark Supreme Court case was **Roe v Wade** legalizing abortion.

In 1972, Nixon was involved in the **Watergate** scandal when members of the Nixon administration broke into the Democratic National Committee headquarters in the Watergate Hotel to plant listening devices. The result was the first resignation of an American president.

Not only did Nixon resign, but his Vice President **Spiro Agnew** had as well—for tax evasion.

Gerald Ford was the first Vice President selected under the Twenty-fifth Amendment. Ford was appointed by Nixon and approved by Congress. When Nixon resigned, Ford became the 38th President. He pardoned Nixon and appointed **Nelson Rockefeller** as his Vice President.

The challenges that faced his administration included:

- Depressed economy
- Inflation
- Energy shortages
- *Détente* or lessening aggression

He tried to reduce the role of the federal government. He reduced business taxes and lessened the government controls on business. His international focus was on preventing a major war in the Middle East. He negotiated with Russia regarding limitations on nuclear weapons.

Jimmy Carter is the first U.S. president to win the Nobel Peace Prize. When he took office in 1977, he inherited unemployment, a budget deficit, inflation and high interest rates. Carter's presidency is known for:

- National energy policy
- Removing price controls from domestic petroleum production
- Pursuing Camp David Accords
- Pursuing Panama Canal Treaties
- **Strategic Arms Limitation Talks (SALT)**
- **Iran hostage crisis**
- Botched helicopter rescue effort
- Deregulation of trucking and airline industries
- Appointment of women and minorities to government jobs

> http://www.defenselink.mil/news/newsarticle.aspx?id=31346
> America Remembers Desert One

Egyptian President **Anwar el-Sadat** and Israeli Prime Minister **Menachem Begin** met at presidential retreat **Camp David** in 1978 and agreed to sign a formal treaty of peace between the two countries. The Camp David Accords led directly to the 1979 Israel-Egypt peace treaty.

In 1979, 53 American **hostages** were captured in Iran. The Shah had been deposed, and control of the government and the country was in the hands of Islamic cleric **Ayatollah Ruhollah Khomeini.**

In 1953 Iran's **Mossadegh** government was overthrown in a *coup d'état*, sponsored by the CIA known as **Operation AJAX**. The CIA trained Shah Mohammad Reza Pahlavi's secret police force, and when the exiled Shah was allowed into the U.S. for medical treatment, 52 U.S. diplomats were held hostage for 444 days by Iranian college students who supported the revolution. President Carter froze all Iranian assets in the U.S., set up trade restrictions, and approved a risky rescue attempt. The helicopters met with a sandstorm; the dust cloud raised by rotors was disorienting, and the ensuing crash, explosion, and fire resulted in the deaths of U.S. eight servicemen.

Khomeini ignored U.N. requests for releasing the Americans, and Europeans refused to support the embargo so as not to risk losing access to Iran's oil. The hostages were released on the day of **President Ronald Reagan**'s inauguration.

Presidents of the 1980s

Ronald Reagan was the first president whose career including being a professional actor. He was also the first divorced president, and he was the oldest president, elected at the age of 69. A two-term president, the Reagan Administration is know for:

- "Reagonomics," or supply-side or "trickle-down" economics
- Curbing inflation
- Increasing employment – following the peak unemployment rate of 10.8 percent in December 1982
- Signing **Economic Recovery Tax Act of 1981** (also known as **ERTA** or the **Kemp-Roth Tax Cut** - resulted in one percent decrease in government revenues or three percent of GDP
- Nominating **Sandra Day O'Connor,** first female justice on the Supreme Court.
- Contributing to **Iran-Contra** scandal
- Making war on **Grenada**
- Negotiation with Soviet Premier **Mikahail Gorbachev** to reduce nuclear weapons
- Experiencing assassination attempt by **John Hinkley, Jr**.
- Breaking union of **air traffic controllers**
- Increasing **national debt** from $600 billion to $3 trillion or 48.1% of GDP
- Ending of Cold War
- Stock market crash of 1987
- War on Drugs – "Just Say No"
- Appearance of AIDS

Employment and Inflation – When Reagan took office, inflation stood at 11.83% and unemployment at 7.1%. Increases in federal budget deficits and the national debt were used to reduce these numbers.

Defense Spending. Defense spending increased by 40 percent between 1981 and 1985. Much of the budget was to fund the B-1 bomber program, the MX "Peacekeeper" Missile, and the Strategic Defense Initiative (SDI, also known as "Star Wars").

Savings & Loan Crisis. The savings and loan industry (S&L) was deregulated and began to make greater loans along with other financial activities. More than 1,000 savings and loan institutions failed.

> http://www.nysscpa.org/cpajournal/old/08033828.htm
> The S&L Crisis:Putting Things In Perspective by Walter M. Primoff *CPA Journal*

Iran-Contra Affair. U.S. involvement in the domestic revolutions of El Salvador and Nicaragua continued into Reagan's second term. Congress held televised hearings on the **Iran-Contra Affair**, and not only were members of his administration selling arms to Iran, but there was also drug dealing. The cover-up was exposed, showing that profits from secretly selling military hardware to Iran had been used to give support to rebels, called Contras, who were fighting in Nicaragua.

Air Traffic Controllers Strike
Reagan said that the striking air traffic controllers had to report to work within 48 hours or "they have forfeited their jobs and will be terminated". On August 3, 1981, Reagan broke the union and fired 11,345 striking air traffic controllers.

Attack on Peacekeeping Forces - In 1983 in **Lebanon**, 241 American Marines who were serving as part of a peacekeeping force in Beirut were killed when an Islamic suicide bomber drove an explosive-laden truck into U.S. Marines headquarters located at the airport in Beirut. This tragic event came as part of the unrest and violence between the Israelis and the **Palestinian Liberation Organization** (PLO) forces in southern Lebanon.

Granada
In the same month, 1,900 U.S. Marines landed on the island of **Grenada** to rescue a small group of American medical students and depose the leftist government.

George H. W. Bush served as Vice President under President Reagan. His prior career included Dresser, a maker of oil supplies; and Zapata, an oil company. Nixon asked Bush to chair the Republican National Committee. After that he served as Chief of the U.S. Liaison Office in China and then as Director of the CIA. He then became chairman of the First International Bank in Houston and adjunct professor at Rice University.

When Bush ran against the Massachusetts governor Michael Dukakis, his **"Thousand points of light"** speech moved him forward in the pools

During the Reagan administration, Bush held responsibility for anti-drug programs and federal deregulation

Some events that occurred during the Bush Administration:

- Invasion of Panama Canal and capture of dictator **Manuel Noriega**
- Iraq's invasion of Kuwait
- Gulf War, known as **Desert Storm**
- Fall of the Berlin Wall
- Unification of Germany
- Break-up of Soviet Union
- Establishment of independent nations
- Tiananmen Square Massacre in Beijing
- Exxon *Valdez* oil spill of 11 million gallons of crude oil
- First World Wide Web page created
- Ruby Ridge confrontation with the Weaver family and federal agents
- Seizure of Lincoln Savings and Loan, a company that cost taxpayers about $200 billion

> http://www.pbs.org/newshour/indepth coverage/law/corruption/history.html
> **PBS News Hour –**
> **Washington Corruption Probe**

President Bush sent U.S. troops to invade **Panama** in December of 1989, and arrest the Panamanian dictator, **Manuel Noriega**. Although he had periodically assisted CIA operations with intelligence information, Noriega also laundered money from drug-smuggling and gun-running through Panama's banks.. When a political associate tried unsuccessfully to depose him, and an off-duty U.S. Marine was shot and killed at a roadblock, Bush acted. Noriega was brought to the U.S. where he stood trial in Miami and was convicted on eight out of ten drug and racketeering charges.

During the Iraq-Iran war, the U.S. and most of Iraq's neighbors supported Iraq. In a five-year period, **Saddam Hussein** received from the U.S. $500 million worth of American technology, including lasers, advanced computers, and special machine tools used in missile development. Iraq also received $14 billion from its supportive neighbor Kuwait.

The Iraq-Iran war resulted in a stalemate with a U.N. truce ending it.

Iraq intended to pay off its war debt with oil earnings by raising the prices of oil. However, Kuwait, a member of the OPEC, prevented a global increase in petroleum prices by increasing its own petroleum production, thus lowering the price and preventing recovery of the war-crippled Iraqi economy.

The drop in oil prices upset Hussein, who was deeply in debt from the war and totally dependent on oil revenues. Iraq invaded Kuwait on August 2, 1990. Consequently, the U.S. made extensive plans to carry out **Operation Desert Storm**, the liberation of Kuwait. It was a joint effort of many nations with the backing of the UN.

Operation Desert Storm began with airstrikes on January 16, 1991. The next day

> http://www.gwu.edu/~nsarchiv/
> NSAEBB/NSAEBB39/
> **National Security Archive:**
> **Operation Desert Storm**

Iraq shot **scud missiles** into Israel. The U.S. persuaded Israel not to do the same in return. When the Iraqi soldiers retreated from Kuwait on February 28, they set fire to Kuwaiti oil fields.

William Clinton won the election against Bush, and **Ross Perot**. He was the first baby-boomer president. Despite his being only the second president to be impeached after President Andrew Johnson, he left office with a high approval rating. He was the first president to return to Vietnam where he had served in the Army.

Some actions during his two terms include:

- Family and Medical Leave Act
- The "Don't Ask, Don't Tell" policy
- First female Secretary of State
- North American Free Trade Agreement (NAFTA)
- Brady Bill
- Earned Income Tax Credit
- The Elián González affair
- Policy of "regime change" against Iraq,
- Operation Allied Force with NATO in Bosnia
- Oslo Accords
- Defense of Marriage Act
- **Extraordinary rendition** and **irregular rendition approval**

- Loss of the seven crew members of the NASA space shuttle "**Challenger**"
- Waco Siege

Clinton's domestic accomplishments include the lowest inflation in thirty years, the lowest unemployment rate, the highest rate of home ownership, lower crime rates in many places, smaller welfare rolls, a balanced budget, and a budget surplus.

Clinton sent U.S. troops to **Haiti** to protect the efforts of **Jean-Bertrand Aristide**, former Roman Catholic priest who had been elected President of Haiti and was overthrown by a military coup.

He also sent troops to Bosnia to assist U.N. peacekeeping forces in 1992 to 1995.

He also inherited from the Bush administration the problem of **Somalia** in East Africa, where U.S. troops had been sent in December 1992 to support U.N. efforts to end the starvation of the Somalis and restore peace. The efforts were successful at first, but eventually failed due to the severity of the intricate political problems within the country. After U.S. soldiers were killed in an ambush along with 300 Somalis, American troops were withdrawn and returned home.

In Waco, Texas, in 1993, the FBI held a 51-day siege on the **Branch Davidian Seventh Day Adventist Church** headed by **David Koresh** after the Bureau of Alcohol, Tobacco and Firearms had attempted to serve a warrant on the group. On April 19th, 76 residents along with 21 children died in a fire.

The **Murrah Federal Building** was a terrorist attack on April 19, 1995, that killed 168 in Oklahoma City.

Numerous **savings and loans institutions** were in serious jeopardy when hundreds of these failed and others went into bankruptcy due to customer default on loans and mismanagement. Congressional legislation helped rebuild the industry costing taxpayers billions of dollars.

> www.fdic.gov/bank/analytical/banking/2000dec/brv13n2_2.pdf
> **The Cost of the Savings and Loan Crisis: Truth and Consequences**

The Environment

The population of the U.S. had greatly increased, and along with it, the nation's industries and the resulting harmful pollution of the environment. Factory smoke, automobile exhaust, waste from factories all combined to create hazardous air, water, and ground pollution which, if not brought under control and significantly diminished, would severely endanger all life on earth.

The **Exxon Valdez** oil spill off the Alaskan coast, the nuclear accident and melt-down at the Ukrainian nuclear power plant at **Chernobyl,** near-disaster at **Three Mile Island** Nuclear Plant in Pennsylvania are some prominent events in environmental threats.

.Changing policies and legislation

"**Minority rights**" encompasses two ideas. The first is the *individual* rights of members of ethnic, racial, class, religious or sexual minorities. The second is *collective* rights of minority groups. Various civil rights movements have sought to guarantee that the individual rights of persons are not denied on the basis of being part of a minority group. The effects of these movements may be seen in guarantees of minority representation and affirmative action quotas.

Since 1941 a number of anti-discrimination laws have been passed by the Congress. These acts have protected the civil rights of several groups of Americans. These laws include:

- Fair Employment Act of 1941
- Civil Rights Act of 1964
- Immigration and Nationality Services Act of 1965
- Voting Rights Act of 1965
- Civil Rights Act of 1968
- Age Discrimination in Employment Act of 1967
- Age Discrimination Act of 1975
- Pregnancy Discrimination Act of 1978
- Americans with Disabilities Act of 1990
- Civil Rights Act of 1991
- Employment Non-Discrimination Act

Numerous groups have used various forms of protest, attempts to sway public opinion, legal action, and congressional lobbying to obtain full protection of their civil rights under the Constitution.

The **disability rights** movement resulting in a guaranteed access to public buildings and transportation; equal access to education and employment; and equal protection under the law in terms of access to insurance, and other basic rights of American citizens. Public buildings and public transportation must be accessible to persons with disabilities. Discrimination in hiring or housing on the basis of disability is also illegal.

A "**prisoners' rights**" movement has helped to ensure the basic human rights of persons incarcerated for crimes. **Immigrant rights** movements have provided for employment and housing rights, as well as preventing abuse of immigrants through hate crimes. In some states, immigrant rights movements have led to bi-lingual education and public information access.

Another group movement seeking to obtain equal rights is the lesbian, gay, bisexual and transgender social movement. This movement seeks equal housing, freedom from social and employment discrimination, and equal recognition of relationships under the law.

The **women's rights movement** is concerned with the freedoms of women that are at times suppressed or prohibited in a culture.

- The right to vote
- The right to work
- The right to fair wages
- The right to bodily integrity and autonomy
- The right to own property
- The right to an education
- The right to hold public office
- Marital rights
- Parental rights
- Religious rights
- The right to serve in the military
- The right to enter into legal contracts

http://www.now.org/
National Organization for Women

By the 1960s the word **feminism** came to describe the movement. The **National Organization for Woman (NOW)** began in 1966 with the purpose of getting the **Equal Rights Amendment** passed, which said: "equality of rights under the law shall not be denied or abridged by the United States or any state on account of sex." In 1982, the amendment died, however, because not enough states had ratified it.

Some of the most famous leaders in the women's movement American history are:

- Abigail Adams
- Harriet Tubman
- Susan B. Anthony
- Elizabeth Cady Stanton
- Margaret Sanger
- Elizabeth Blackwell
- Sojourner Truth
- Amelia Bloomer
- Lydia Pinkham
- Charlotte Perkins Gilman
- Shirley Chisolm
- Coretta Scott King
- Katha Pollett
- Betty Friedan
- Gloria Steinem
- Adrienne Rich
- Naomi Wolf
- Ana Castillo

Domain II: **World History**

Skill 2.1a   Human Society to approximately 3000 B.C.E.

Prehistory is defined as the period of human achievement prior to the development of writing.   Three different periods are:

- **Lower Paleolithic Period** - use of crude tools;
- **Upper Paleolithic Period** - a greater variety of better-made tools and implements, the wearing of clothing, highly organized group life, and skills in art
- **Neolithic Period** - domesticated animals; food production; the arts of knitting; spinning and weaving cloth; starting fires through friction; building houses rather than living in caves; the development of institutions including the family, religion, and government or origin of the state.

ANTHROPOLOGY is the scientific study of human culture and humanity and the relationship between humans and their culture. Anthropologist Eric Wolf defined it as: "the most scientific of the humanities, and the most humanistic of the sciences."

Anthropologists study different groups; how groups relate to other cultures; patterns of behavior; and similarities and differences among cultures. Research is two-fold: **cross-cultural** and **comparative**. The major method of study is referred to as "**participant observation.**" An anthropologist studies and learns about the people by living among them and participating with them in their daily lives. Anthropology is divided into: biological and cultural anthropology, archaeology, and linguistics

ARCHAEOLOGY is the scientific study of past human cultures by studying the remains they left behind including pottery, bones, buildings, tools, and artwork.

Archaeologists locate and examine any evidence to help explain the way people lived in past times. They use special equipment and techniques to gather the evidence, keeping detailed records of their findings. Research may result in destruction of the remains being studied.

The first step is to locate an archaeological site. Next, surveying the site takes place starting with a detailed description of the site with notes, maps, photographs, and collecting artifacts from the surface. Excavating follows, either by digging for buried objects or by diving and working in submersible decompression chambers when underwater. They record and preserve the evidence for eventual classification, dating, and evaluating their find.

Sources of knowledge about early humans include fossils derived from burial pits, occasional bones found in rock deposits, archaeological excavations of tools, pottery, paintings, and studying living primitives. Although written records go back only about 4,500 years, scientists have pieced together evidence that documents the existence of humans (or "man-apes) as many as 600,000 years ago. The first man-like primates arose about one million years ago. These primates developed and discovered fire and tools. They had human-sized brains and produced the **Cro-Magnon** (25,000 years ago) from which **Homo sapiens** descended.

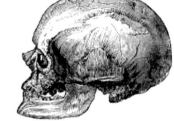

Primitive humans demonstrated wide behavior patterns and great adaptability. Little is known of details, including when language began to develop. They are

believed to have lived in small communities that developed on the basis of the need to hunt. **Cave paintings** suggest a belief that magic pictures of animals could conjure up real ones. Some figurines indicate belief in fertility gods and goddesses. Belief in an afterlife is indicated by burial formalities.

Archaeological evidence points to the use of hatchets, awls, needles and cutting tools in the **Lower Paleolithic** or Old Stone Age (one million years ago). Artifacts of the **Upper Paleolithic** or New Stone Age (6,000-8,000 BCE) include indications of polished tools, domesticated animals, the wheel, and some agriculture. Pottery and textiles have been found dating to the end of the New Stone Age (**Neolithic** period). The discovery of metals in the **Bronze Age** (3,000 BCE) is concurrent with the establishment of what are believed to be the first civilizations. The **Iron Age** rapidly developed next.

> http://www.culture.gouv.fr/culture/arcnat/lascaux/en/
> **Cave of Lascaux**

By 4,000 BCE humans lived in villages, engaged in animal husbandry, grew grains, sailed in boats, and practiced religions. Civilizations arose earliest in the fertile river valleys of the Nile, Mesopotamia, the Indus, and the Hwang Ho.

Prerequisites of civilization include 1) use of metals rather than stone for tools and weapons, 2) a system of writing, 3) a calendar, 4) and a territorial state.

The earliest known civilizations developed in the **Tigris-Euphrates** valley of Mesopotamia (modern Iraq) and the Nile valley of Egypt between 4000 BCE and 3000 BCE. The **Fertile Crescent** was bounded on the West by the Mediterranean, on the South by the Arabian Desert, on the north by the Taurus Mountains, and on the east by the Zagros Mountains. Geography and the physical environment played a critical role in the rise and the survival of civilizations. They are also known as **fluvial civilizations**.

Rivers provided a source of water that would sustain life. The hunters had ample access to a variety of animals, to provide food, hides, bones, and antlers from which clothing, tools, and art could be made. Proximity to water enabled domesticating animals which could be herded and husbanded to provide a stable supply of food and animal products. Rivers flooded, leaving behind a deposit of very rich soil. The soil was fertile and water was readily available to produce sizeable harvests. In time, the people developed systems of irrigation that channeled water to the crops.

The term "**Fertile Crescent**" came from James Breasted, University of Chicago archaeologist to describe the part of the Near East that extended from the Persian Gulf to the Sinai Peninsula. It included Mesopotamia, Syria, and Palestine.

This region was marked by invasions and migrations. The invaders and migrants may have destroyed existent cultures or absorbed and supplement the civilization that existed before their arrival. In the Fertile Crescent, civilization developed quickly into an advanced culture.

Advanced ancient civilizations

Egypt made numerous significant contributions including construction of the great pyramids; development of hieroglyphic writing; preservation of bodies after death; making paper from papyrus; contributing to developments in arithmetic and geometry; the invention of the method of counting in groups of 1-10 (the decimal system); completion of a solar calendar; and laying the foundation for science and astronomy.

The ancient civilization of the **Sumerians** invented the wheel; developed irrigation through use of canals, dikes, and devices for raising water; devised the system of cuneiform writing; learned to divide time; and built large boats for trade.

The **Babylonians** devised the famous **Code of Hammurabi**, a code of laws.

The ancient **Assyrians** are considered to have been warlike and aggressive with a highly organized military that used horse-drawn chariots.

The **Hebrews**, also known as the ancient Israelites, instituted "monotheism", which is the worship of one God, Yahweh, who provided The Ten Commandments.

The ancient **Persians** developed an alphabet; contributed the religions/philosophies of **Zoroastrianism**, **Mithraism**, and **Gnosticism**; and allowed conquered peoples to retain their own customs, laws, and religions.

The **Minoans** used a writing system of symbols to represent syllables in words. They built palaces with multiple levels with many rooms, water and sewage systems with flush toilets, bathtubs, hot and cold running water, and bright paintings on the walls.

The **Mycenaeans** changed the Minoan writing system to **Linear Script B** which preceded classical Greek by 700 years. Tablets show that the Mycenaeans were involved in trade, agriculture, industry, and war and that they worshipped Zeus and the other gods and goddesses of Mount Olympus.

The **Phoenicians** were sea traders well-known for manufacturing skills in glass, and metals, and for the development of their famous purple dye. Proficient in the skill of navigation, they were able to sail by the stars at night. Further, they devised an alphabet using symbols to represent single sounds, which was an extension of the Egyptian writing system.

> http://www.gisdevelopment.net/applicati on/archaeology/site/archs0001.htm
> **The Saraswati: Where lies the mystery**
> **Saswati Paik**
> **GIS Devlopment**

In **India**, the principle of **zero** in mathematics was identified, the major religion of Hinduism was begun, and the caste system developed. The Indus Valley culture was primarily urban and traded with Sumer. Along the now-dry banks of the Saraswati River, archaeologists are discovering many ancient towns and cities.

Ancient China began along the Yangtze River as long ago as half a million years. Neolithic China was far wetter than today. Silk production was active, and the Yangshao had the pottery wheel. The Lungshan created black pottery. Millet was grown south of the Yellow River.

> http://library.thinkquest.org/23062/
> ThinkQuest Ancient China

Skill 2.1b Development of Early Civilizations (Circa 3000–1500 B.C.E.)

In the 1500 years between 3000 BCE and 1500 BCE, cultures developed all over the world:

Mesopotamia in the Middle East
Egypt and Kush in Africa
Greece in Southern Europe
India in Asia
China in Asia
Japan in Asia
Americas in the Western Hemisphere

The civilizations of the Sumerians, Amorites, Hittites, Assyrians, Chaldeans, and Persians controlled various areas of the land we call **Mesopotamia**. The culture of **Mesopotamia** was autocratic: top-heavy, with a single ruler at the head of the government who, in many cases, was also the head of the religion. With few exceptions, tyrants and military leaders controlled trade, religions, and law.

Sumer was composed of 12 city-states, which had their own gods, with the city-state's leader doubling as the high priest. Sumerians developed astronomy and mathematics, the potter's wheel, the sailboat, and the first pictograph writing system.

> http://history-world.org/sumeria.htm
> **Sumer History**

Ur, an ancient city in Sumer was at one time led by Ur-Nammu who developed the *Codes*, which preceded the *Codes of Hammarubi* by about 300 years. The third dynasty of Ur was taken over by the **Elamites** in about 1950 BCE.

> http://www.crystalinks.com/elam.html
> **Kingdom of Elam**

Sumer was the southern half of Mesopotamia; **Akkad** was the northern half.

Sargon of Akkad is known for conquering these areas in the south: **Syria, Anatolia**, and **Elam**, and Sargon is also known for establishing the first **Semitic** dynasty. Semites include **Akkadians, Phoenicians, Hebrews**, and **Arabs.**

> http://history-world.org/sargon_the_great.htm
> **Sargon the Great**

Legacies handed down include:

- First use of writing
- The wheel
- Banking (Sumer)
- First written set of laws
- First epic story (*Gilgamesh*)
- First library dedicated to preserving knowledge (instituted by the Assyrian leader Ashurbanipal)
- Hanging Gardens of Babylon (built by the Chaldean Nebuchadnezzar)

Kush

The earliest historical record of **Kush** is in Egyptian sources. Kush (also known as Cush) was located in the southern part of modern Egypt and the northern part of Sudan. During the time when it ranged from near Khartoum to the Mediterranean Sea, it was the largest empire on the Nile River. In Greece, it was called Ethiopia, but that does not refer to modern-day Ethiopia

The Neolithic civilization of Kush was characterized by a settled way of life in fortified mud-brick villages with hunting and fishing, herding cattle, and raising grain.

Skeletal remains suggest that the people were a blend of Negroid and Mediterranean peoples. The Kush spoke **Nilo-Saharan** languages. The capital city was Kerma, a major trading center.

Descent of the king was determined through the mother's line (as in Egypt), and the Kushites were ruled by a series of female heads of state called **Kandake** or **Kentake**.

The Kushite religion was polytheistic, including all of the primary Egyptian gods. There were, however, regional gods which were the principal gods in their regions. Along with other African cultures, there was a lion warrior god.

In about 2900 BCE Kush invaded the Empire of Persia and established the Kingdom of Elam east of the Tigris and Euphrates Rivers. Kush was conquered by the Nubian Kingdom around 800 B.C.E.

http://wysinger.homestead.com/chronology.html
Chronology of Ancient Egypt and Nubia
http://www.nubianet.org/ - Nubia

The **Minoan civilization** developed on the island Crete about 2700 BCE and lasted until approximately 1450 BCE. This occurred during the Bronze Age. They developed a writing system known as Linear A and B, but A is not yet translatable. Minoans were traders. Archaeologists are examining Minoan ruins and ancient palaces. In about 2000, there was destruction of Minoan settlements There is evidence of earthquakes as well as volcanoes.

- 2000-1550 - Middle Bronze Age
- 1600-1627 Eruption of Thera volcano
- 1600-1100 Late Bronze Period
- 1500 – 1100 - Late Helladic Period

India

In ancient times India had the shining light of Mohenjo-Daro, which was a planned community with wide, straight streets and modern plumbing, among other what we would consider "modern" innovations. Indian goods also found their way to western ports through trade with the ancient Mediterranean civilizations.
The twin great religions of Hinduism and Buddhism had their genesis in India. The Hindu doctrine of reincarnation made it nearly impossible for anyone to change his or her fortune.

Indo-European languages. The northern Indian languages evolved from Old Indo-Aryan such as Sanskrit. Indo-Uralic languages are being examined. The Finno-Ugric languages are separate from the Indo-sources.

China

China is considered by some historians to be the oldest, uninterrupted civilization in the world. Chinese writing goes back to 1500 BCE. The Neolithic age is traced back 10,000 years, and agriculture goes back 7,000 years. The Yellow River Valley is where the earliest settlements are found. Cliff carvings dating back 6,000 years have been discovered at Ningxia.

Ancient Americans

An agricultural society existed in Peru more than 5,000 years ago. It is called the Norte Chico civilization, and it included 20 communities.

> http://www.precolumbia.com/bearc/CAAS/ancient_america.html
> **Center for Ancient America**

Skill 2.1c Ancient Empires and Civilizations Circa 1700 B.C.E.–500 C.E.

Ancient civilizations were those cultures that developed to a great degree and are considered advanced.

The **Mycenaean** civilization was Europe's first major civilization. It was home to **Sparta, Metropolis**, and **Corinth**--and a target for the **Persian War**. The writing, Linear B, as it continues to be transcribed reveals more about this ancient culture. Along with the text, archaeology has continued to turn up information. For example, it has been discovered that in **Peloponnesus** a town of the **Bronze Age** was deserted in about 1150 and then was reborn 125 years later.

The **Greek Dark Ages** were from 1100 BCE to 750 BCE.

There is evidence of the palaces and cities of the Mycenaean being destroyed around 1200 BCE, about the same time that the **Hittite** culture was destroyed (located in what is now Turkey). The ancient Greek writer **Homer** puts the date for the destruction of Troy at 1220 BCE. **Hisarlik** is the name today for the site where it is thought that if there really was an ancient Troy, it was in this area.

It is assumed that the destruction was because of a **Dorian invasion**, but the answer is not known. In Hittite records, it indicates that destruction occurred by "the people of the Aegean." The Dorian invasion is spoken about as "return of the sons of Heracles" when Greek invaders came in from the north. We do know that only Athens was spared. The destruction is also blamed upon the "Sea People," and there are numerous conjectures as to who they might be.

The Greek city-states located on the coast of Asia Minor were under the control of the **Lydian** king, **Croesus** in the middle of the sixth century BCE. When the Persians under Cyrus conquered the Lydians, then the Persians had control over all the subject states also. Miletus, a Greek city-state under the leader Aristagoras went to persuade the Spartans and Athenians to help him, but the Athenians went to the Sardis, the capital of Lydian, and conquered it. Other city states on the coast of Asia Minor then joined in—until Persia put an end to it.

Cleisthenes of Athens is responsible for the birth of democracy in 510 BCE. He created a system that gave every man a vote. After time, however, there was the **Peloponnesian War in** which Athens was against Sparta and the other Peloponnese cities.

> http://eawc.evansville.edu/grpage.htm
> **Ancient Greece**

Greece was responsible for the rise of independent, strong city-states.   Other important areas that the Greeks are credited with influencing include drama, epic

http://www.ling.ohio-state.edu/~bjoseph/articles/gancient.htm Ancient Greece

and lyric poetry, fables, myths centered on the many gods and goddesses, science, astronomy, medicine, mathematics, philosophy, art, architecture, and recording historical events.

The tradition of theater was born in Greece, with the plays of **Aristophanes** and others. In the field of mathematics, **Pythagoras** and **Euclid** laid the foundation of geometry and **Archimedes** calculated the value of *pi*. **Herodotus** and **Thucydides** were the first to apply research and interpretation to written history.

In sculpture, the Greeks achieved an idealistic aesthetic that had not been perfected before that time. The Greek alphabet was derived from the Phoenician letters which formed the basis for the Roman alphabet and our present-day alphabet. Extensive trading and colonization resulted in the spread of the Greek

civilization. The conquests of **Alexander the Great** spread Greek ideas to the areas he conquered.

Alexander the Great. Philip II of Macedon was his father, and **Aristotle** was Alexander's tutor. Not only did Alexander conquer Egypt and the **Achaemenid Persian Empire** that spanned three continents, but he went to India and to the Iberian Peninsula. He was 32 years old when he died. **Ptolemy**, general under Alexander who was appointed satrap of Egypt and was the founder of the Great Library of Alexandria, called himself King, and his family ruled Egypt until the Romans came.

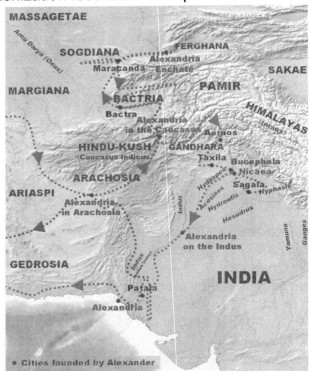

The civilizations of the **Sumerians**, **Amorites**, **Hittites**, **Assyrians**, **Chaldeans**, and **Persians** controlled various areas of the land we call **Mesopotamia**. With few exceptions, tyrants and military leaders controlled trade, religions, and the laws.

Each Sumerian city-state had its own god, with the city-state's leader doubling as the high priest. Subsequent cultures had a handful of gods as well although they had more of a national worship structure, with high priests centered in the capital city as advisors to the tyrant.

Trade was vastly important to these civilizations since they had access to some but not all of the things that they needed to survive. Some trading agreements led to occupation, as was the case with the Sumerians, who did not build walls to protect their wealth of knowledge. Egypt and the Phoenician cities were powerful and regular trading partners of the various Mesopotamian cultures.

Legacies handed down to us from these early societies include:

- Use of writing
- Wheel
- Banking (Sumer)
- Written set of laws (Code of Hammurabi)
- Epic story (*Gilgamesh*)
- The first library dedicated to preserving knowledge (instituted by the Assyrian leader Ashurbanipal)
- Hanging Gardens of Babylon (built by the Chaldean Nebuchadnezzar)

The ancient civilization of the **Sumerians** invented the wheel; developed irrigation through use of canals, dikes, and devices for raising water; devised the system of cuneiform writing; learned to divide time; and built large boats for trade.

The **Babylonians** devised the famous **Code of Hammurabi**, a code of laws.

Egypt built the great pyramids. In Egypt, there was also the development of hieroglyphic writing; preservation of bodies after death; making paper from papyrus; contributing to developments in arithmetic and geometry; the invention of the method of counting in groups of 1-10 (the decimal system); completion of a solar calendar; and the laying of a foundation for science and astronomy. The Egyptian civilization encompassed many cities up and down the Nile River in northeastern and east-central Africa. Egyptian goods flowed from ports and trade centers to locations all over the Mediterranean area and into central Asia. The **pharaohs** who were in command of all aspects of the lives of the Egyptian people were also heads of the various religions. Even though each Egyptian god had its own temple and each temple had its own priests, the pharaoh was the liaison between the people and their gods

The first empire was probably in Mesopotamia--the **Akkadians** led by **Sargon**, conqueror of Sumer. The **Amorite** leader **Hammurabi** who wrote the famous Code was emperor from about 1810 BCE.

Nebuchadnezzar, leader of the Chaldeans, is remember for building the **Hanging Gardens of Babylon** and the **Babylonian Captivity** near the turn of the century in 597 BCE when he conquered Judah and Jerusalem, destroyed the Temple, and banished Jews to Babylon.

The Hittite empire, centered in what is now Turkey, extended from Mesopotamia to Palestine and Syria. They conquered the Babylonians yet over time

http://www.specialtyinterests.net /hittites.html   Hittites

adopted Babylonian laws and religion. The height of the Hittite empire was 1600 to 1200 BCE. The Hittite rulers were less despotic than other rulers in the region, and their religious tolerance included see all gods as legitimate and incorporating them into their religion. Their war with the Egyptians was weakening. Hittite cities continued until 700 BCE when they were taken over by the Assyrians.

The **Assyrians** ruled the northern Mesopotamia by about 1300 BCE. Their empire ultimately included Egypt and the Fertile Crescent. Their empire preceded the Persian Empire. Agriculture and breeding horses were important, but more known perhaps is their record of impaling and beheading enemies.

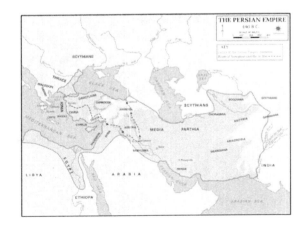

The Medean Empire (600 BCE) reached from the Black Sea to Afghanistan and Central Asia. It was the first Iranian empire and was combined into the Persian Empire of **Cyrus the Great** who took Egypt in 539 BCE and was followed by **Darius** who became king in 522. Darius remade the ancient trade route into the Persian "**Royal Road**" When Darius died, the Persian Empire was at its zenith. The Persians and Greeks engaged in the **Persian Wars** (499-448 BCE). This struggle includes the battles of **Marathon**, which the Greeks won despite being vastly outnumbered; **Thermopylae**, in which **Spartans** held off thousands of Persian warriors for several days; **Salamis,** a naval battle that the Greeks won despite being outgunned and outnumbered; and **Plataea**, in which the Greeks outnumbered the Persians. These victories convinced the Persians not to attempt another invasion of Greece, but it didn't mean the end of the Persian Empire.

That end came at the hands of **Alexander the Great**, a Macedonian general who conquered Greece, Persia--and eventually Egypt, Phoenician cities, and part of India. He created an empire that was staggering in its geography and impact and cultural exchange. This was known as **Hellenization**, and it brought the Greek way of life to people in the East while also bringing exotic goods and customs of the East to Greece.

Until this time, the East and West exchanged goods and customs in small ways, but Alexander changed all that--bringing both sides together under one banner and beginning an exchange of ideas, beliefs, and goods that would capture the imagination of rulers for years after his death.

The **Maurya Empire** lasted from 322 to 185 BCE. **Chandragupta** brought the subcontinent of India together after the Alexander the Great's armies withdrew. There was a common economic system. Waterworks were built, and trade with the selling silk goods, spices, and exotic foods to the Greeks and others. Their trade extended into Southeast Asia. Private corporations were common. Religion developed with Buddhism and Jainism. Not only was their protection of civil and social rights, but there was protection of animals.

Chinese Empires

In 221 BCE China became unified into an empire under Qin Shi Huang.

Empires in China:

Qin Dynasty – 221 BCE – 206 BCE
Han Dynasty - 206 BCE-220 CE
Jin Period – 265-420
Southern and Northern Dynasties – 420-589
Sui Dynasty – 581-618
Tang Dynasty – 618-907
Five Dynasties and Ten Kingdoms – 907-960
Song Dynasty and Liao, Jin, Western Xia - 960–1279 CE
Yuan Dynasty -1271-1368
Ming Dynasty – 1368-1644
Qing Dynasty – 1644 CE - 1911

China expanded, rivaling even Rome in breadth and accomplishments by the time of the famous Han Dynasty. The Great Wall of China was built to keep out invaders. A strong "government of one", was the rule of law.

Chinese were proficient at producing and exporting beautiful artworks and silks. China was also home to many of the inventions, including paper, printing, paper money, and gunpowder.

Rome built itself from one town that borrowed from its Etruscan neighbors into a worldwide empire--from the wilds of Scotland to the shores of the Middle East. The ancient civilization of **Rome** lasted approximately 1,000 years including the periods of Roman Republic and Roman Empire. It began with two kings—Remus and Romulus, and Romulus slew Remus.

Building on the principles of Hellenization, Rome imported and exported goods and customs galore, melding the production capabilities and the belief systems of all it conquered into a heterogeneous, yet distinctly, Roman civilization. Trade, religion, science, political structure—all were incorporated into the Roman Empire with all of the benefits that assimilation brought being passed on to the Empire's citizens.

The **Roman Empire** which began in 27 BCE ended in about 476 CE—when Emperor Romulus Augustus was deposed.

http://www.crystalinks.com/romanempire.html
Roman Empire

There was a sharp contrast between the curious, imaginative, inquisitive Greeks and the practical, simple, down-to-earth, no-nonsense Romans. The population of the city of Rome may have reached a million or more, but 80 percent of Roman citizens lived in smaller communities and in rural areas, and there were many slaves.

In government, Rome used an autocratic form of government but with a **limited administrative system**. That meant that officials were local people in the provinces, and this might be a key to the length of survival for the empire.

A link to Roman History Questions:
http://www.funtrivia.com/quizzes/history/ancient_history/roman_history.html

http://www.pbs.org/empires/romans/educators/lesson8.html
PBS - Romans

Rome fought three wars against Carthage, known as the **Punic Wars**. Rome destroyed Carthage in 146 BCE—and then refounded it because it had an excellent position on the Mediterranean.

Some Roman Empire wars include:

- Germanic Wars
- Roman Conquest of Britain
- Parthian Wars
- Jewish Wars
- Civil Wars
- Gothic Invasions

Splitting of the Empire in the early fourth century had tipped the balance in favor of the eastern part of the Empire, closer to Asia, farther away from Germany, and easier to defend.

The early **religion of the Roman Empire** had been one of many gods and goddesses, representing the various parts of Nature and the skies. As Rome had conquered various people with various religions, the Empire had assimilated the religions of those people.

By the time that the Eastern Empire was created, the Empire as a whole contained a wide variety of religious beliefs and faiths. Constantine founded Constantinople in 330 CE, and the Eastern Empire became The **Byzantine Empire**. It was close to the Middle East and included traditions of Mesopotamia and Persia. This was in contrast to the Western Empire, which inherited the traditions of Greece and Carthage.

Byzantium was known for exquisite artwork including the famous church **Hagia Sophia**. Uniquely situated at the gateway to both West and East, Byzantium could control trade going in both directions. The Eastern Empire was much more centralized and rigid in its enforcement of its policies than the feudal West. The **Byzantines** made important contributions in art and the preservation of Greek and Roman achievements including architecture (especially in eastern Europe and Russia) and the **Code of Justinian**—with Roman law collected into a clear and well-stated system of laws.

The Byzantine Empire (1353-1453) was the successor to the Roman Empire in the

East and protected Western Europe from invaders such as the Persians and Ottomans. The Byzantine Empire was a Christian incorporation of Greek philosophy, language, and literature along with Roman government and law. It is regarded as having had a strong infantry, cavalry, and engineering corps along with excellent morale among its soldiers.

The Conference of Nicea was held in 325 CE, and one matter was the "Trinity." A uniform Christian doctrine was created with the **Nicene Creed**. After the the Council of Chaledon in 451, there was no more debate-- to speak out against the Trinity was now considered blasphemy or heresy.

Skill 2.1d   Disruption and Reversal Circa 500–1400 C.E.

The **fall of the Western Roman Empire** was due to a variety of factors, including:

- Increasing sprawl of the Empire
- Resilience of the Germanic and other "barbarian" foes
- Spread of dissatisfaction of the Empire's residents themselves with the administration of the vast social, economic, and political network

Germanic tribes controlled most of Europe. The five major tribes were the **Visigoths, Ostrogoths, Vandals, Saxons,** and the **Franks**. The Ostrogoths, Viligoths, and Vandals converted to Arianism which does not adhere to the **Nicene Creed**, so the Roman Catholic Church viewed them as heretics.

The **Franks** successfully stopped the invasion of southern Europe by Muslims by defeating them under the leadership of Charles Martel at the Battle of Tours in 732 CE. In 768 the grandson of Charles Martel, **Charlemagne**, became King of the Franks. A man of war, Charlemagne also respected and encouraged learning. He is remembered for efforts to rule fairly and ensure just treatment for the people. After war upon the Roman Empire, when the leader Theodoric died in 526, Ostrogoths and Visigoths separated. Byzantine Emperor Justinian I declared war on the Vandals, and afterward they fled or became slaves. The Saxons invaded Britannia in the fifth century along with fellow tribe the Angles. They immigrated onto the island that became known as England. This later had them fighting against invading Vikings.

A problem developed regarding the iconoclasm issue: **Emperor Leo III** (685-741 CE) ordered that the image of Jesus on the Chalke Gate at the entrance to the Constantinople Palace be replaced with a cross and order that all icons across the empire be destroyed. **Pope Gregory III** (731-741) called a synod, and it was agreed to take strong measures against anyone who would destroy images of Jesus, Mary, or the saints. Leo then attempted to kidnap the Pope, but a storm destroyed Leo's ships.

In 711, Spain was conquered by the **Muslims**. In 805, they captured Rhodes and Cyprus; in 816 the island of Corsica; in 969, Egypt. In 1099, the **Crusaders** captured Jerusalem.

Highlights of the Period

In the tenth century in the Americas it was the end of the Classic **Maya** period, and it marked the rise of the **Toltecs**. The Vikings settled in Northern France, becoming the **Normans** instead of the Norse. The tenth century is viewed as the low point in Western history; it was also a low point in Chinese history who used gunpowder in a battle for the first time, but for the Muslims, the **Puebloans** , and the **Byzantine Empire**, this century was zenith.

http://www.fordham.edu/halsall/sbook1k.html
Crusades: Medieval Sourcebook

In the eleventh century the German emperor of Rome, Henry IV (1050-1106) clashed with Pope Gregory VII. He insisted upon the right of a ruler to appoint members of the clergy to their offices. This is known as the **Investiture Controversy** and resulted in 50 years of civil war in Germany.

The **Byzantine-Arab Wars** began in 629 CE and lasted until the twelfth century. The eleventh century is regarded as the beginning of the **High Middle Ages**. Part of what happened was that the **Crusades** began. The Byzantine Empire collapsed when Constantinople fell to the Ottoman Turks in 1453.

http://www.accd.edu/sac/history/keller/Mongols/empsub1.html
Ghengis Khan

Mongol **Ghengis Khan** born in about 1167 grew up to be a warrior, and he overran China, then moved on to to battle in Caucasia, with Russians and Turks. His legacy went on after his death. His grandsons founded dynasties—in Russia, in Persia, in China, and his descendants continued to rule for centuries

The **Vikings** had spread their ideas and knowledge of trade routes and sailing, accomplished first through their conquests and later through trade. They were Scandinavian seafaring warriors who raided and colonized wide areas of Europe from the eighth to the eleventh century. Overpopulation at home, ease of conquest abroad, and their extraordinary capacity as shipbuilders and sailors inspired their adventures.

In 865 Vikings conquered major centers in England--which, under **Alfred the Great**, made a truce in 878 that led to Danish control of much of England. Alfred and his successors retook many of the lands, although renewed Viking raids in 980 brought England into the empire where it remained until 1042, when the Vikings were finally pushed out. The Vikings

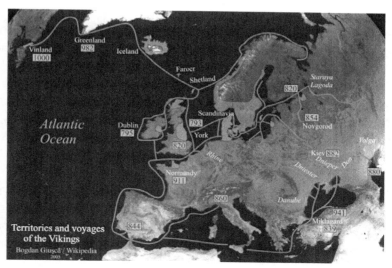

permanently affected English social structure, dialect, and names, and subsequently European cultures at large. In the western seas, Vikings had settled in Iceland by 900, after which they traveled to Greenland and North America. As traders they made commercial treaties with the Byzantines and served as mercenaries in Constantinople. Viking activity came to an end in the eleventh century.

Feudalism

During the Middle Ages, the system of **feudalism** became a dominant feature of the economic and social system in Europe. Feudalism began as a way to ensure that a king or nobleman could raise an army when needed. In exchange for the promise of loyalty and military service, **lords** would grant a section of land, called a **fief** to a **vassal**, as those who took this oath of loyalty were called. The vassal was then entitled to work the land and benefit from its proceeds or to grant it in turn as a fief to another. At the bottom of this ladder were **peasants** or **serfs** who actually worked the land. At the top was the king to whom all lands might legally belong. The king could ensure loyalty among his advisors by giving them use of large sections of land which they in turn could grant as fiefs.

It was a system of loyalty and protection. The strong protected the weak who returned the service with farm labor, military service, and loyalty. Improved tools and farming methods made life more bearable although most never left the manor nor traveled from their village during their lifetime. The lord or noble, in return for the serfs' loyalty, offered them his protection.

In practical effect, the serf was considered property owned by his lord with little or no rights at all. The lord's sole obligation to the serfs was to protect them so they could continue to work for him (in most cases, though not all, lords were men). This system would last for many centuries. In Russia it would last until the 1860s. **Manorialism**, which also arose during the Middle Ages is similar to feudalism in structure, but consisted of self-contained manors that were often owned outright by a nobleman. Some manors were granted conditionally to their lords, and some were linked to the military service and oaths of loyalty found in feudalism, meaning that the two terms overlapped somewhat.

Manors usually consisted of a large house for the lord and his family, surrounded by fields and a small village that supported the activities of the manor. The lord of the manor was expected to provide certain services for the villagers and laborers associated with the manor including the support of a church.

Also coming into importance at this time was the era of **knighthood** and its code of chivalry because knighthood rewarded good manners including loyalty to the king. Knighthood was not inherited. There was also tremendous influence of the Roman Catholic Church.

Until the Renaissance, the Church was the only place where people could be educated. The Bible and other books were hand-copied by monks in the monasteries. Cathedrals were built and were decorated with art depicting religious subjects.

With the increase in trade and travel, cities sprang up and began to grow. Craft workers in the cities developed their skills to a high degree, eventually organizing **guilds** to protect the quality of the work and to regulate the buying and selling of their products. City government developed and flourished centered on strong town councils. Active in city government and the town councils were the wealthy businessmen who made up the rising middle class.

The end of the feudal manorial system was sealed by the outbreak and spread of the infamous **Black Death**, which killed over one-third of the total population of Europe. The **Black Death** resulted in a look back to ancient Greece since prayers were not working. Those who survived and were skilled in any job or occupation were in demand, and many serfs or peasants found freedom and, for that time, a decidedly improved standard of living. Strong nation-states became powerful and people developed a renewed interest in life and learning.

Crusades

The **Crusades** were a series of military campaigns beginning in the eleventh century against the encroaching Muslim Empire, particularly in the holy land of Palestine and the city of Jerusalem. They continued into the thirteenth century as Jerusalem and other holy cities changed hands between Christian and Muslim forces. Several crusades took place within Europe, as well, such as the efforts to re-conquer portions of the Muslim-occupied Iberian Peninsula. Not only were the Crusades against Muslims but also against Greek Orthodox Christians and pagan Slaves.

The Christian Byzantine Empire was centered in Constantinople. The empire was under attack from Seljuk Turk forces who had taken Palestine. The eastern emperor, Alexius I called on his western counterpart, **Pope Urban II** for assistance. Urban saw the situation as an opportunity to reunite Christendom, which was still in the throes of schism between the Eastern Orthodox and the Western Catholic sects, and to invest the papacy with religious authority.

In 1095, Urban called on all Christians to rally behind the campaign to drive the Turks out of the Holy Land. Participation in the crusade, Urban said, would count as full penance for sin in the eyes of the Church.
A force of crusaders marched to Jerusalem and captured it, massacring the inhabitants. Along the way, several small Crusader states were established. A second crusade was led against Damascus in 1145, but was unsuccessful.

In 1187, **Saladin**, the Sultan of Egypt recaptured Jerusalem, and a third Crusade was called for by Pope Gregory VIII. This Crusade was joined by the combined forces of France, England, and the Holy Roman Empire, but fell short of its goal to recapture Jerusalem. The fourth Crusade took place in 1202, under Pope Innocent III. The intention of the fourth Crusade was to enter the Holy Land through Egypt. The plan was changed, however, and forces diverted to Constantinople.
One result of the Crusades was to establish and reinforce the political and military authority of the Catholic Church and the Roman Pope. The religious fervor spurred on by the Crusades would eventually culminate in such movements as the **Inquisition** in Spain and the expulsion of the **Moors** from Europe.

The marches of the crusaders also opened new routes between Europe and the East along which culture, learning and trade could travel.

Asia and Africa

Between the fourth and ninth centuries, Asia was a story of religions and empires, of kings and wars, and of increasing and decreasing contact with the West.

India began this period recovering from the invasion of **Alexander the Great**. One strong man who met the great Alexander was **Chandragupta Maurya**, who began one of his country's most successful dynasties. Chandragupta conquered most of what we now call India. His grandson, **Asoka**, was more of a peaceful ruler but powerful nonetheless. He was also a great believer in the practices and power of Buddhism, sending missionaries throughout Asia to preach the ways of the Buddha. Succeeding the Mauryas were the Guptas, who ruled India for a longer period of time and brought prosperity and international recognition to their people.

The **Guptas** were great believers in science and mathematics, especially their uses in production of goods. They invented the decimal system and had a concept of zero, two things that put them ahead of the rest of the world on the mathematics timeline. They were the first to make cotton and calico, and their medical practices were much more advanced than those in Europe and elsewhere in Asia at the time. These inventions and innovations created high demand for Indian goods throughout Asia and Europe.

The idea of a united India continued after the Gupta Dynasty ended. It was especially favorable to the invading Muslims, who took over in the eleventh century, ruling the country for hundreds of years through a series of sultanates. The most famous Muslim leader of India was **Tamerlane**, who founded the Mogul Dynasty and began a series of conquests that expanded the borders of India. Tamerlane's grandson **Akbar** is considered the greatest Mogul. He believed in freedom of religion and is perhaps most well-known for the series of buildings that he had built, including mosques, palaces, forts and tombs, some of which are still standing today. During the years that Muslims ruled India, Hinduism continued to be respected, although it was a minority religion; Buddhism, however, died out almost entirely from the country that begot its founder, **Siddhartha Gautama**.

Taj Mahal

The imposing mountains to the north of India served as a deterrent to Chinese expansion. India was more vulnerable to invaders who came from the west or by sea from the south. The Indian people were also vulnerable to the powerful monsoons, which came driving up from the south a few times every year, bringing howling winds and devastation in their wake.

The story of **China** during this time is one of dynasties controlling various parts of what is now China and Tibet. The **Tang Dynasty** was one of the most long-lasting and the most proficient, inventing the idea of civil service and the practice of block printing. Next was the Sung Dynasty, which produced some of the world's greatest paintings and porcelain pottery but failed to unify China in a meaningful way. This would prove instrumental in the takeover of China by the Mongols, led by Genghis Khan and his most famous grandson, Kublai.

Genghis Khan was known as a conqueror, and Kublai was known as a uniter. They both extended the borders of their empire, however; and at its height, the Mongol Empire was the largest the world has ever seen, encompassing all of China, Russia, Persia, and central Asia.

Following the Mongols were the Ming and Manchu Dynasties, both of which focused on isolation. As a result, China at the end of the eighteenth century knew very little of the outside world, and vice versa. **Ming** artists created beautiful porcelain pottery, but not much of it saw its way into the outside world until much later. The **Manchus** were known for their focus on farming and road-building, two practices that were instituted in greater numbers in order to try to keep up with expanding population. Confucianism, Taoism, and ancestor worship—the staples of Chinese society for hundreds of years—continued to flourish during all this time.

The other major power in Asia was **Japan**, which developed independently and tried to keep itself that way for hundreds of years. Early Japanese society focused on the emperor and the farm, in that order. Japan was often influenced early on by China, from which it borrowed many things, including religion (Buddhism), a system of writing, calendar, and even fashion. The Sea of Japan protected Japan from Chinese invasion, including the famous Mongol attempted invasion that was blown back by by the famed **kamikaze** or "divine wind." Japan was thus free to continue to develop itself as it saw fit and to refrain from interacting with the West, especially. This isolation, and thus the feudal system, lasted until the nineteenth century.

Feudalism developed in Japan later than it did in Europe and lasted longer as well. The power of the emperor declined as it was usurped by the era of the **Daimyo** and his loyal soldiers, the **samurai**. Japan flourished economically and culturally during many of these years, although the policy of isolation the country developed kept the rest of the world from knowing such things. Buddhism and local religions were joined by Christianity in the sixteenth century, but it wasn't until the mid-nineteenth century that Japan rejoined the world community.

From its beginnings, Japan had morphed into an imperial form of government, with the divine emperor being able to do no wrong and, therefore, serving for life. **Kyoto**, the capital, became one of the largest and most powerful cities in the world. Slowly, though, as in Europe, the rich and powerful landowners, the nobles, grew powerful. Eventually, they had more power than the emperor. A change of attitude in the minds of the Japanese people was required.

The nobles were lords of great lands and were called **Daimyos**. They were of the highest social class and had working for them people of lower social classes, including the lowly peasants, who had few privileges other than being allowed to work for the great men that the Daimyos told everyone they were. The Daimyos had warriors serving them known as **samurai**, who were answerable only to the Daimyo. The samurai code of honor was an exemplification of the overall Japanese belief that every man was a soldier and a gentleman.

The main economic difference between imperial and feudal Japan was that the money that continued to flow into the country from trade with China, Korea, and other Asian countries and from good, old-fashioned plundering on the high seas made its way no longer into the emperor's coffers but rather the pockets of the Daimyos.

African civilizations during these centuries were few and far between. Most of northern coastal Africa had been conquered by Moslem armies. The preponderance of deserts and other inhospitable lands restricted African settlements to a few select areas. The city of Zimbabwe became a trading center in south-central Africa in the fifth century but didn't last long. More successful was **Ghana**, a Muslim-influenced kingdom that arose in the ninth century and lasted for nearly 300 years. Ghanaians had large farming areas and also raised cattle and elephants. They traded with people from Europe and the Middle East.

Eventually overrunning Ghana was Mali, whose trade center **Timbuktu** survived its own empire's demise and blossomed into one of the world's caravan destinations. Iron, tin, and leather came out of Mali with a vengeance. The succeeding civilization of the Songhai had relative success in maintaining the success of their predecessors. Religion in all of these places was definitely Muslim, and even after extended contact with other cultures technological advancements were few and far between.

Islam

A few years after the death of the Emperor Justinian, Mohammed was born (570 CE) in a small Arabian town near the Red Sea. Before this time, Arabians played only an occasional role in history. Except for the coastal areas on the Red Sea, Arabia was a vast desert of rock and sand. It was populated by nomadic wanderers called **Bedouins** who lived in scattered tribes near oases where they watered their herds. Tribal leaders engaged in frequent war with one another. The family, or tribe, was the social and political unit under the authority of the head of the family.

Although there was regular contact with Christians and Jews through trading interactions, the idea of monotheism was foreign. What vague unity there was within the religion took place in small temples such as a square temple called **the Kaaba** (Cube) located in the town of **Mecca**. Arabs came from all parts of the country in annual pilgrimages to Mecca during the sacred months when warfare was prohibited. For this reason, Mecca was considered the center of Arab religion.

In about 610, **Mohammed** came to prominence. He called his new religion **Islam** (submission to the will of God) and his followers were called **Moslems**. His first converts were members of his family and his friends. As the new faith began to grow, it remained a secret society. When they began to make their faith public, they met with opposition and persecution from the pagan Arabians who feared the new religion and the possible loss of the profitable trade with the pilgrims who came to the Kaaba every year.

But Islam slowly gained ground although persecutions of Moslems became more severe around Mecca. In 622, Mohammed and his close followers fled the city and found refuge in **Medina** to the North. His flight is called the **Hegira**. This event marks the beginning of the Moslem calendar. Mohammed took advantage of the ongoing feuds between Jews and Arabs in the city and became the rulers of Medina, making it the capital of a rapidly growing state.

In the years that followed, Islam grew significantly. The group survived by raiding caravans on the road to Mecca and plundering nearby Jewish tribes. It attracted many converts from the Bedouin tribes. By 630, Mohammed conquered Mecca and made it the religious center of Islam, toward which all Moslems turned to pray, and the *Kaaba,* the most sacred **Mosque** or temple. Medina remained the political capital. By the time of Mohammed's death in 632 CE, most of the people of Arabia had become at least nominal adherents of Islam.

Mohammed left behind a collection of divine revelations (**surahs**) he claimed were delivered by the angel Gabriel. These were collected and published in a book called the **Koran (**Qur'an), which is the holy scripture of Islam. The revelations were not kept in chronological order. After the prophet's death they were organized by length (in diminishing order). The Koran contains phonetic and thematic structures and rhyme and was written down in the classical Arabic, based on the Medieval language of Quraysh, Mohammed's tribe

Islam has five basic principles, known as the **Pillars of Islam**:

- The oneness and omnipotence of God – **Allah**.
- Mohammed is the prophet of Allah to whom all truth has been revealed by God.
- To each of the previous prophets (Adam, Noah, Abraham, Moses and Jesus) a part of the truth was revealed.
- One should **pray five times a day** at prescribed intervals, facing Mecca,
- **Charity** – for the welfare of the community.
- **Fasting** from sunrise to sunset every day during the holy month of **Ramadan** to cleanse the spirit.
- **Pilgrimage to Mecca** should be made if possible and if no one suffers thereby.

The moral principles of Islam are:

- Practice the virtues of charity, humility and patience
- Enemies are to be forgiven
- Avarice, lying and malice are condemned
- Drinking alcohol, eating pork, and gambling are prohibited

In Islam on the Day of Judgment all souls will be judged. The infidel will be condemned to a **gehennem** with perpetual fire, and the good/faithful will go to Paradise, a beautiful place of cool waters, sensual delights, and ease. The Koran elevated the level of women. A man could marry as many as four wives if he loved them equally. Divorce was easy, but the wife had to be given a dowry.

Mohammed died with neither a political nor a religious succession plan. His cousin, Ali, who had married Mohammed's daughter, Fatima, believed his kinship and his heroism as a warrior gave him a natural claim to leadership. But Moslems in Medina thought one of their own should succeed Mohammed. **Abu Bakr** was finally chosen. He took the title of **Caliph**. The title was retained throughout the duration of the Moslem Empire.

These Moslem Arabians immediately launched an amazing series of conquests which, in time, extended the empire from the Indus to Spain. It has often been said that these conquests were motivated by religious fanaticism and the determination to force Islam upon the infidel. However, the motives were economic and political.

During the period of expansion a brief civil war occurred because Ali was proclaimed Caliph at Medina. He was opposed by an aristocratic family of Mecca called the **Umayyad**. Ali was assassinated in 661, and the Umayyads emerged supreme, handing the caliphate down in their family for nearly a century. Because their strongest support was in Syria, they moved the capital from Medina to Damascus. Finally, in the middle of the thirteenth century, they were overcome by a fresh invasion from Asia–the Mongols. The Abbasid caliphate disappeared.

Despite these political divisions, the Moslem world maintained strong economic, religious and cultural unity throughout this period. Mohammed had taught that all Moslems are brothers, equal in the sight of God. Conversion to Islam erased the differences between peoples of different ethnic origin.

A blending of cultures, facilitated by a common language, a common religion, and a strong economy, created learning, literature, science, technology and art that surpassed anything found in the Western Christian world during the Early Middle Ages. Interestingly, the most brilliant period of Moslem culture was from the eighth century through the eleventh, coinciding with the West's darkest cultural period. Reading and writing in Arabic, the study of the Koran, arithmetic, and other elementary subjects were taught to children in schools attached to the mosques. In larger and wealthier cities, the mosques offered more advanced education in literature, logic, philosophy, law, algebra, astronomy, medicine, science, theology and the tradition of Islam. Books were produced for the large reading public. The wealthy collected private libraries and public libraries arose in large cities.

The most popular subjects were theology and the law, but the more important field of study was philosophy. The works of the Greek and Hellenistic philosophers were translated into Arabic and interpreted with commentaries. These were later passed on to the Western Christian societies and schools in the twelfth and thirteenth centuries. The basis of Moslem philosophy was Aristotelian and Neo-platonic ideas, which were essentially transmitted without creative modification.

The Moslems were also interested in natural science. They translated the works on Galen and Hippocrates into Arabic and added the results of their own experience in medicine. **Avicenna** was regarded in Western Europe as one of the great masters of medicine. They also adopted the work of the Greeks in the other sciences and modified and supplemented them with their own discoveries. Much of their work in chemistry was focused on alchemy, the attempt to transmute base metals into gold.

Adopting the heritage of Greek mathematics, the Moslems also borrowed a system of numerals from India. This laid the foundation for modern arithmetic, geometry, trigonometry and algebra.

Moslem art and architecture tended to be mostly uniform in style, allowing for some regional modification. They borrowed from Byzantine, Persian and other sources. The floor plan of the mosques was generally based on Mohammed's house at Medina. The notable unique elements were the tall minarets from which the faithful were called to prayer. Interior decoration was the style now called *arabesque*. Because Mohammed had banned paintings or other images of living creatures, they continued to be absent from mosques, although they occasionally appeared in book illustration and secular contexts. But their skilled craftsmen produced the finest art in jewelry, ceramics, carpets, and carved ivory.

The Moslems also produced sophisticated literature in both prose and poetry. The flexibility of the Arabic language was very well adapted to poetry. Little, however, of their poetry or prose has been translated into Western languages. The best-known works of this period are the short stories known as the **Arabian Nights** and the poems of **Omar Khayyam.**

The Ottoman Empire

The Ottoman strength in Anatolia grew by 1400, and their power was being felt in the Byzantine territory—in Macedonia and Bulgaria. They struggled to take Constantinople again and again, and finally in 1453, they were successful and renamed it **Istanbul.**

The Ottoman Empire is noted for its ability to unite a highly varied population as it grew through conquest and treaty arrangement. This ability is to be attributed to military strength, a policy of strict control of recently invaded territories, and an Islamic-inspired philosophy that stated that all Muslims, Christians, and Jews were related because they were all "People of the Book."

The major religious groups were permitted to construct their own semi-autonomous communities. Conquering armies immediately repaired buildings, roads, bridges, and aqueducts or built them where needed. They also built modern sanitary facilities and linked the city to a supply structure that was able to provide for the needs of the people. This religious and ethnic tolerance was the basis upon which a heterogeneous culture was built. It quickly transformed a Turkish empire into the Ottoman Empire.

The attitude of tolerant blending and respect for diverse ethnic and cultural groups, in time produced a rich mix of people that was reflected in multi-cultural and multi-religious policies that were based on recognition and respect for different perspectives. Ottoman architecture, although influenced by Seljuk, Byzantine, and Arab styles, developed a unique style of its own. Music was important to the elites of the empire. Two primary styles of music that developed were Ottoman classical music and folk music. Again, both styles reflect a basis in the diversity of influences that came together in the unified empire.

Government had an absolute authority in the monarch or sultan. The Ottomans viewed justice as distributive justice, a justice of fairness, and that it is vital to build a just government and just laws.

Skill 2.1e   Emerging Global Interactions

The word "**Renaissance**" literally means "rebirth", and signaled the rekindling of interest in the glory of ancient classical Greek and Roman civilizations. It was the period in human history marking the start of many ideas and innovations leading to our modern age. A combination of a renewed fascination with the classical world and new infusion of money into the hands of those who were fascinated brought on the Renaissance. In the areas of art, literature, music, and science, the Western world grew.

The Renaissance began in Italy with many of its ideas starting in Florence, controlled by the infamous **Medici** family. Education, especially for some of the merchants, then required reading, writing, math, the study of law, and the writings of classical Greek and Roman writers.

Most famous are the Renaissance artists, The more important artists were Giotto and his development of perspective in paintings; **Leonardo da Vinci** who was not only an artist but also a scientist and inventor; **Michelangelo** who was a sculptor, painter, and architect; and others including Raphael, Donatello, Titian, and Tintoretto. All of these men pioneered a new method of painting and sculpture—that of portraying real events and real people as they really looked, not as the artists imagined them to be. Michelangelo's *David* illustrates this.

Literature grew during the Renaissance. **Humanists**, a group which included **Petrarch, Boccaccio, Erasmus**, and **Sir Thomas More**, advanced the idea of being interested in life here on earth and the opportunities it can bring, rather than constantly focusing on heaven and its rewards.

The monumental works of **Shakespeare, Dante,** and **Cervantes** found their origins in these ideas as well as the ones that drove the painters and sculptors. All of these works, of course, owe much of their existence to the invention of the **printing press**, which occurred during the Renaissance.

The Renaissance changed music as well. No longer just a religious experience, music could be fun and composed for its own sake, to be enjoyed in fuller and more humanistic ways than in the Middle Ages. Musicians worked for themselves, rather than for the churches, as before, and so could command good money for their work, increasing their prestige.

Science advanced considerably during the Renaissance, especially in the area of physics and astronomy. **Copernicus, Kepler,** and **Galileo** led a Scientific Revolution in proving that the earth was round and certainly not perfect, an earth-shattering revelation to those who clung to medieval ideals of a geocentric, church-centered existence.

All of these things encouraged people to see the world in a new way, more real, more realized, and more realistic than ever before. Other contributions of the Italian Renaissance period were in:

- **Political philosophy** - the writings of **Machiavelli**

- **Literature** - the writings of **Petrarch** and **Boccaccio**

- **Medicine** - the work of Brussels-born **Andrea Vesalius** earned him the title of "father of anatomy" and had a profound influence on the Spaniard **Michael** Servetus and the Englishman **William Harvey**

In Germany, **Gutenberg**'s invention of the printing press with movable type facilitated the rapid spread of Renaissance ideas, writings and innovations, thus ensuring the enlightenment of most of Western Europe. Contributions were also made by **Durer** and **Holbein** in art and by **Paracelsus** in science and medicine.

The effects of the Renaissance in the Low Countries can be seen in the literature and philosophy of **Erasmus** and the art of **van Eyck** and **Breughel the Elder**. **Rabelais** and **de Montaigne** in France also contributed to literature and philosophy. In Spain, the art of **El Greco** and **de Morales** flourished, as did the writings of **Cervantes** and **De Vega**. In England, Sir Thomas More and **Sir Francis Bacon** wrote and taught philosophy and were inspired by **Vesalius**. **William Harvey** made important contributions in medicine. The greatest talent was found in literature and drama and given to mankind by **Chaucer, Spenser, Marlowe, Jonson**, and the incomparable Shakespeare.

The Renaissance ushered in a time of curiosity, learning, and incredible energy. It sparked a desire for trade for exotic products and better, faster, cheaper trade routes. Geographers, astronomers and mapmakers made important contributions, and many studied and applied the work of such men as Hipparchus of Greece, Ptolemy of Egypt, Tycho Brahe of Denmark, and Fra Mauro of Italy.

The Reformation

The Reformation period consisted of two phases: the Protestant Revolution and the Catholic Reformation.

The **Protestant Revolution** came about because of religious, political, and economic reasons.

The **religious reasons** stemmed from abuses in the Catholic Church including the clergy and their lifestyles; the sale of religious offices, indulgences, and dispensations; different theologies within the Church; and frauds involving sacred relics.

The **political reasons** for the Protestant Revolution involved the increase in the power of rulers who were considered "absolute monarchs." They desired all power and control, especially over the Church. The growth of "nationalism" or patriotic pride in one's own country was another contributing factor.

Economic reasons included the greed of ruling monarchs to possess and control all lands and wealth of the Church, the deep animosity against the burdensome papal taxation, the rise of the affluent middle class and its clash with medieval Church ideals, and the increase of an active system of mercantilism.

The Protestant Revolution began in Germany with the revolt of **Martin Luther** against Church abuses. It spread to Switzerland where it was led by **John Calvin** (Jean Cauvin). It began in England with the efforts of **King Henry VIII** to have his marriage to Catherine of Aragon annulled so he could wed another for a male heir. The results were the increasing support given not only by the people but also by nobles and some rulers. The Church attempted to stop it.

The **Catholic Reformation** was undertaken by the Church in response to the Protestant Revolution. The major efforts to this end were supplied by the **Council of Trent** and the **Jesuits**. Six major results of the Reformation included:

- Religious freedom
- Religious tolerance
- More opportunities for education
- Power and control of rulers limited
- Increase in religious wars
- An increase in fanaticism and persecution

The Scientific Revolution and the Enlightenment

The Scientific Revolution and the Enlightenment were two of the most important movements in the history of civilization, resulting in a new sense of self-examination and a wider view of the world than ever before.

The **Scientific Revolution** was, above all, a shift in focus from **belief to evidence**. Scientists and philosophers wanted to see the proof, not just believe what other people told them. It was an exciting time for forward-looking thinkers.

A Polish astronomer, **Nicolaus Copernicus**, began the **Scientific Revolution**. He crystallized a lifetime of observations into a book that was published about the time of his death. In this book, *Revolutions of the Celestial Spheres*, Copernicus argued that the Sun, not the Earth, was the center of a solar system and that other planets revolved around the Sun, not the Earth. This flew in the face of established, Church-mandated doctrine. The Church wielded tremendous power at this time, including the power to banish people or sentence them to prison or even death for heresy.

The Danish astronomer **Tycho Brahe** was the first to catalog his thousands of observations of the night sky. Building on Brahe's data, German scientist **Johannes Kepler** communicated his Laws of Planetary Motions. Using Brahe's data, Kepler confirmed Copernicus's observations and argument that the Earth revolved around the Sun.

The most famous defender of this idea was **Galileo Galilei**, an Italian scientist who conducted many famous experiments in the pursuit of science. He is most well-known for his defense of the **heliocentric** (sun-centered) idea. He wrote a book comparing the two theories, but most readers could tell easily that he favored the new one. He was convinced of this mainly because of what he had seen with his own eyes. He had used the relatively new invention of the telescope to see four moons of Jupiter. Those moons did not revolve around the Earth, so why should everything else? Galileo's ideas were not favored by the Church. The Church ordered Galileo to be placed under house arrest.

Galileo died under house arrest, but his ideas didn't die with him. The English scientist **Isaac Newton** became perhaps the most famous scientist of all. He is known as the discoverer of gravity and a pioneering voice in the study of optics (light), calculus, and physics. Newton argued for a **mechanistic** view of the world. People can see how the world works and prove how the world works through observation.

Then came the **Enlightenment**, a period of intense self-study that focused on ethics and logic. More so than at any time before, scientists and philosophers questioned widely held beliefs in an attempt to discover the world within. "I think, therefore I am" ("*Cogito ergo sum*" in Latin) was said by **Rene Descartes**, a French scientist-philosopher whose dedication to logic and the rigid rules of observation were a blueprint for the thinkers who came after him.

England's **David Hume** was a pioneer of the doctrine of **empiricism**, a theory of experience as truth. Hume believed in the value of **skepticism**. He was suspicious of things that other people told him to be true and constantly set out to discover the truth for himself. These two related ideas influenced many thinkers after Hume, and his writings continue to inspire philosophers to this day.

Immanuel Kant of Germany was both a philosopher and a scientist. He wrote the famous essay, "Answering the Question: What Is Enlightenment?" and he answered his famous question with the motto "Dare to Know." Kant believed that humans were rational and capable of creative thought and intense self-evaluation. He encouraged self-examination and observation of the world. Kant believed that the source of morality lay not in the nature of the grace of God but in the human soul itself. He believed that man believed in God for practical, not religious or mystical, reasons.

The idea of **social contract**--the belief that government existed because people wanted it to, that the people had an agreement with the government that they would submit to it as long as it protected them and didn't encroach on their basic human rights--was an idea first made famous by the Frenchman **Jean-Jacques Rousseau** but was also adopted by England's **John Locke** and America's **Thomas Jefferson**.

Skill 2.1f Political and Industrial Revolutions, Nationalism (1750–1914)

The period from the 1700s to the 1800s was characterized in Western countries by opposing political ideas of democracy and nationalism. This resulted in strong nationalistic feelings and people of common cultures asserting their belief in the right to have a part in their government.

The **American Revolution** resulted in the successful efforts of the English colonists in America to win their freedom from Great Britain. After more than one hundred years of mostly self-government, the colonists resented the increased British meddling and control, they declared their freedom, won the Revolutionary War with aid from France, and formed a new independent nation.

The **French Revolution** was the revolt of the middle and lower classes against the gross political and economic excesses of the rulers and the supporting nobility. Conditions leading to revolt included extreme taxation, inflation, lack of food, and

the total disregard for the impossible, degrading, and unacceptable condition of the people on the part of the rulers, nobility, and the Church. Coming at the end of the eighteenth century, it ended the thousand-year rule of kings in France and established the nation as a republic, the first in a series of French Republics.

The revolution began in 1789, after **King Louis XVI** had convened the French parliament to deal with an enormous national debt. The common people's division of the parliament declared itself the true legislature of France, and when the king seemed to resist, a crowd destroyed the royal prison, the **Bastille**. A constitutional monarchy was set up, but after King Louis and his queen, **Marie Antoinette**, tried to flee the country, they were arrested, tried for treason, and executed on the guillotine.

Control of the government passed to **Robespierre** and other radicals - the extreme Jacobins--and the **Reign of Terror** followed from 1793-1794, when thousands of French nobles and others considered enemies of the revolution were executed. After the Terror, Robespierre himself was executed, and a new ruling body, the Directory, came into power. Its incompetence and corruption allowed **Napoleon Bonaparte** to emerge in 1799 as dictator and, eventually, to become emperor. Napoleon's ascent to power is considered the official end of the revolution.

The American Revolution and the French Revolution were similar yet different, liberating their people from unwanted government interference and installing a different kind of government. They were both fought for the liberty of the common people, and they both were built on writings and ideas that embraced such an outcome; yet there is where the similarities end. Both Revolutions proved that people could expect more from their government and that such rights as self-determination were worth fighting--and dying--for.

Several important differences need to be emphasized:

First, the British colonists were striking back against unwanted taxation and other sorts of "government interference."

Second, the American Revolution involved a years-long campaign, of often bloody battles, skirmishes, and stalemates.

Third, the American Revolution resulted in a representative government which marketed itself as a beacon of democracy for the rest of the world.

The French people were starving and, in many cases, destitute and were striking back against an autocratic regime that cared more for high fashion and courtly love than bread and circuses.

The French Revolution was bloody to a degree but mainly an overthrow of society and its outdated traditions.

The French Revolution resulted in a **consulship**, a generalship, and then an emperor—probably not what the perpetrators of the Revolution had in mind when they first struck back at the king and queen.

Still, both Revolutions are looked back on as turning points in history, as times when the governed stood up to the governors and said, "Enough."

Until the early years of the twentieth century Russia was ruled by a succession of **Czars**. The Czars ruled as autocrats or, sometimes, despots. Society was essentially feudalistic and was structured in three levels.

- The top level was held by the Czar.
- The second level was composed of the rich nobles who held government positions and owned vast tracts of land.
- The third level of the society was composed of the remaining people who lived in poverty as peasants or serfs.

There were several unsuccessful attempts to revolt during the nineteenth century, caused largely by discontent among these three levels, especially the peasant, but they were quickly suppressed. The two revolutions of the early twentieth century in 1905 and 1917, however, were quite different.

Discontent with the social structure, with the living conditions of the peasants, and with working conditions despite industrialization were among the causes of the **1905 Revolution**.

This general discontent was aggravated by the **Russo-Japanese War** (1904-1905) with inflation and rising prices.

Peasants who had been able to eke out a living began to starve. Many of the fighting troops were killed in battles Russia lost to Japan because of poor leadership, lack of training, and inferior weaponry. Czar Nicholas II refused to end the war despite setbacks, and in January 1905 Port Arthur fell.

A trade union leader, Father Gapon, organized a protest to demand an end to the war, industrial reform, more civil liberties, and a constituent assembly. Over 150,000 peasants joined a demonstration outside the Czar's **Winter Palace**. Before the demonstrators even spoke, the palace guard opened fire on the crowd.

This destroyed the people's trust in the Czar. Illegal trade unions and political parties formed and organized strikes to gain power.

The strikes eventually brought the Russian economy to a halt. This led Czar Nicholas II to sign the **October Manifesto** which created a constitutional monarchy, extended some civil rights, and gave the parliament limited legislative power.

But in a very short period of time, the Czar disbanded the parliament and violated the promised civil liberties. His violation of the October Manifesto would help foment the **1917 Revolution**.

There were other factors as well. Defeats on the battlefields during WWI caused discontent, loss of life, and a popular desire to withdraw from the war. The war had also caused another surge in prices and scarcity of many items. Most of the

peasants could not afford to buy bread. In addition, the Czar's behavior triggered more unrest. The Czar continued to appoint unqualified people to government posts and handle the situation with general incompetence. The Czar also listened to his wife Alexandra's advice.

Alexandra was strongly influenced by **Rasputin**. This caused increased discontent among all levels of the social structure.

Workers in Petrograd went on strike in 1917 over the need for food. The Czar again ordered troops to suppress the strike. This time, however, the troops sided with the workers. The revolution then took a unique direction. The parliament created a provisional government to rule the country. The military and the workers also created their own governments called **soviets** (popularly elected local councils). The parliament was composed of nobles who soon lost control of the country when they failed to comply with the wishes of the populace. The result was chaos.

The most significant differences between the 1905 and 1917 revolutions were the formation of political parties and their use of propaganda and the support of the military and some of the nobles in 1917. The political leaders who had previously been driven into exile returned. **Lenin**, Stalin and Trotsky won the support of the peasants with the promise of "Peace, Land, and Bread." The parliament, on the other hand, continued the country's involvement in the war. Lenin and the Bolshevik party gained the support of the **Red Guard** and together overthrew the provisional government. In short order they had complete control of Russia and established a new communist state.

The conditions in Russia in previous centuries led up to this. Russia's harsh climate, tremendous size, and physical isolation from the rest of Europe, along with the brutal, despotic rule and control of the tsars over enslaved peasants, contributed to the final conditions leading to revolution. Despite the tremendous efforts of **Peter the Great** to bring his country up to the social, cultural, and economic standards of the rest of Europe, Russia always remained a hundred years or more behind. Autocratic rule, the existence of the system of serfdom or slavery of the peasants, lack of money, defeats in wars, lack of enough food and food production, and little if any industrialization--all of these contributed to conditions ripe for revolt.
As succeeding Marxist or communist leaders came to power, the effects of this violent revolution were felt all around the earth.

The foreign policies of all free Western nations were directly and immensely affected by the Marxist-Communist ideology. Its effect on Eastern Europe and the former Soviet Union was felt politically, economically, socially, culturally, and geographically. The people of ancient Russia simply exchanged one autocratic dictatorial system for another, and its impact on all of the people on the earth is still being felt to this day.

The Industrial Revolution

The **Industrial Revolution**--which began in Great Britain and spread elsewhere--was the development of power-driven machinery (fueled by coal and steam) leading to the accelerated growth of industry with large factories replacing homes and small workshops as work centers. The lives of people changed drastically. A largely agricultural society changed to an industrial one. In Western Europe, the period of empire and colonialism began.

The industrialized nations seized parts of Africa and Asia in an effort to control and provide the raw materials needed to feed the industries and machines in the "mother country."

Next developed power based on electricity and internal combustion replacing coal and steam. That resulted in even greater changes in human civilization and even greater opportunities for trade, increased production, and the exchange of ideas and knowledge.

The **first phase** of the Industrial Revolution (1750-1830) saw the mechanization of the textile industry, vast improvements in mining, with the invention of the steam engine, and numerous improvements in transportation, with the development and improvement of turnpikes, canals, and the invention of the railroad.

The **second phase** (1830-1910) resulted in vast improvements in a number of industries that had already been mechanized through such inventions as the Bessemer steel process and the invention of steam ships. New industries arose as a result of the new technological advances--photography, electricity, and chemical processes. New sources of power were harnessed and applied, including petroleum and hydroelectric power. Precision instruments were developed and engineering was launched. It was during this second phase that the Industrial Revolution spread to other European countries, to Japan, and to the United States.

The **political results** included the growth of complex government run by technical experts and the centralization of those governments, including the rise of regulatory administrative agencies. For democracies, the industrial revolution held both advantages and disadvantages.

Some of the advantages to democratic development include:

- the extension of franchise or the right to vote to the male middle class-- and later to all elements of the population
- mass education to meet the needs of an industrial society
- the development of media of public communication, including radio, television, and cheap newspapers—and broad internet access

Some of the dangers to democracy include:

- the risk of manipulation of the media of mass communication
- facilitation of dictatorial centralization and totalitarian control
- efforts to achieve uniformity, conformity, social depersonalization

The **economic results** were numerous, but most of them can be viewed as a struggle between differing economic forces and philosophies. For example:

- the conflict between free trade and low tariffs and protectionism
- the issue of free enterprise against government regulation
- the struggles between labor and capital
- the trade-union movement

All were all the result of the industrial revolution. By the same token, the rise of socialism and the utopian socialists--as well as the rise of Marxian or scientific socialism--can be traced to the revolution.

The **social results** of the Industrial Revolution included the transformation of a rural society into the modern age we recognize today. This occurred as a result of:

- an increase of population, especially in industrial centers,
- advances in science applied to agriculture,
- sanitation and medicine,
- the growth of great cities.

At the same time, these changes led to the disappearance of the difference between city dwellers and farmers as well as a faster tempo of life--and increased stress from the monotony of the work routine. The emancipation of women, the decline of religion, the rise of scientific materialism, and even Darwin's theory of evolution were influenced by the industrial revolution.
Increased mobility produced knowledge and new ideas. Increased mobility also resulted in wide-scale immigration to industrialized countries.

Cultures clashed and cultures melded.

The direct results of the industrial revolution--particularly as they affected **industry, commerce,** and **agriculture**--were increases in productivity, world trade, giant business conglomerates, and monopolies. On one hand, there was specialization and division of labor. On the other hand, there was a standardization of parts plus mass production. The industrial revolution also fostered a **Second Agricultural Revolution** facilitated by the steam engine, machinery, chemical fertilizers, processing, canning, and refrigeration.

Nationalism

During the eighteenth and especially the nineteenth centuries, **nationalism** emerged as a powerful force in Europe and elsewhere in the world. Strictly speaking, nationalism was a belief in one's own nation and people. More so than in previous centuries, the people of the European nations began to think in terms of a nation of people who had similar beliefs, concerns, and needs. This was partly a reaction to a growing discontent with the autocratic governments of the day and also just a general realization that there was more to life than the individual. People could feel a part of something like their nation, making themselves more than just an insignificant soul struggling to survive.

The time from 1830 to 1914 especially is characterized by the extraordinary growth and spread of patriotic pride in a nation along with intense, widespread imperialism. Loyalty to one's nation included national pride, extending and maintaining sovereign political boundaries, and unification of smaller states with common language, history, and culture into a more powerful nation. As part of a larger multicultural empire, there were smaller groups who wished to separate into smaller, political nations with their own culture.

Nationalism also brought large groups of people together--for example, the unifications of Germany and Italy. What it did not do, however, is provide sufficient outlets for this sudden rise in national fervor.

Especially in the 1700s and 1800s, European powers and peoples began looking to Africa and Asia in order to find colonies: rich sources of goods, trade, and cheap labor. Africa, especially, suffered at the hands of European imperialists, bent on expanding their reach outside the borders of Europe. Asia, too, suffered colonial expansion, most notably in India and Southeast Asia. This colonial expansion would come back to haunt the European imperialists when colonial skirmishes spilled over into alliance that brought the European powers into World War I. Some of these colonial battles were still being fought with the start of World War II.

In the United States, territorial expansion westward marched under the banner of "Manifest Destiny." The U.S. was involved in the War with Mexico, the Spanish-American War, and support of the Latin American colonies of Spain in their revolt for independence.

In Latin America, the Spanish colonies were successful in their own fight for independence and self-government.

In Europe, Italy and Germany were each totally united into one nation from many smaller states. There were revolutions in Austria and Hungary, the Franco-Prussian War, the dividing of Africa among the strong European nations, interference and intervention of Western nations in Asia, and the breakup of Turkish dominance in the Balkans.

In Africa, France, Great Britain, Italy, Portugal, the Netherlands, Spain, Germany, and Belgium controlled the entire continent except Liberia and Ethiopia. In Asia and the Pacific Islands, only China, Japan, and present-day Thailand (Siam) kept their independence. The others were controlled by the strong European nations.

An additional reason for European imperialism was the harsh, urgent demand for the raw materials needed to fuel and feed the great Industrial Revolution. These resources were not available in the huge quantity so desperately needed which necessitated (and rationalized) the partitioning of the continent of Africa and parts of Asia. In return, these colonial areas would purchase the finished manufactured goods.

Skill 2.1g   Conflicts, Ideologies, and Evolutions 20th Century 1900–1991

Europe-World War I: 1914 to 1918

Emotions ran high in early twentieth century Europe, and minor disputes magnified into major ones--and sometimes quickly led to threats of war. Especially sensitive to these conditions was the area of the states on the Balkan Peninsula.

Along with the imperialistic colonization for industrial raw materials, military build-up (especially by Germany), and diplomatic and military alliances, the conditions for one tiny spark to set off the explosion were in place. In July 1914, a Serbian national assassinated **Archduke Ferdinand**, the Austrian heir to the throne, and his wife as they visited Sarajevo.

There were a few attempts to keep war from starting, but these efforts were futile. War began. Eventually nearly 30 nations were involved, and the war went on until 1918.

One of the major causes of the war was the tremendous surge of **nationalism** during the 1800s and early 1900s. People of the same nationality or ethnic group sharing a common history, language or culture began uniting or demanding the right of unification, especially in Eastern Europe—Russia, the Ottoman Empire and the Austria-Hungary Empire.

Other causes were the increasing strength of military capabilities, massive colonization for raw materials needed for industrialization and manufacturing, and military and diplomatic alliances.

World War I saw the introduction of such warfare as use of tanks, airplanes, machine guns, submarines, poison gas, and flame throwers. Fighting on the Western front was characterized by a series of **trenches** that were used throughout the war until 1918. The atrocities of war took everyone by surprise, and led to much of the animosity that marked the terms of the end of the war. It would lead to ban on certain weapons, particularly poison gas, and leave the nations of Europe unwilling to go to war again.

The Beginning

On June 28 1914, a Bosnian Serb student named **Gavrilo Princip** assassinated **Archduke Frantz Ferdinand**, heir to the Austria-Hungarian throne, and his wife, Sophie Chotek while on a formal visit to Sarajevo. Princip was a member of the Black Hand, a Serbian Nationalist Secret Society whose activities had been on the up rise. Ferdinand had already survived one assassination attempt earlier that day.

Three weeks later, Austria-Hungary issued a reaction to the death of Ferdinand, their heir, in the form of a remarkable ultimatum to Serbia. The terms of the ultimatum were so severely stated that Austria-Hungary's anticipation was that Serbia would reject the terms, thus giving Austria-Hungary a cause for launching a limited war against Serbia. Ferdinand's death set in motion a series of reflexive events that culminated in the world's first global war, WW I. What Austria-Hungary intended as a brief war against Serbia rapidly escalated into a conflict between all the major world powers.

Countries

- **Austria-Hungary** - unhappy with Serbia's response to their ultimatum immediately declared war on Serbia

- **Russia** - bound by its treaty to Serbia initiates recruitment of its immense army in her defense

- **Germany** - allied to Austria-Hungary by treaty, and viewed the Russian mobilization as an act of war against Austria-Hungary; declared war on Russia

- **France** - bound by treaty to Russia; found itself at war against Germany

- **Japan** - honored a military agreement with Britain and declared war on Germany, though largely for its own interests. Austria-Hungary responded by declaring war on Japan

- **Britain** - allied to France by a loosely worded treaty which stated a "moral obligation" to defend France; soon declared war against Germany

- Britain's colonies and dominions (**Australia, Canada, India, New Zealand, and the Union of South Africa)** offered financial and military assistance

- **Italy** - committed to both Germany and Austria-Hungary, which allowed them to remain neutral for a short period of time. Eventually Italy joined the conflict by choosing to side with the Allies fighting against her two former allies.

- **United States** - President Woodrow Wilson declared the United States absolutely neutral, but finally entered the war in 1917 on the side of the Allies.

Staying true to the military alliances, the **Allies**; chiefly, Britain, France, and Russia, opposed the **Central Powers**; primarily Austria-Hungary, Germany, and Turkey. Eventually, the war spread outside of Europe as the warring continent looked to its colonies and allies for assistance, including the United States.

Trench Warfare

Much of the fighting in World War I took place along the Western Front which ran from the North Sea to the border Switzerland. On the Eastern Front were the vast eastern plains. The two opposing fronts were comprised of a complex system of opposing manned trenches and fortifications, separated by unoccupied land called "no man's land." By the war's end, each side had dug at least 12,000 miles of trenches.

A line of trenches soon stretched along the war's Western Front from the Swiss Alps to the English Channel. The first major trench lines were completed in late November 1914. At their peak, the trenches built by both sides extended nearly 400 miles from Nieuport, on the Belgian coast, to the Swiss border.

The Allies used several "lines" of trenches. The front-line (firing and attack) was situated 50 yards to one mile of the German's front line. A support trench was dug another several hundred yards, and then an emergency reserve trench was dug another several hundred feet back. Communication trenches connected these trenches which allowed the movement of supplies, messages, and men. German trench construction was much different then the Allies. Their tunnel and trench structures were elaborate and sophisticated, sometimes consisting of living quarters more than 50 feet below the surface. These living quarters had electricity, beds, toilets, and other necessities of life that contrasted harshly with the open-air trenches of the Allies.

By 1917, in order to break the stalemate, both sides began to implement new technologies which allowed the construction of formidable static defenses which included poison gases, barbed wire, machine artillery, and tanks. Before the official **Armistice** was declared on November 11, 1918, nine million people had died on the battlefields. The Allies had defeated the Central Powers, but the conflicts underlying the war had not been equally vanquished.

World War I seriously damaged the economies of the European countries, both the victors and the defeated, leaving them deeply in debt. There was difficulty on both sides paying off war debts and loans. It was difficult to find jobs, and some countries like Japan and Italy found themselves without enough resources. Solving these problems by expanding the territory merely set up conditions for war later.

Germany suffered from runaway inflation, which ruined the value of its money and wiped out the savings of millions. Despite the U.S. loans to Germany which helped the government to restore some order and which provided a short existence of some economic stability in Europe, the Great Depression only served to undo any good that had been done.

Mass unemployment, poverty, and despair greatly weakened the democratic governments that had been formed and greatly strengthened the increasing power and influence of extreme political movements such as **Communism, Fascism, and Socialism**.

Communism and Socialism

Socialism is a fairly recent political phenomenon though its roots can be traced pretty far back. At the core, both socialism and communism are fundamentally economic philosophies that advocate public rather than private ownership, especially over means of production, yet even here, there are many distinctions.

Karl Marx concentrated his attention on the industrial worker and on state domination over the means of production. Socialism by contrast, usually occurs when industry has already been developed, and it has concerned itself more with the welfare of the individual and the fair distribution of whatever wealth is available.

This distinction in philosophy, of course, makes for an immense conflict in methods. Communism, believing that revolution is inevitable, works toward it by emphasizing class antagonisms. Socialism, while seeking change, insists on the use of democratic procedures within the existing social order of a given society. In it, the upper classes and capitalists are not to be violently overthrown but instead to be won over by logical persuasion.

This tendency was especially found in the **Utopian-Socialists** of the early nineteenth century, whose basic aim was the repudiation of the private-property system with its economic inefficiency and social injustice. Their criticisms rather than any actual achievements would linger after them. Like Marx, they envisioned industrial capitalism as becoming more and more inhumane and oppressive. They could not imagine the mass of workers prospering in such a system.

It was in London in 1864 that the first **Socialist International** was organized by Karl Marx. This radical leftist organization died off after limping along for twelve years, by which time its headquarters had moved to New York. After the passage of about another twelve years, the **Second Socialist International** met in Paris to celebrate the anniversary of the fall of the Bastille in the French Revolution. By this time, serious factions were developing. There were the **Anarchists**, who wanted to tear down everything, **Communists** who wanted to tear down the established order and build another in its place, and the **Democratic-Socialist** majority who favored peaceful political action.

Struggling for internal peace and cohesion right up to the First World War, socialism would remain largely ineffectual at this critical international time. Peace brought them all together again in Bern, Switzerland, but by this time the Soviet Union had been created and the Russian Communists refused to attend the meeting on the grounds that the Second Socialist International opposed the type of dictatorship it saw as necessary in order to achieve revolutions.

Thus the **Communist International** was created in direct opposition to the Socialist International. The socialists went on to advocate the "triumph of democracy, firmly rooted in the principles of liberty." The main objective of this new Socialist International was to maintain the peace--an ironic and very elusive goal in the period between the two world wars.

The Nazi attack on Poland in September, 1939, completely shattered the organization. In 1946, however a new Socialist Information and Liaison Office were set up to reestablish old contacts and in 1951 the Communist International was revived with a conference in Frankfurt, Germany. It adopted a document entitled "Aims and Tasks of Democratic Socialism". A summary of these objectives gives a good picture of modern Democratic-Socialism as it exists on paper in its ideal form.

The decade following World War II saw tremendous growth in socialism. Economic planning and the nationalization of industry was undertaken in many countries, though a subsequent return to self-confidence in the private business community and among voters, in general, has frequently weakened the socialist majority or reduced it to the status of an opposition party. This political balance leaves most industrialized countries with a mixed socialist-capitalist economy.

Fascism

The effects of the Depression were very strong throughout Europe, which was still rebuilding after the devastation of World War I. Germany was especially hard hit, as US reconstruction loans dried up. Unemployment skyrocketed in Germany, leaving millions out of work.

During the Depression in Germany, large numbers of urban workers found themselves unemployed and dissatisfied with the government. Communist and Fascist paramilitary organizations arose, promising dramatic action and economic restructuring. These organizations found a receptive audience among the disgruntled German workers. It was out of this climate that the **Nazi Party** emerged.

After a failed attempt at a coup, many of the Nazi leaders, including **Adolf Hitler**, were jailed. Upon his release, Hitler was able to take leadership again. Hitler built the fascist Nazi party into a political organization with seats in the German Parliament. Then Hitler was named Chancellor of Germany, from which position he implemented his policies of military expansion and aggression that culminated in the Second World War.

Fascist movements often had socialists' origins. For example, in Italy, where fascism first arose in place of socialism, **Benito Mussolini**, sought to impose what he called **corporativism**. A fascist "corporate" state would, in theory, run the economy for the benefit of the whole country like a corporation. It would be centrally controlled and managed by an elite who would see that its benefits would go to everyone.

Fascism has always declared itself the uncompromising enemy of communism, with which, however, fascist actions have much in common.

In fact, many of the methods of organization and propaganda used by fascists were taken from the experience of the early Russian communists, along with the belief in a single strong political party. Secret police were another shared feature. The propertied interests and the upper classes, fearful of revolution, often gave their support to fascism on the basis of promises by the fascist leaders to maintain the status quo and safeguard property.

Once established, a fascist regime ruthlessly crushes communist and socialist parties as well as all democratic opposition. It regiments the propertied interests to its national goals and wins the potentially revolutionary masses to fascist programs by substituting a rabid nationalism for class conflict. Thus fascism may be regarded as an extreme defensive expedient adopted by a nation faced with the sometimes illusionary threat of communist subversion or revolution. Under fascism, capital is regulated as much as labor and fascist contempt for legal or constitutional guarantees effectively destroys whatever security the capitalistic system had enjoyed under pre-fascist governments.

The Soviet-German Ribbentrop–Molotov pact of 1939 stated that if either country went to war, both countries would be neutral and refrain from acts of aggression against each other. There was a secret clause about partitioning Poland with Stalin taking the east and Hitler the west. Of course, quite soon when Hitler invaded Poland, the agreement was over.

During the period of alliance created by the treaty, Italy and Germany and their satellite countries ceased their anti-Communist propaganda. They emphasized their own revolutionary and proletarian origins and attacked the so-called plutocratic western democracies.

The fact that fascist countries sought to control national life by methods identical to those of communist governments make such nations vulnerable to communism after the fascist regime is destroyed.

Europe: World War II: 1939 to 1945

World War I had seriously damaged the economies of the European countries, both the victors and the defeated, leaving them deeply in debt. There was difficulty on both sides paying off war debts and loans. It was difficult to find jobs and some countries like Japan and Italy found themselves without enough resources and more than enough people. Solving these problems by expanding the territory merely set up conditions for war later. Germany suffered horribly with runaway inflation ruining the value of its money and wiping out the savings of millions. Even though the U.S. made loans to Germany, which helped the government to restore some order and which provided a short existence of some economic stability in Europe, the Great Depression only served to undo any good that had been done. Mass unemployment, poverty, and despair greatly weakened the democratic governments that had been formed and greatly strengthened the increasing power and influence of extreme political movements, such as communism, fascism, and national-socialism. These ideologies promised to put an end to the economic problems.

The extreme form of patriotism called nationalism that had been the chief cause of World War I grew even stronger after the war ended in 1918. The political, social, and economic unrest fueled nationalism and it became an effective tool enabling dictators to gain and maintain power from the 1930s to the end of World War II in 1945. In the Soviet Union, **Joseph Stalin** succeeded in gaining political control and establishing a strong harsh dictatorship. **Benito Mussolini** and the Fascist party, promising prosperity and order in Italy, gained national support and set up a strong government. In Japan, although the ruler was considered Emperor **Hirohito,** actual control and administration of government came under military officers. In Germany, the results of war, harsh treaty terms, loss of territory, great economic chaos and collapse all enabled **Adolf Hitler** and his National Socialist, or **Nazi,** party to gain complete power and control.

Germany, Italy, and Japan initiated a policy of aggressive territorial expansion with Japan being the first to conquer. In 1931, Japanese forces seized control of **Manchuria**, a part of China containing rich natural resources, and in 1937 began an attack on the rest of China, occupying most of its eastern part by 1938. Italy invaded **Ethiopia** in Africa in 1935, having complete control by 1936. The Soviet Union did not invade or take over any territory but along with Italy and Germany, actively participated in the **Spanish Civil War**, using it as a proving ground to test tactics and weapons setting the stage for World War II.

In Germany, almost immediately after taking power, in direct violation of the World War I peace treaty, Hitler began the buildup of the armed forces. He sent troops into the Rhineland in 1936, then invaded Austria in 1938 and united it with Germany. In 1938, he seized control of the Sudetenland, part of western Czechoslovakia and containing mostly Germans, followed by the rest of Czechoslovakia in March 1939. Despite his territorial designs, the other nations of Europe made no moves to stop Hitler.

Preferring not to embark on another costly war, the European powers opted for a policy of **Appeasement**, believing that once Hitler had satisfied his desire for land he would be satisfied, and war could be averted. Then, on September 1, 1939, Hitler began World War II in Europe by invading **Poland**.

By 1940, Germany had invaded and controlled Norway, Denmark, Belgium, Luxembourg, the Netherlands, and France. Germany military forces struck in what came to be known as the **blitzkrieg**, or "lightning war." A shock attack, it relied on the use of surprise, speed, and superiority in firepower. The German blitzkrieg coordinated land and air attacks to paralyze the enemy by disabling its communications and coordination capacities.

When France fell in June 1940, the Franco-German armistice divided France into two zones: one under German military occupation and one under nominal French control (the southeastern two-fifths of the country). The National Assembly, summoned at Vichy, France ratified the armistice and granted **Philippe Pétain** control of the French State. The **Vichy** government then collaborated with the Germans, eventually becoming little more than a rubber stamp for German policies. Germany would occupy the whole of France in 1942, and by early 1944 a **Resistance** movement created a period of civil war in France. The Vichy regime was abolished after the liberation of Paris.

With Europe safely conquered, Hitler turned his sights to England. The **Battle of Britain** (June 1940 – April 1941) was a series of intense raids directed against Britain by the **Luftwaffe**, Germany's air force. Intended to prepare the way for invasion, the air raids were directed against British ports and Royal Air Force (**RAF**) bases. In September 1940, London and other cities were attacked in the "**blitz**," a series of bombings that lasted for 57 consecutive nights. Sporadic raids until April 1941. The RAF was outnumbered but succeeded in blocking the German air force, and eventually Hitler was forced to abandon his plans for invasion, Germany's first major setback in the war.

After success in North Africa and Italy, and following the D-Day Invasion, the Allied forces faced a protracted campaign across Europe. Each gain was hard won, and both the weather and local terrain at times worked against them. The **Battle of the Bulge**, also known as Battle of the Ardennes (December 16, 1944-January 28, 1945) was the largest World War II land battle on the Western Front, and the last major German counteroffensive of the war. Launched by Adolf Hitler himself, the German army's goal was to cut Allied forces in half and to retake the crucial port of Antwerp. Secretly massed Panzer tank-led units launched their assault into the thinnest part of the Allied forces.

Though surprised and suffering tremendous losses, Allied forces still managed to slow the Germans. American tanks moved swiftly to counterattack and cut German supply lines. The attack resulted in a bulge seventy miles deep into Allied lines, but all forward momentum for the Germans was essentially stopped by Christmas. It took another month before the Allies could push back to the original line. Both sides suffered great casualties, but the Germans' losses were a crushing blow, as the troops and equipment lost were irreplaceable.

Major consequences of the war included horrendous death and destruction, millions of displaced persons, the gaining of strength and the spread of Communism and Cold War tensions. World War II ended more lives and caused more devastation than any other war.
 Besides the losses of millions of military personnel, the devastation and destruction directly affected civilians. Cities, houses, and factories were reduced to ruin and rubble, and communication and transportation systems were destroyed. Millions of civilian deaths, especially in China and the Soviet Union, were the results of famine.

More than 12 million people were uprooted by the war's end, having no place to go. Some had been in concentration and slave labor camps; some were orphans, and some had escaped war-torn areas and invading armies. Changing national boundary lines also caused the mass movement of displaced persons.

Genocide & The Holocaust

Genocide, or the intended extinction of one people by another, is not a new concept. However, in the 20th Century, it has reached great heights—and depths.

The first organized genocide in the 1900s was the **Armenian genocide**, an attempted extermination of a huge number of Armenians at the hands of the **Young Turks** who inherited Turkey from the Ottoman Empire. More than one million Armenian people (nearly half of their population) died between 1915 and 1917. The Armenians were blamed for early defeats at the hands of Russia and its allies.

Armenians were forcibly moved and kept in harsh conditions elsewhere. Twenty-five concentration camps are believed to have existed. Turkish authorities claimed that the Armenian people had agitated for separation from the Ottoman Empire and that the relocation fulfilled the goals of both. Others disagree. Some sources blame other causes for these deaths, but most scholars agree that it was a determined attempt to exterminate an entire group of people.

The most well-known genocide of the twentieth century is the **Holocaust** of Jews before and during World War II. Much of this took place in Germany, although the practice increased throughout German-occupied countries throughout the war. German authorities capitalized on hundreds of years of distrust of the Jewish people and invented what they saw as "the **Final Solution** of the Jewish Question"--extermination of the Jewish people.

Germans in charge of this "Final Solution" constructed a vast, complicated system of transport systems and concentration camps where Jews were imprisoned, forced to work, and killed in increasingly large numbers. This Holocaust was known especially for its efficiency and its extensive record keeping. Thousands of pages of documents describe in excruciating detail how thorough and determined Nazi authorities were in pursuing their goals.

German doctors also carried out experiments on their Jewish prisoners, pursuing radical cures for diseases and, more often than not, new methods of torture and mistreatment of prisoners of war. The deadly fingers of torture and killing were not at all restricted to able-bodied people. Youngsters, the elderly, the disabled, the mentally ill, and the near dead were all subject to the harshest treatment imaginable. One common practice was the forced march from one location to another, miles away, without food or sustenance. These "**death marches**" left many of the prisoners dead or near death.

The number of Jews killed during the Holocaust is generally said to be six million. This figure includes people from all over Europe. The Holocaust didn't kill just Jews, however. Gypsies, communists, homosexuals, Jehovah's Witnesses, Catholics, psychiatric patients, and even common criminals were systematically incarcerated and, in many cases, killed for being "enemies of the state." The number of concentration camps in Nazi-controlled lands during World War II was more than 40. Not all of them were death camps. The most famous ones, including **Auschwitz**, were.

The Holocaust ended with Germany's defeat in World War II. The liberating troops of the West and East uncovered the concentration camps and the lists of killings that the Nazis had done. Much of the meticulous record-keeping was intact, preserving for the entire world the horrors that the Nazis had wrought.

International organizations received sharp criticism during WWII for their failure to act to save the European Jews. The Allied Powers, in particular, were accused of gross negligence. Many organizations and individuals did not believe reports of the abuse and mass genocide that was occurring in Europe. Many nations did not want to accept Jewish refugees. The International Red Cross was one of the organizations that discounted reports of atrocities.

One particular point of criticism was the failure of the Allied Powers to bomb the death camp at Auschwitz-Birkenau or the railroad tracks leading there. Military leaders argued that their planes did not have the range to reach the camp; they also argued that they could not provide sufficiently precise targeting to safeguard the inmates. Critics have claimed that even if Allied bombs killed all inmates at Auschwitz at the time, the destruction of the camp would have saved thousands of other Jews. Regardless of post-facto arguments, it is very likely that even if the Allies had destroyed the camp, the Nazis would have turned to other methods of extermination.

It was not until after the war that genocide was accepted by the United Nations as a crime against humanity. Also after the war, there was recognition that the United Nations charter was insufficiently precise as to the rights it protected. The U.N. then unanimously passed the **Universal Declaration of Human Rights**. The **Nuremberg Trials** redefined morality on a global scale. The phrase "crimes against humanity" attained popular currency, and individuals, rather than governments, were held accountable for war crimes.

This has not led to an end to genocide, however. **Ethnic cleansing** in Yugoslavia occurred in Kosovo in the 1990s. The country was a melting pot of ethnic peoples, all of whom were struggling for meager resources and living space. People who had the most power, including control of the government and the army, were the Serbs.

In 1989 the Serbian president, **Slobodan Milosevic**, abrogated the constitutional autonomy of Kosovo. He and the minority of Serbs in Kosovo had long bristled at the fact that Muslim Albanians were in control of an area considered sacred to Serbs. The Serbian government expelled ethnic Albanians from the province. The Serbian officials also confiscated all identity documentation from those who were expelled so that any attempt to return could be refused by claiming that without documents to prove Serbian citizenship the people must be native Albanians. The effort even went so far as to destroy archival documents that proved citizenship.

Growing tensions led in 1998 to armed clashes between Serbs and the Kosovo Liberation Army (**KLA**), which had begun killing Serbian police and politicians. The Serbs responded with a ruthless counteroffensive, inducing the UN Security Council to condemn the Serbs' excessive use of force, including ethnic cleansing (killing and expulsion), and to impose an arms embargo, but the violence continued.

After diplomatic efforts broke down, **NATO** responded with an 11-week bombing campaign that extended to Belgrade and significantly damaged Serbia's infrastructure. NATO and Yugoslavia signed an accord in June 1999 outlining Serbian troop withdrawal and the return of nearly 1,000,000 ethnic Albanian refugees as well as 500,000 displaced within the province. Bosnia is now its own country, as is Croatia and Serbia and Montenegro. The leaders of this genocide have been convicted of their crimes, as were the Nazi perpetrators before them.

Rwandan Genocide was the 1994 mass extermination of hundreds of thousands of ethnic **Tutsis** and moderate **Hutu** sympathizers in Rwanda and was the largest atrocity during the Rwandan Civil War. This genocide was mostly carried out by two extremist Hutu militia groups April 6 through mid-July 1994. Hundreds of thousands of people were slaughtered.

In the wake of the Rwandan Genocide, the United Nations and the international community drew severe criticism for its inaction. Despite international news media coverage of the violence as it unfolded, most countries, including France, Belgium, and the United States, declined to intervene or speak out against the massacres. Canada continued to lead the UN peacekeeping force in Rwanda. However, the UN Security Council did not authorize direct intervention or the use force to prevent or halt the killing.

The genocide ended when a Tutsi-dominated expatriate rebel overthrew the Hutu government and seized power. Fearing reprisals, hundreds of thousands of Hutu and other refugees fled into eastern **Zaire** (now the **Democratic Republic of the Congo**). People who had actively participated in the genocide hid among the refugees, fueling the First and Second Congo Wars. Rivalry between Hutu and Tutsi tribal factions is also a major factor in the Burundi Civil War.

During WWII, Allied forces flew extensive bombing raids deep into German territory. Launching from bases in England, both American and RAF bomber squadrons bombed German factories and cities. Although the raids were dangerous--with many planes and lives lost both to the Luftwaffe and ant-aircraft artillery--the raids continued throughout the war. German cities were reduced to rubble by war's end. The impact on Germany's production capacity and transportation lines helped swing the tide of war.

Before war in Europe had ended, the Allies had agreed on a military occupation of Germany. It was divided into four zones each one occupied by Great Britain, France, the Soviet Union, and the United States with the four powers jointly administering Berlin. After the war, the Allies agreed that Germany's armed forces would be abolished, the Nazi Party outlawed, and the territory east of the Oder and Neisse Rivers taken away. Nazi leaders were accused of war crimes and brought to trial at **Nuremburg**.

Major consequences of the war included horrendous death and destruction, millions of displaced persons, the gaining of strength and spread of Communism and Cold War tensions as a result of the beginning of the nuclear age. World War II ended more lives and caused more devastation than any other war.

Besides the losses of millions of military personnel, the devastation and destruction directly affected civilians, reducing cities, houses, and factories to ruin and rubble and wrecking communication and transportation systems.

Millions of civilian deaths, especially in China and the Soviet Union, were the results of famine. More than 12 million people were uprooted by wars end and had no place to live. Included in those numbers were prisoners of war, those that survived Nazi concentration camps and slave labor camps, orphans, and people who escaped war-torn areas and invading armies. Changing national boundary lines also caused the mass movement of displaced persons.

Germany and Japan were completely defeated; Great Britain and France were seriously weakened; and the Soviet Union and the United States became the world's leading powers. Although allied during the war, the alliance fell apart as the Soviets pushed Communism in Europe and Asia. In spite of the tremendous destruction it suffered, the Soviet Union was stronger than ever.

During the war, it took control of Lithuania, Estonia, and Latvia and by mid-1945 parts of Poland, Czechoslovakia, Finland, and Romania. It helped Communist governments gain power in Bulgaria, Romania, Hungary, Czechoslovakia, Poland, and North Korea. China fell to **Mao Zedong**'s Communist forces in 1949.

Until the fall of the Berlin Wall in 1989 and the dissolution of Communist governments in Eastern Europe and the Soviet Union, the United States and the Soviet Union faced off in what was called a Cold War. The possibility of the terrifying destruction by nuclear weapons loomed over both nations.

The world after World War II was a complicated place. The Axis powers, Nazi German, Fascist Italy and the Empire of Japan were defeated, but the Cold War had sprung up in its place. Many countries struggled to get out of the debt and devastation that their Nazi occupiers had wrought.

The American **Marshall Plan** helped the nations of Western Europe get back on their feet. The Soviet Union helped the Eastern European nations return to greatness, with Communist governments at the helm. The nations of Asia were rebuilt as well, with Communism taking over China and Americanization taking over Japan and Taiwan. East and West struggled for control in this arena, especially in Korea and Southeast Asia. When Communism fell in the USSR and Eastern Europe, it remained in China, North Korea, and Vietnam. Vietnam's neighbors, however set their own path to government.

The kind of nationalism that Europe saw in the nineteenth century spilled over into the mid-twentieth century, with former colonies of European powers declaring themselves independent all the time, especially in Africa. India, a longtime British protectorate, also achieved independence at this time. With independence, these countries continued to grow. Some of these nations now experience severe overcrowding and dearth of precious resources. Some who can escape do; others have no way to escape.

The Middle East has been an especially violent part of the world since the war and the inception of the State of Israel. The struggle for supremacy in the Persian Gulf area has brought about a handful of wars as well. Oil, needed to power the world's devastatingly large transportation and manufacturing engines, is king of all resources.

The **United Nations**, a more successful successor to the League of Nations (which couldn't prevent World War II), began in the waning days of the war. It brought the nations of the world together to discuss their problems, rather than fight about them. Another successful method of keeping the peace since the war has been the atomic bomb. On a more specific note, UNICEF, a worldwide children's fund, has been able to achieve great things in just a few decades of existence. Other peace-based organizations like the Red Cross and Doctors Without Borders have seen their membership and their efficacy rise during this time as well.

Decolonization refers to the period after World War II when many African and Asian colonies and protectorates gained independence from the powers that had colonized them. The independence of India and Pakistan from Britain in 1945 marked the beginning of an especially important period of decolonization that lasted through 1960. Several British colonies in eastern Africa and French colonies in western Africa and Asia also formed as independent countries during this period.

Colonial powers had found it efficient to draw political boundaries across traditional ethnic and national lines, thereby dividing local populations and making them easier to control. With the yoke of colonialism removed, many new nations found themselves trying to reorganize into politically stable and economically viable units. The role of nationalism was important in this reorganization, as formerly divided peoples had opportunity to reunite. **Nationalism** is most simply defined as the belief that the nation is the basic unit of human association, and that a nation is a well-defined group of people sharing a common identity. This process of organizing new nations out of the remains of former colonies was called nation building.

Nation building in this fashion did not always result in the desired stability. Pakistan, for example, eventually split into Bangladesh and Pakistan along geographic and religious lines. Ethnic conflicts in newly formed African nations arose, and are still flaring in some areas. As the United States and the Soviet Union emerged as the dominant world powers, these countries encouraged dissent in post-colonial nations such as Cuba, Vietnam and Korea, which became arenas for Cold War conflict.

With the emergence of so many new independent nations, the role of **international organizations** such as the newly formed United Nations grew in importance. The United Nations was formed after World War II to establish peaceful ties between countries. Dismayed by the failure of the former League of Nations to prevent war, the organizers of the United Nations provided for the ability to deploy peacekeeping troops and to impose sanctions and restrictions on member states. Other international organizations arose to take the place of former colonial connections. The British Commonwealth and the French Union, for example, maintained connections between Britain and France and their former colonies.

Global migration saw an increase in the years during and following World War II. During the war years, many Jews left the hostile climate under Nazi Germany for the United States and Palestine.

Following the war, the Allied countries agreed to force German people living in Eastern Europe to return to Germany, affecting over 16 million people. In other parts of the world, instability in post-colonial areas often led to migration. Colonial settlers who had enjoyed the protection of a colonial power sometimes found themselves in hostile situations as native peoples gained independence and ascended to power, spurring migration to more friendly nations. Economic instability in newly forming countries created incentive for people to seek opportunity in other countries.

Korean War 1950 to 1953

Korea was under control of Japan from 1895 to the end of the Second World War in 1945. At war's end, the Soviet and U.S. military troops moved into Korea with the U.S. troops in the southern half and the Soviet troops in the northern half with the 38 degree North Latitude line as the boundary.

The General Assembly of the U.N. in 1947 ordered elections throughout all of Korea to select one government for the entire country. The Soviet Union would not allow the North Koreans to vote, so they set up a communist government there. The South Koreans set up a democratic government, but both claimed the entire country. At times, there were clashes between the troops from 1948 to 1950. After the U.S. removed its remaining troops in 1949 and announced in early 1950 that Korea was not part of its defense line in Asia, the communists decided to act and invaded the south.

Participants were: North and South Korea, United States of America, Australia, New Zealand, China, Canada, France, Great Britain, Turkey, Belgium, Ethiopia, Colombia, Greece, South Africa, Luxembourg, Thailand, the Netherlands, and the Philippines. It was the first war in which a world organization played a major military role, and it presented quite a challenge to the U.N. (which had only been in existence five years).

The war began June 25, 1950. In 1950, after General MacArthur had led troops to the Chinese border, China entered into the war, and the troops retreated south. By the winter of 1951, troops were fighting along the 38th parallel, and MacArthur threatened to attack China. President Truman relieved MacArthur from duty.

The U A truce was drawn up and an armistice agreement was signed ending the fighting July 27, 1953. A permanent treaty of peace has never been signed, and the country remains divided between the Communist North and the Democratic South. It was a very costly and bloody war destroying villages and homes and displacing and killing millions of people.

The Vietnam War

Though ostensibly an American war, conflict in the region began with what is often called the French Indochina War, which waged from 1946-1954. This conflict involved France, which had ruled Vietnam as its colony (French Indochina), and the newly independent Democratic Republic of Vietnam under **Ho Chi Minh**. On May 7, 1954, at a French military base known as **Dien Bien Phu**, Vietminh troops emerged victorious after a 56-day siege, leading to the end of France's involvement in Indochina. The war ended in Vietnamese victory and the country was then divided into the communist-dominated north and the U.S.-supported south. Almost inevitably, war soon broke out between the two.

In the fighting that ensued, fighters trained in the north (the **Viet Cong**) fought a guerrilla war against U.S.-supported South Vietnamese forces. North Vietnamese forces would later join the fighting, supported by Soviet advisors and equipment. At the height of U.S. involvement, there were more than half a million U.S. military personnel in Vietnam. The **Tet Offensive** of 1968, in which the Viet Cong and North Vietnamese attacked thirty-six major South Vietnamese cities and towns, marked a turning point in the war. Many in the U.S. had come to oppose the war on moral and practical grounds, and President Lyndon B. Johnson decided to shift to a policy of "de-escalation."

Peace talks were begun in Paris. Between 1969 and 1973 U.S. troops were withdrawn from Vietnam, although the war had by that time expanded to Cambodia and Laos in 1970. Peace talks, which had reached a stalemate in 1971, started again in 1973, producing a cease-fire agreement. Fighting continued, and there were numerous truce violations. In 1975 the North Vietnamese launched a full-scale invasion of the South. The South surrendered later that year, and in 1976 the country was reunited as the Socialist Republic of Vietnam. More than 2,000,000 people (including 58,000 Americans) died over the course of the war, about half of them civilians.

In related conflict, **Cambodia** experienced its own civil war between communists and non-communists during that period, which was won by the communist **Khmer Rouge** in 1975. After several years of horrifying atrocities under **Pol Pot**, the Vietnamese invaded in 1979 and installed a puppet government. Fighting between the Khmer Rouge and the Vietnamese continued throughout the 1980s; Vietnam withdrew its troops by 1989. In 1993 UN-mediated elections established an interim government, and Cambodia's monarchy was reestablished. In **Laos**, North Vietnam's victory over South Vietnam brought the communist **Pathet Lao** into complete control in Laos.

Skill 2.1h Contemporary Trends 1991–Present

Globalism is defined as the principle of the interdependence of all the world's nations and their peoples. Within this global community, every nation, in some way to a certain degree, is dependent on other nations. Since no one nation has all of the resources needed for production, trade with other nations is required to obtain what is needed for production, to sell what is produced, to buy finished products, and/or to earn money to maintain and strengthen the nation's economic system.

Those nations not part of an international trade organization not only must make those economic decisions of what to produce, how and for whom, but must also deal with the problem of tariffs and quotas on imports. Regardless of international trade memberships, economic growth and development are vital and affect all trading nations. Businesses, labor, and governments share common interests and goals in a nation's economic status. International systems of banking and finance have been devised to assist governments and businesses in setting the policy and guidelines for the exchange of currencies.

Historiographers place the origins of the global economy in the early twentieth century, with the advent of the **airplane**, which made travel and trade easier and less time-consuming than ever. They can reduce days-long trips to hours, resulting in not only shorter tourist trips, but also shorter trade trips. This means that goods (especially perishable foods) can travel farther and wider than ever before. Being able to ship goods quickly and efficiently means that businesses can do business overseas much more than they ever could.

Trucks, trains, and ships carry cargo all over the world. Trains travel faster than ever, as do ships. Roads are more prevalent and usually in better repair than they have ever been, making truck and even car travel not the dead-end option that it once was.

An increase in demand for something is not always a good thing, however, especially if what is being demanded has a limited supply.

Nonrenewable resources (coal and oil) are in worldwide demand these days, and the supplies won't last forever. Making it easier to ship goods all over the world has made demand grow at high rates, raising concerns about supply. Because resources like this have a limited supply (although the day when that limit is reached seems far away still), they are in danger of becoming extinct without being replaced.

Globalization has also brought about developments in the field of epidemiology. Vaccines and other cures for diseases can be shipped quickly all around the world. This has made it possible for HIV vaccines to reach the remotest areas of the world. Unfortunately, the preponderance of global travel has also meant that the threat of spreading a disease to the world by an infected person traveling on an international flight is real.

The most recent example of technology contributing to globalization is the development of the **Internet**. Instant communication between people thousands of miles apart is possible just by plugging in a computer and connecting to the Internet.

The Internet is an extension of the telephone and cell phone revolutions; all three are developments that have brought faraway places closer together. All three allow people to communicate no matter the distance. This communication can facilitate friendly chatter--or trade. Businesses use cell phones and the Internet while also using computers to track goods and receipts quickly and efficiently.

Globalization has also brought financial and cultural exchange on a worldwide scale. A large number of businesses have investments in countries around the world. Financial transactions are conducted using a variety of currencies. People elsewhere in the world, through the wonders of television and the Internet, can view other cultures. Not only goods but belief systems, customs, and practices are being exchanged.

With the exchange of money, goods, and culture has come an increase in immigration. Many people who live in less-developed nations see what is available in other places and want to move there in order to fully take advantage of all that more-developed nations have to offer. Depending on the numbers of people who want to immigrate and the resources available, this could become a problem. The technological advances in transportation and communications have made such immigration easier than ever.

The Middle East

The **Middle East** is defined by its name and its geographic position. It is in the middle of the globe, a position that enables it to exert tremendous influence on not only the trade that passes through its realm of influence, but also the political relations between its countries and those of different parts of the world. From the beginnings of civilization, the Middle East has been a destination for attackers, for adventure-seekers, for those starving for food, and a technologically-advanced series of other resources, from iron to oil. The countries of the Middle East continue to play an important role in the economics of the world.

First and foremost is the importance of **oil**. Saudi Arabia, most notably, but also Iran, Iraq, Kuwait, Qatar, Dubai, and the United Arab Emirates are huge exporters of oil. In some cases, the amount of oil that one of these countries exports exceeds 90 percent of its total economic outflow. The nations that make up the **Organization of the Petroleum Exporting Countries** or **OPEC** (not all of them in the Middle East) are:

- Algeria
- Angola
- Indonesia
- Iran
- Iraq
- Kuwait
- Libya
- Nigeria
- Qatar
- Saudi Arabia
- United Arab Emirates
- Venezuela
- Ecuador

Most of the world requires oil in large quantities to run machines, especially transportation vehicles such as cars, trucks, airplanes, and buses. Oil is also the product that plastic is created from. The vast majority of the world's developed nations would be helpless without oil, and so nations will pay nearly any price to keep that oil flowing from the Middle East into their countries.

The oil-rich exporters of the Middle East can hold the rest of the world hostage by increasing the price of oil even slightly, since the consumption for even a small-developed nation numbers in the billions of gallons every month.

Muslims claimed Jerusalem, capital of the ancient civilization of Israel, as a holy city in the same way that Jews and Christians did. Muslims held **Palestine** and **Jerusalem** for many years, prompting Christian armies from Europe to join the Crusades to "regain the Holy Land." For hundreds of years after Christendom's failure, these lands were ruled by Muslim leaders and armies. In recent centuries, Palestine was made a British colony and then divided, creating a modern state of Israel in 1948.

The addition of **Israel** to the Middle East presents a religious conflict not only with the Palestinians, but also with the Arab peoples of neighboring Egypt and Syria. In the last 40 years, Israel has won two major wars with its neighbors. Nearly daily conflict continues.

Governmental structures differ around the world. For example, a unitary state is one where the central government can create, change powers, or abolish sub-governmental units In federal systems, however, the constitution determines functions that cannot be changed by the central government, and a process is required to make changes. The U.S. has a federal system; most of the nations in the world have a unitary system.

Domain III.   Government/Civics/Political Science

Skill 3.1a   Political Theory

Political Science is the study of government, international relations, political thought and activity, and comparison of governments. It is tied to:

- History
- Anthropology (how government affects a group's culture and relationship with other groups)
- Economics (governmental influence and regulation of producing and distributing goods and products)
- Sociology (insight into how social developments affect political life)

The study of political science is crucial to understanding political processes and the influence of government, civic duties, and responsibilities of people.

Politic Science is the study of political life, different forms of government including elections, political parties, and public administration. In addition, political science studies include values such as justice, freedom, power, and equality. There are six main fields of political-study in the United States:

- Political theory and philosophy
- Comparative governments
- International relations
- Political behavior
- Public administration
- American government and politics

Aristotle and Plato were Greek philosophers who believed that political order was to be the result of political science and that this political order would ensure maximum justice while at the same time ensuring stability.

Saint Thomas Aquinas elaborated on Aristotle's theories and adapted them to Christianity, emphasizing certain duties and rights of individuals in the governmental processes. He also laid emphasis on government rule according to those rights and duties. Aquinas helped lay the foundation of the idea of **modern constitutionalism** by stating that government was limited by law.

Niccolò Machiavelli was a famous politician and writer (*The Prince*) from Florence, Italy, who disregarded the ideals of Christianity in favor of realistic power politics.

http://plato.stanford.edu/entries/machiavelli/
Stanford Encyclopedia of Philosophy - Niccolò Machiavelli

Thomas Hobbes believed that a person's life was a constant, unceasing search for power and believed in the state's supremacy to combat this. His most famous work was **Leviathan** (651)**,** which was actually written as a reaction to the disorders caused by the English civil wars which had culminated with the execution of King Charles I. Hobbes perceived people as rational beings, but unlike Locke and Jefferson, he had no faith in their abilities to live in harmony with one another without a government. The trouble was, as Hobbes saw it, people were selfish and the strong would take from the weak. However, the weak being rational would in turn band together against the strong. For Hobbes, the state of nature became a chaotic state in which every person becomes the enemy of every other. It became a war of all against all, with terrible consequences for all.

John Locke was an important thinker on the nature of democracy. He regarded the mind of man at birth as a tabula rasa, a blank slate upon which experience imprints knowledge and behavior. He did not believe in the idea of intuition or theories of innate knowledge. Locke also believed that all men are born good, independent and equal, that it is their actions that will determine their fate. Locke's views, espoused in his most important work, **Two Treatises of Civil Government** (1690) attacked the theory of the divine right of kings and the nature of the state as conceived by Thomas Hobbes. Locke argued that sovereignty did not reside in the state, but with the people. The state is supreme, but only if it is bound by civil and what he called "**natural'** law.

Many of Locke's political ideas, such as those relating to natural rights, property rights, the duty of the government to protect these rights and the rule of the majority, were embodied in the Constitution of the United States. He further held that revolution was not only a right, but also often an obligation and advocated a system of checks and balances in government. A government comprised of three branches of which the legislative is more powerful than either the executive or the judicial. He also believed in the separation of the church and state. All of these ideas were to be incorporated in the Constitution of the United States. As such Locke is considered in many ways the true founding father of our Constitution and government system. He remains one of history's most influential political thinkers to this day.

Montesquieu and Rousseau were proponents of "liberalism", the willingness to change ideas, policies, and proposals to solve current problems. They also believed that individual freedom was just as important as any community's welfare. Rousseau especially was one of the most famous and influential political theorists before the French Revolution. His most important and most studied work is *The Social Contract* (1762). He was concerned with what should be the proper form of society and government. However, unlike Hobbes, Rousseau did not view the state of nature as one of absolute chaos.

The problem as Rousseau saw it was that the natural harmony of the state of nature was due to people's intuitive goodness not to their actual reason. Reason only developed once a civilized society was established. The intuitive goodness was easily overwhelmed however by arguments for institutions of social control, which likened rulers to father figures and extolled the virtues of obedience to such figures. To a remarkable extent, strong leaders have, in Rousseau's judgment, already succeeded not only in extracting obedience from the citizens that they ruled, but also more importantly, have managed to justify such obedience as necessary.

Rousseau's most direct influence was upon the **French Revolution** (1789-1815). In the *Declaration of the Rights of Man and The Citizen* (1789), it explicitly recognized the sovereignty of the general will as expressed in the law. In contrast to the American **Declaration of Independence**, it contains explicit mention of the obligations and duties of the citizen, such as assenting to taxes in support of the military or police forces for the common good. In modern times, ideas such as Rousseau's have often been used to justify the ideas of authoritarian and totalitarian systems.

David Hume and Jeremy Bentham believed that "the greatest happiness of the greatest number was the goal of politics." Hume was a pioneer of the doctrine of empiricism: believing things only when you've seen the proof for yourself. Hume was also a prime believer in the value of skepticism; in other words, he was naturally suspicious of things that other people told him to be true and constantly set out to discover the truth for himself.

John Stuart Mill wrote extensively of the liberal ideas of his time. He was a progressive British philosopher and economist, whose ideas came closer to socialism than to the classical capitalist ideas of Adam Smith. Mill constantly advocated for political and social reforms, including emancipation for women, labor organizations, and farming cooperatives

Johann Gottlieb Fichte and **Friedrich Hegel** were German philosophers who contributed significantly in the eighteenth century. Johann Gottlieb Fichte and Friedrich Hegel supported a liberalism, which included ideas about nationalism and socialism.

Various civil rights acts, notably the **Voting Rights Act of 1965**, sought to eliminate the remaining features of unequal suffrage in the United States.

Most recently, the question has revolved around the issue of "**gerrymandering**", which involves the adjustment of various electoral districts in order to achieve a predetermined goal. Gerrymandering sometimes creates odd and unusual looking districts in the adjustment for political favoritism, often an ethnic adjustment. This has led to questioning whether the practice is fair.

Skill 3.1b United States Government and Politics

In the United States, there are three branches of the federal government, the **Executive**, the **Legislative**, and the **Judicial**.

Legislative – Article I of the Constitution establishes the legislative or law-making branch of the government called Congress. It is made up of two houses, the House of Representatives and the Senate. Voters in all states elect the members who serve in each respective House of Congress. The legislative branch is responsible for:

- making laws
- raising and printing money
- regulating trade
- establishing the postal service
- establishing federal courts
- approving president's appointments
- declaring war
- supporting the armed forces

Congress also has the power to amend the Constitution (with state ratification) and to **impeach** (bring charges against) the president. Charges for impeachment are brought by the House of Representatives and are tried in the Senate.

Executive – Article II of the Constitution creates the executive branch of the government. This branch is headed by the President who recommends new laws, and can veto bills passed by the legislative branch. As chief of state, the president is responsible for:

- carrying out the laws of the country
- carrying out treaties and declarations of war passed by the legislative branch
- appointing federal judges
- serving as commander-in-chief of the military when it is called into service
- appointing cabinet members
- appointing ambassadors

Other members of the executive branch include the Vice President, also elected, and various presidential advisors, members of the armed forces, and other appointed and civil servants of government agencies, departments and bureaus. Although the president appoints them, they must be approved by the legislative branch.

Judicial – Article III of the Constitution establishes the judicial branch of government headed by the Supreme Court. The Supreme Court has the power to rule that a law passed by the legislature or an act of the executive branch is illegal and unconstitutional. Citizens, businesses, and government officials can ask the Supreme Court to review a decision made in a lower court if someone believes that the ruling by a judge is unconstitutional.

The judicial branch also includes the federal district courts established by Congress. These courts try lawbreakers and review cases referred from other courts.

Powers delegated to the federal government

1. To tax
2. To borrow and coin money
3. To establish postal service
4. To grant patents and copyrights
5. To regulate interstate & foreign commerce
6. To establish courts
7. To declare war
8. To raise and support the armed forces
9. To govern territories
10. To define and punish felonies and piracy on the high seas
11. To fix standards of weights and measures
12. To conduct foreign affairs

Powers reserved to the states

1. To regulate intrastate trade
2. To establish local governments
3. To protect general welfare
4. To protect life and property
5. To ratify amendments
6. To conduct elections
7. To make state and local laws

Concurrent powers of the federal government and states

1. Both Congress and the states may tax
2. Both may borrow money
3. Both may charter banks and corporations
4. Both may establish courts
5. Both may make and enforce laws
6. Both may take property for public purposes
7. Both may spend money to provide for the public welfare

Implied powers of the federal government

1. To establish banks or other corporations implied from delegated powers to tax, borrow, and regulate commerce
2. To spend money for roads, schools, health, insurance, etc. implied from powers to establish post roads, to tax to provide for general welfare and defense, and to regulate commerce
3. To create military academies, implied from powers to raise and support an armed force
4. To locate and generate sources of power and sell surplus, implied from powers to dispose of government property, commerce, and war powers
5. To assist and regulate agriculture, implied from power to tax and spend for general welfare and regulate commerce

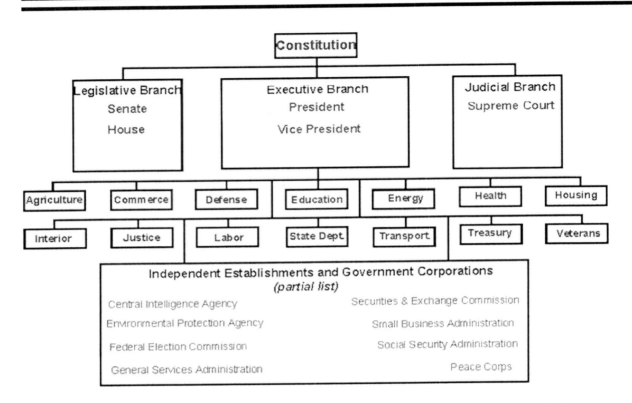

The terms "**civil liberties**" and "**civil rights**" are often used interchangeably, but there are some fine distinctions between the two terms.

Civil liberties implies that the state has a positive role to play in assuring that all citizens will have equal protection and justice under the law. The term implies equal opportunities to exercise privileges of citizenship and to participate fully in the life of the nation, regardless of race, religion, sex, color or creed.

Civil rights refers to rights described as guarantees specified against the state authority, implying limitations on the actions of the state to interfere with citizens' liberties.

Although the term "civil rights" has been identified with the ideal of equality and the term "civil liberties" with the idea of freedom, the two concepts are really inseparable and interacting. Equality implies the proper ordering of liberty in a society so that one individual's freedom does not infringe on the rights of others.

The beginning of civil liberties and the idea of civil rights in the United States goes back to ideas of the Greeks. The political philosophies of the ancient Greeks backed the early British struggle for civil rights, the same philosophies that led many people to come to the New World in the first place. Religious freedom, political freedom, and the right to live one's life as one sees fit are basic to the American ideal. These ideas were embodied in the Declaration of Independence and the Constitution.

All these ideas found their final expression in the Constitution's first ten amendments, known as the **Bill of Rights**. In 1789, the first Congress passed these first amendments. By December 1791, three-fourths of the states had ratified them. James Madison, who wrote the amendments, said that the Bill of Rights does not give Americans these rights. People, Madison said, already have these rights. They are natural rights that belong to all human beings. The Bill of Rights simply prevents the governments from taking away these rights.

Summary of Bill of Rights:

The **First Amendment** guarantees the basic rights of freedom of religion, freedom of speech, freedom of the press, and freedom of assembly.

The next **three amendments** came out of the colonists' struggle with Great Britain. For example, the **Third Amendment** prevents Congress from forcing citizens to keep troops in their homes. Before the Revolution, Great Britain tried to coerce the colonists to house soldiers. The **Second Amendment** guarantees the right to bear arms; the **Fourth Amendment** is protection from unreasonable search and seizure.
Amendments **five through eight** protect citizens who are accused of crimes and are brought to trial. Every citizen has the right to due process of law. Due process means that the government must follow the same fair rules for everyone brought to trial. These rules include the right to a trial by an impartial jury, the right to be defended by a lawyer, and the right to a speedy trial.

The last **two amendments** limit the powers of the federal government to those expressly stated in the Constitution. Any rights not expressly mentioned in the Constitution belong to the states or to the people.

Freedom of Religion: Religious freedom has not been seriously threatened in the United States historically. The policy of the government has been guided by the premise that church and state should be separate. When religious practices have been at cross-purposes with prevailing attitudes at particular times, restrictions have been placed on these practices.

One is restrictions against polygamy, supported by certain religious groups. Animal sacrifice promoted by some religious beliefs is generally prohibited. The use of mind-altering, illegal substances sometimes used in religious rituals is restricted.

All recognized religious institutions are tax-exempt, and therefore, there have been many quasi-religious groups that have tried to take advantage of tax-exemption.

Freedom of Speech, Press, and Assembly: These rights historically have been given wide latitude been but have been limited on occasion. The classic limitation on freedom of speech is the famous precept that an individual is prohibited from yelling "Fire!" in a crowded theatre. This prohibition is an example of the state saying that freedom of speech does not extend to speech that might endanger other people.

There is also a prohibition against slander, or knowingly stating a deliberate falsehood against someone.

Many regulations regard freedom of the press. For example, there are laws against libel, the printing of a known falsehood.

In times of national emergency, various restrictions can be placed on the rights of press, speech, and sometimes assembly. Speech that would incite people to overthrow the government or resist lawful authority are restricted.

The legal system has also undergone a number of serious changes with the interpretation of some constitutional guarantees. A number of organizations are champions for civil liberties and civil rights in this country. Criticism, however, is raised against these groups questioning whether they are really protecting rights, or are attempting to create new rights. Rights come with responsibility and respect for the public order.

How best to move forward with ensuring civil liberties and civil rights for all continues to dominate the national debate. In recent times, issues seem to revolve not around individual rights, but group rights. At the forefront of the debate is whether some specific remedies like affirmative action, quotas, or gerrymandering are fair or unfair.

It is a testament to the American system that it has shown itself able to enter into these debates and to find solutions to come out stronger. That the United States has the longest single constitutional history in the modern era is just one reason to be optimistic about the future of American liberty.

Voting

The terms **suffrage** and **franchise** refer to voting or right to vote. Although elections are associated with democratic practices, various limitations have been placed on the right to vote throughout history. These have included property qualifications, poll taxes, residency requirements, race, and gender

In 1787, the Constitution of the United States provided for the election of the chief executive in Article II, Section I, and members of the national legislature in Article I, Section II. A number of election abuses, however, led to the adoption of what was known as the **Australian or secret ballot** and the practice of registering voters prior to the election.

Voting machines were first used in the United States in 1892. During the nineteenth century, the electorate in the United States grew considerably. Most of the states franchised all white male adults, although the so-called poll tax was retained. The poll tax was abolished by the Twenty-fourth Amendment to the Constitution, ratified in 1964. The Fifteenth Amendment ratified in 1870 extended the vote to the former black slaves. In the period after the Civil War known as Reconstruction, many blacks were elected to high office for the first time in American history.

Average citizens can participate in the political process by voting. Since the passing of the Twenty-third Amendment in 1965, US citizens who are at least 18 years old are eligible to vote. Elections are held at regular intervals at all levels of government, allowing citizens to weigh in on local matters as well as those of national scope.

Citizens wishing to engage in the political process to a greater degree have several paths open, such as participating in local government, including the **caucus**. Counties, states, and cities and towns are governed by locally-elected boards or councils that meet publicly. Citizens are usually able to bring their concerns and express their opinions. Citizens may run for local elections, join a governing board, or seek support for higher office.

Political parties endorse certain platforms that express social and political goals, and support member candidates in election campaigns. Political parties use volunteer labor, with supporters making telephone calls, distributing printed material, and campaigning for the causes and candidates. Political parties solicit donations. and contributing money to a political party is another form of participation citizens can undertake.

Another form of political activity is to **support an issue-related political group**. Several political groups work actively to sway public opinion on various issues or on behalf of a segment of American society. These groups may have representatives who meet with state and federal legislators to "lobby" them - to provide them with information on an issue and persuade them to take favorable action.

Campaigning

Volunteers on a **political campaign** are plentiful, but campaigns also need to pay campaign specialists.

Money is also needed to buy or rent all of the tangible and intangible things that are needed to power a political campaign: office supplies, meeting places, transportation vehicles, and advertising.

Television is the most expensive kind of advertising, but it also has the potential to reach the widest audience. TV commercials have the potential to reach perhaps millions of viewers. Other forms of advertising include radio and Web ads, signs, billboards, and good old-fashioned flyers.

A candidate might have a significant amount of money in his or her own **personal coffers**. In rare cases, the candidate finances the entire campaign. However, the most prevalent source of money is **outside donations**.

The largest source of campaign finance money, however, comes from so-called "**special interests**." A large company, such as an oil company or a manufacturer of electronic goods, will want to keep prices or tariffs down and so will want to make sure that laws lifting those prices or tariffs aren't passed. To this end, the company will contribute money to the campaigns of candidates who are likely to vote to keep those prices or tariffs down. A candidate is not obligated to accept such a donation, of course, and further is not obligated to vote in favor of the interests of the special interest.

An anti-abortion group, for example, will provide money to candidates who agree and promise to work on the issue. Social groups have many dedicated individuals who organize themselves into political action committees, attend meetings and rallies, and work to make sure that their message gets out to a wide audience. Methods of spreading the word often include media advertising on behalf of their chosen candidates. This kind of expenditure is no doubt welcomed by the candidates, who will get the benefit of the exposure.

The Media

A **free press** is essential to maintaining responsibility and civic-mindedness in government and in the rest of society. The broadcast, print, and electronic media serve as societal and governmental watchdogs.

First and foremost, the media reports on the actions taken and encouraged by leaders of the government. In many cases, these actions are common knowledge. Policy debates, discussions on controversial issues, struggles against foreign powers in economic and wartime endeavors—all are fodder for media reports. The First Amendment guarantees media in America the right to report.

Owners of large companies and charities and recognizable figures in popular entertainment are continually under scrutiny for signs of questionable actions or behavior. In the same way that lawmakers are responsible for public legislative policy, many company owners are responsible for public economic policy. If a corporation is stealing money from its employees or shareholders, then those employees and shareholders and the American public at large need to know about it. Such reporting is not only informative, but also usually leads to indictments, prosecutions, and jail terms for the perpetrators of such economic crimes.

Public officials will hire one person, a department of employees, or perhaps an entire business to conduct **public relations**, efforts. The firm will write press releases, arrange media events, and do everything else to keep the politician's name in front of the public for name recognition.

Evaluating Internet Sources

Internet opportunities include news websites as well as personal web sites. A site might not have undergone the same sort of scrutiny as comparable efforts released by major media outlets to newspapers, radio, and television. Those media processes have editors and fact checkers who will verify information before it is released. In contrast, bloggers seldom use editors or or fact checkers before publishing. Looking for scholarly sites can be helpful.

Skill 3.1c Comparative Government and Politics

Forms of Government

Anarchism - Political movement believing in the elimination of all government and its replacement by a cooperative community of individuals. Sometimes it has involved political violence such as assassinations of important political or governmental figures. The historical banner of the movement is a black flag.

Communism - A belief, as well as a political system, characterized by the ideology of class conflict and revolution, one party state and dictatorship, repressive police apparatus, and government ownership of the means of production and distribution of goods and services. Communism supports a revolutionary ideology preaching the eventual overthrow of all other political orders and the establishment of one world communist government. The historical banner of the movement is a red flag with a variation of stars and hammer and sickles, representing the various types of workers.

Dictatorship - The rule by an individual or small group of individuals (Oligarchy) that centralizes all political control in itself and enforces its will with a terrorist police force.

Fascism - A belief, as well as a political system, opposed ideologically to Communism, though similar in basic structure with a one party state, centralized political control, and a repressive police system. It does tolerates private ownership of the means of production, though it maintains tight overall control. Central to its belief is the idolization of the leader, a "Cult of the Personality", and most often an expansionist ideology. Examples have been German Nazism and Italian Fascism.

Monarchy - The rule of a nation by a monarch (a non-elected usually hereditary leader) most often a king or queen. It may or may not be accompanied by some measure of democratic open institutions and elections at various levels. A modern example is Great Britain, where it is called a constitutional monarchy.

Parliamentary System - A system of government with a legislature that usually involves a multiplicity of political parties and often coalition politics. There is division between the head of state and head of government. Head of government is usually known as a Prime Minister who is usually the head of the largest party. The head of government and cabinet usually both sit and vote in the parliament. Head of state is most often an elected president, though in the case of a constitutional monarchy like Great Britain, the sovereign may take the place of a president as head of state. A government may fall when a majority in parliament votes "no confidence" in the government.

Presidential System - A system of government with a legislature can involve few or many political parties with no division between head of state and head of government. The President serves in both capacities. The President is elected either by direct or indirect election. A president and cabinet usually do not sit or vote in the legislature, and the president may or may not be the head of the largest political party. A president can thus rule even without a majority in the legislature. He can only be removed from office before an election for major infractions of the law.

Socialism - Political belief and system in which the state takes a guiding role in the national economy and provides extensive social services to its population. It may or may not own outright means of production, but even where it does not, it exercises tight control. It usually promotes democracy (Democratic Socialism), though the heavy state involvement produces excessive bureaucracy and usually inefficiency. Taken to an extreme, it may lead to Communism as government control increases and democratic practice decreases. Ideologically the two movements are very similar in both belief and practice, as Socialists also preach the superiority of their system to all others and that it will become the eventual natural order. It is also considered for that reason a variant of Marxism. It also has used a red flag as a symbol.

A **totalitarian** system doesn't recognize the right for any aspect of society to be outside the influence of the state. Such a government sees itself as having a legitimate concern with all levels of human existence. Not only in regards to freedom of speech, or press, but even to social and religious institutions, it tries to achieve a complete conformity to its ideals. Thus, those ideologies that presume to speak to all of society's ills, such as Communism and Fascism, look to this model for what they attempt to create in society.   As Benito Mussolini said, "Nothing outside of the state; nothing instead of the state." A totalitarian government is **authoritarian**, but an authoritarian system does not have to be totalitarian.

An **authoritarian** system may leave some autonomous institutions alone, such as the Church so long as they do not interfere with the state authority. This model can be seen in the history of Central and South America, where regimes, usually representing the interests of the upper classes, came to power and instituted dictatorships that seek to concentrate all political power in a few hands.

Democracy comes from the Greek "for the rule of the people." The two most prevalent types are **direct** and **indirect** democracy. Direct democracy usually involves all the people in a given area coming together to vote and decide on issues that will affect them. It is used only when the population involved is relatively small, for instance a local town meeting. An **indirect democracy** involves much larger areas and populations and involves the sending of representatives to a legislative body to vote on issues affecting the people. Such a system can be comprised of a **Presidential** or **Parliamentary** system. In the United States, we follow an indirect or representative democracy of the presidential type.

Skill 3.1d   International Relations

There are many theories of international relations, all of which seek to describe how sovereign countries interact, or should interact, with one another. Four of the primary schools of thought in international theory are Realism, Liberalism, Institutionalism and Constructivism.

Realism is an international theory that holds the nation-state as the basic unit and recognizes no international authority above individual nations. Realism is based on the assumption that nations act only in their own self-interest to preserve their own security. Realism holds that international relations are based on the relative military and economic power between nations, and that nations are inherently aggressive.

Liberalism allows for the cooperation of several states working in common interest. Instead of the Realist belief that states act based on their capabilities, Liberalism holds that states act based on their preferences. The term Liberalism was first used critically by Realist thinkers to describe the international theories of Woodrow Wilson.

Institutionalism is a theory of international relations that holds that there is a structure to the interactions of nations that determine how they will act. The rules that nations follow in making international decisions are called institutions. Institutions can give structure, distribute power and provide incentives for international cooperation.

Constructivism is similar to Liberalism in philosophy, but recognizes the role that ideas and perceptions play in international relations. Constructivism makes note of traditional relations between countries and their relative goals, identities and perceived threats. Constructivism recognizes, for instance, that a country building up its military is likely to be taken as more of a threat by that country's traditional antagonists than by its allies.

In practice, international relations are often conducted through **diplomacy.** Nations that formally recognize one another, station a group of diplomats, led by an ambassador, in one another's countries to provide formal representation on international matters.

Diplomats convey official information on the policies and positions of their home countries to the host countries where they are stationed. Diplomats are also involved in negotiating international agreements on issues such as trade, environmental issues, and conflict resolutions. Countries sometimes engage in informal diplomacy between private individuals when they wish to discuss common issues without taking official positions.

Diplomacy also takes place within international organizations such as the United Nations. Member nations send diplomatic representation to the U.N. and have input into forming international policy. While member countries agree to abide by U.N. resolutions as a condition of membership, in practice there is often dissent.

The U.N. has the ability to impose economic and other sanctions on its members for failing to follow its decisions, but other types of enforcement have been problematic. The U.N. has the ability to raise military forces from its member countries, and these forces have historically been limited to peacekeeping missions, not active military campaigns.

The world continues to change with immigration, terrorism, advances in communication, and environmental impacts. Current events include politicians being arrested for a variety of offenses, activists arrested and jailed, journalists covering wars murdered. For example:

- Mayors, state legislators, and school board officials from Atlantic, Essex and Passaic counties in New Jersey
- Alberto Ken'ya Fujimori, former president of Peru
- Nelson Mandela in South Africa
- 58 journalists killed in the Algerian conflict from 1993 to 1996.

Domain IV: _____ Geography

Skill 4.1a   The World in Spatial Terms

GEOGRAPHY involves studying location and how living things and earth's features are distributed throughout the earth. It includes where animals, people, and plants live and the effects of their relationship with earth's physical features. Geographers also explore the locations of earth's features and how they came to be.

Some of the more important geographers include **Eratosthenes,** an ancient Greek mathematician who calculated the circumference of the earth; **Strabo** who wrote _Geographica_, a 17-volume description of the ancient world; and **Ptolemy** contributed his skills in mapping and theories from studies in astronomy to geographic knowledge.

Explorers have contributed to the study of geography as well. **Christopher Columbus** was known for his famous first voyage sailing west to find the riches of the east and finding the Western Hemisphere instead. **Marco Polo, Vasco da Gama, and Magellan** were three of many explorers and colonizers who contributed to geographic knowledge.

The National Geographic Society is publisher of the _National Geographic_ magazine and the funding of expeditions and other activities furthering geographic education.

What geographers study can be broken down into four parts:

- **Location**: Being able to find the exact site of anything on the earth
- **Spatial relations**: Relationships of earth's features, places, and groups of people with one another due to their location
- **Regional characteristics**: Characteristics of a place such as landform and climate, types of plants and animals, kinds of people who live there, and how people use the land
- **Forces that change the earth**: Human activities and natural forces.

Geographical studies are also divided into four categories:

- **Regional**: Elements and characteristics of a place or region
- **Topical**: One earth feature or one human activity occurring throughout the entire world
- **Physical**: Earth's physical features, what creates and changes them, their relationships to each other as well as human activities
- **Human**: Human activity patterns and how they relate to the environment including political, cultural, historical, urban, and social geographical fields of study.

Geography is the study of the earth, its people, and how people adapt to life on earth and how they use its resources. It is undeniably connected to history, economics, political science, sociology, anthropology, and even a bit of archaeology. Geography not only deals with people and the earth today but also:

- How did it all begin?
- What is the background of the people of an area?
- What kind of government or political system do they have?
- How does that affect their ways of producing goods and the distribution of them?
- What kind of relationships do these people have with other groups?
- How is the way they live their lives affected by their physical environment?
- In what ways do they effect change in their way of living?

The vast majority of people live in areas that are hospitable. Yes, people live in the Himalayas and in the Sahara, but the populations in those areas are small indeed when compared to the seacoasts of China, India, Europe, Australia, and the United States.

We can examine the spatial organization of the places where people live. For example, in a city, where are the factories and heavy industry buildings? Are they near airports or train stations? Are they on the edge of town, near major roads? What about housing developments? Are they near these industries, or are they far away? Where are the other industry buildings? Where are the schools and hospitals and parks? What about the police and fire stations? How close are homes to each of these things? Towns and especially cities are routinely organized into neighborhoods, so that each house or home is near to most things that its residents might need on a regular basis. This means that large cities have multiple schools, hospitals, grocery stores, fire stations.

Related to this is the distance between cities, towns, villages, or settlements. Population settlement patterns achieve **megalopolis** standards, with no clear boundaries from one town to the next. Other, more sparsely populated areas have towns that are few and far between and have relatively few people in them.

Flight has made possible global commerce and goods exchange on a level never before seen. Foods can be flown around the world and, with the aid of refrigeration techniques, be kept fresh enough to sell in markets nearly everywhere. The same is true of medicine and weapons.

The Use of Maps

We use **illustrations** because it is often easier to demonstrate a given idea visually instead of orally. Among the more common illustrations used are various types of **maps, graphs, and charts**, and photographs and **globes** are useful as well.

The disadvantage of a map is that maps are flat and the Earth is a sphere. It is impossible to reproduce exactly on a flat surface an object shaped like a sphere. In order to put the earth's features onto a map they must be stretched in some way. This stretching is called **distortion.**

Cartographers, or mapmakers, understand the problems of distortion. They design maps so that there is as little distortion as possible.

The process of putting the features of the Earth onto a flat surface is called **projection**. Map projections are made in a number of ways projecting onto a cylinder, cone, or plane

Cylindrical Projections - These are made by taking a cylinder of paper and wrapping it around a globe. A light is used to project the globe's features onto the paper. Distortion is least where the paper touches the globe.

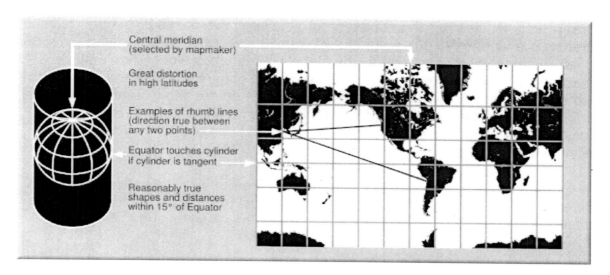

If the paper is wrapped so that it touches the globe at the equator, the mapo from this projection would have just a little distortion near the equator. In moving north or south of the equator, the distortion would increase. The best known and most widely used cylindrical projection is the **Mercator Projection.** It was first developed in 1569 by Gerardus Mercator, a Flemish mapmaker.

Conical Projections - The projection is made onto a cone of paper. The cone is made so that it touches a globe at the base of the cone only. It can be made so that it cuts through part of the globe in two different places. Again, there is the least distortion where the paper touches the globe. If the cone touches at two different points, there is some distortion at both of them. Conical projections are most often used to map areas in the **middle latitudes**. Maps of the United States are most often conical projections because most of the country lies within middle latitudes.

Flat-Plane Projections - These are made with a flat piece of paper that touches the globe at one point only. Areas near this point show little distortion. Flat-plane projections are often used to show the areas of the north and south poles. One such flat projection is called a **Gnomonic Projection**. On this kind of map all meridians appear as straight lines. Gnomonic projections are useful because any straight line drawn between points on it forms a **Great-Circle Route**.

Great-Circle Routes find the shortest route between two points by simply stretching a string from one point to the other. However, if the string was extended in reality, so that it took into effect the globe's curvature, it would then make a great-circle. A great-circle is any circle that cuts a sphere, such as the globe, into two equal parts. Because of distortion, most maps do not show great-circle routes as straight lines. Gnomonic projections, however, do show the shortest distance between the two places as a straight line, and because of this, they are valuable for navigation. They are called Great-Circle Sailing Maps.

To properly analyze a given map, one must be familiar with the various parts and symbols that most modern maps use. For the most part, this is standardized with different maps using similar parts and symbols. These can include:

The Title - All maps should have a title. The title tells you what information is to be found on the map.

The Legend - Most maps have a legend. A legend (also called a *map key*) tells the reader about the various symbols that are used on that particular map and what the symbols represent.

The Grid - A grid is a series of lines that are used to find exact places and locations on the map. There are several different kinds of grid systems in use; however, most maps do use the longitude and latitude system, known as the **Geographic Grid System**.

Directions - Most maps have some directional system to show which way the map is being presented. Often on a map, a small compass will be present with arrows showing the four basic directions: north, south, east, and west.

The Scale - This is used to show the relationship between a unit of measurement on the map versus the real world measure on the earth. Maps are drawn to many different scales. Some maps show a lot of detail for a small area. Others show a greater span of distance. Whichever is being used, one should always be aware of the scale. For instance the scale might be could be 1 inch = 10 miles for a small area or, for a map showing the whole world, it might have a scale in which 1 inch = 1,000 miles.

Maps have four main properties:

- size of the areas shown on the map
- shapes of the areas
- consistent scales
- straight line directions

A map can be drawn so that it is correct in one or more of these properties. No map can be correct in all of them.

Equal areas - In an equal area map, the meridians and parallels are drawn so that the areas shown have the same proportions as they do on the earth. For example, Greenland is about 118th the size of South America; thus, it will be shown as 118th the size on an equal area map. The **Mercator projection** is an example of a map that does not have equal areas. Greenland would appear to be about the same size of South America because Greenland lies near the North Pole.

Conformality (correct shapes) - Conformal Maps are as close as possible to true shapes. The United States is often shown by a Lambert Conformal Conic Projection Map.

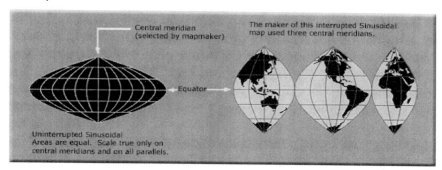

Consistent Scales - Many maps attempt to use the same scale on all parts of the map. Generally, this is easier when maps show a relatively small part of the earth's surface. For example, a map of Florida might be a Consistent Scale Map. Generally, maps showing large areas are not consistent-scale maps. This is so because of distortion. Often such maps will have two scales noted in the key. One scale, for example, might be accurate to measure distances between points along the Equator. Another might be then used to measure distances between the North Pole and the South Pole.

Maps showing physical features often try to show information about the elevation, or **relief,** of the land. **Elevation** is the distance above or below the sea level. The elevation is usually shown with colors. For instance, all areas on a map which are at a certain level will be shown in the same color.

Relief Maps show the shape of the land surface as flat, rugged, or steep. Relief maps usually give more detail than simply showing the overall elevation of the land's surface. Relief is also sometimes shown with colors, but another way to show relief is by using **contour lines**. These lines connect all points of a land surface which are the same height surrounding the particular area of land.

Thematic Maps are used to show more specific information, often on a single **theme**, or topic. Thematic maps show the distribution or amount of something over a certain given area. Population density, climate, economic information, cultural, election or political information, and more can be shown.

Skill 4.1b Places and Regions

The earth's surface is made up of 70 percent water and 30 percent land. Physical features of the land surface include mountains, hills, plateaus, valleys, and plains. Other minor landforms include deserts, deltas, canyons, mesas, basins, foothills, marshes and swamps. Earth's water features include oceans, seas, lakes, rivers, and canals.

Mountains are landforms with rather steep slopes at least 2,000 feet or more above sea level. Mountains are found in groups called mountain chains or mountain ranges. At least one range can be found on six of the earth's seven continents. North America has the Appalachian and Rocky Mountains; South America the Andes; Asia the Himalayas; Australia the Great Dividing Range; Europe the Alps; and Africa the Atlas, Ahaggar, and Drakensburg Mountains.

Hills are elevated landforms rising to an elevation of about 500 to 2000 feet. They are found everywhere on earth including Antarctica where they are covered by ice.

Plateaus are elevated landforms usually level on top. Depending on location, they range from being an area that is very cold to one that is cool and healthful. Some plateaus are dry because they are surrounded by mountains that keep out any moisture. Some examples include the Kenya Plateau in East Africa, which is very cool. The plateau extending north from the Himalayas is extremely dry while those in Antarctica and Greenland are covered with ice and snow.

Plains are described as areas of flat or slightly rolling land, usually lower than the landforms next to them. Sometimes called lowlands (and sometimes located along seacoasts) they support the majority of the world's people. Some are found inland and many have been formed by large rivers. This resulted in extremely fertile soil for successful cultivation of crops and numerous large settlements of people. In North America, the vast plains areas extend from the Gulf of Mexico north to the Arctic Ocean and between the Appalachian and Rocky Mountains. In Europe, rich plains extend east from Great Britain into central Europe on into the Siberian region of Russia. Plains in river valleys are found in China (the Yangtze River valley), India (the Ganges River valley), and Southeast Asia (the Mekong River valley).

Valleys are land areas that are found between hills and mountains. Some have gentle slopes containing trees and plants; others have very steep walls and are referred to as canyons. One famous example is Arizona's Grand Canyon of the Colorado River. An example of a valley is the fertile Central Valley in California.

Deserts are large dry areas of land receiving ten inches or less of rainfall each year. Among the better known deserts are Africa's large Sahara Desert, the Arabian Desert on the Arabian Peninsula, and the desert Outback covering roughly one-third of Australia.

Deltas are areas of lowlands formed by soil and sediment deposited at the mouths of rivers. The soil is generally very fertile and most fertile river deltas are important crop-growing areas. One well-known example is the delta of Egypt's Nile River, known for its production of cotton.

Mesas are the flat tops of hills or mountains usually with steep sides. Sometimes plateaus are also called mesas.

Basins are low areas drained by rivers or low spots in mountains.

Foothills are generally considered a low series of hills found between a plain and a mountain range.

Marshes and swamps are wet lowlands providing growth of rushes and reeds.

Oceans are the largest bodies of water on the planet. The four oceans of the earth are:

- Atlantic Ocean, one-half the size of the Pacific and separating North and South America from Africa and Europe
- Pacific Ocean, covering almost one-third of the entire surface of the earth and separating North and South America from Asia and Australia;
- Indian Ocean, touching Africa, Asia, and Australia
- ice-filled Arctic Ocean, extending from North America and Europe to the North Pole.

The waters of the Atlantic, Pacific, and Indian Oceans also touch the shores of Antarctica. Included in the features of the oceans are coral reefs, atolls, which are formed by corals around the edge of volcanic craters, and volcanic islands.

Seas are usually saline and are smaller than oceans. They are surrounded by land. Some examples include the Mediterranean Sea found between Europe, Asia, and Africa; and the Caribbean Sea, touching the West Indies, South and Central America. The Caspian Sea is the largest sea.

A **lake** is a body of freshwater (usually) surrounded by land. Over 60 percent of lakes are located in Canada. There are more than a dozen types of lakes. Lake Superior in the US is an example of a rift lake.

Rivers, considered a nation's lifeblood, usually begin as very small streams, formed by melting snow and rainfall, flowing from higher to lower land, emptying into a larger body of water, usually a sea or an ocean. Examples of important rivers for the people and countries affected by and/or dependent on them include the Nile, Niger, and Zaire Rivers of Africa; the Rhine, Danube, and Thames Rivers of Europe; the Yangtze, Ganges, Mekong, Hwang He, and Irrawaddy Rivers of Asia; the Murray-Darling in Australia; and the Orinoco in South America.

River systems are made up of large rivers and numerous smaller rivers or tributaries flowing into them. Examples include the vast **Amazon** Rivers system in South America and the **Mississippi** River system in the United States.

Canals are man-made water passages constructed to connect two larger bodies of water. Famous examples include the **Panama Canal** across Panama's isthmus connecting the Atlantic and Pacific Oceans and the **Suez Canal** in the Middle East between Africa and the Arabian Peninsula connecting the Red and Mediterranean Seas.

Communities

Settlements are the cradles of culture, political structure, education, and the management of resources. The relative placement of these settlements or communities are shaped by:

- proximity to natural resources
- movement of raw materials
- production of finished products
- availability of a work force
- delivery of finished products

The composition of communities, at least to some extent, will be determined by:

- shared values
- language
- culture
- religion
- subsistence.

Settlements begin in areas that offer the natural resources to support life – food and water. With the ability to manage the environment, one finds a concentration of populations. With the ability to transport raw materials and finished products comes mobility. With increasing technology and the rise of industrial centers comes a migration of the workforce.

Cities are the major hubs of human settlement. Almost half of the population of the world now lives in cities. These percentages are much higher in developed regions. Established cities continue to grow. The fastest growth, however, is occurring in developing areas. Metropolitan areas are made up of urban and suburban areas. In some places, cities and urban areas have become interconnected into **megalopol**i (e.g., Tokyo-Kawasaki-Yokohama). *Megalopolis* is a Greek word for *Great city*.

North American cities are different from European cities in terms of shape, size, population density, and modes of transportation. While in North America, the wealthiest economic groups tend to live outside the cities; the opposite is true in Latin American cities.

There are also significant differences among the cities of the world in terms of connectedness to other cities. While European and North American cities tend to be well-linked both by transportation and communication connections, in other places in the world communication and transportation have been limited. Now with the cell phone, communications have increased. Rural areas must be connected via communication and transportation in order to provide food and raw materials to urban areas.

Skill 4.1c Physical Systems

Weather is the condition of the air which surrounds the day-to-day atmospheric conditions including temperature, air pressure, wind, and moisture (precipitation) which includes rain, snow, hail, or sleet.

Climate is average weather or daily weather conditions for a specific region or location over a long or extended period of time. Studying the climate of an area includes information gathered on the area's monthly and yearly temperatures and its monthly and yearly amounts of precipitation. In addition, a characteristic of an area's climate is the length of its growing season. Different climates relate to:

- Latitude
- Amount of moisture
- Temperatures in land and water
- Land surface

Regions of climates are divided according to latitudes:

0 - 23 1/2 degrees are the "**low latitudes**"
23 1/2 - 66 1/2 degrees are the "**middle latitudes**"
66 1/2 degrees to the Poles are the "**high latitudes**"

Low latitudes are comprised of the **rainforest**, **savanna**, and **desert** climates.

The tropical **rainforest** climate is found in equatorial lowlands and is hot and wet. There is sun, extreme heat and rain every day. Although daily temperatures rarely rise above 90 degrees F, the daily humidity is always high.

North and south of the tropical rainforests are the tropical grasslands called "**savannas**"--the "lands of two seasons" with a winter dry season and a summer wet season.

Further north and south of the tropical grasslands or savannas are the **deserts**. These areas are the hottest and driest parts of the earth receiving less than ten inches of rain a year. These areas have extreme temperatures between night and day. After the sun sets, temperatures drop by 50 degrees or more.

The middle latitudes contain the Mediterranean climate, humid-subtropical, humid-continental, marine, steppe, and desert climates.

The **Mediterranean climate** is the climate of the lands bordering the Mediterranean Sea; a small portion of southwestern Africa; areas in southern and southwestern Australia; a small part of the Ukraine near the Black Sea; central Chile; and Southern California. Summers are hot and dry with mild winters. The growing season usually lasts all year and what little rain falls, falls during the winter months. The Mediterranean climate occurs between 30 and 40 degrees north and south latitude on the western coasts of countries.

The humid **subtropical climate** is found north and south of the tropics and is moist indeed. The areas with this type of climate are found on the southeastern coastal area of continents and can be found in Japan; mainland China; Australia; Africa; South America; and the United States. Warm ocean currents are found there. The winds that blow across these currents bring in warm moist air all year round. Long, warm summers; short, mild winters; and a long growing season allow for different crops to be grown several times a year. All contribute to the productivity of this climate type which supports more people than any of the other climates.

The **marine climate** is found in Western Europe; the British Isles; the Pacific Northwest; the western coast of Canada; and southern Chile, southern New Zealand; and southeastern Australia. The lands are either near water or surrounded by it. The ocean winds are wet and warm, bringing a mild, rainy climate to these areas. In the summer, the daily temperatures average at or below 70 degrees F. During the winter, because of the warming effect of the ocean waters, the temperatures rarely fall below freezing.

In northern and central United States, northern China, south-central and southeastern Canada, and the western and southeastern parts of the former Soviet Union is the "climate of four seasons," the humid **continental climate**.. Cold winters, hot summers, and enough rainfall to grow a variety of crops are the major characteristics of this climate. In areas where the humid continental climate is found are some of the world's best farmlands, as well as important activities such as trading and mining. Differences in temperatures throughout the year are determined by the distance a place is inland, away from the coasts.

The **steppe** or **prairie** climate is located in the interiors of Asia and North America. The dry flatlands are far from ocean breezes. Although the summers are hot and the winters are cold as in the humid continental climate, the big difference is rainfall. In the steppe climate, rainfall is light and uncertain. Ten to twenty inches a year, mainly in spring and summer, is normal.

In areas of less rain, the steppes or prairies become deserts. These climates exist in the Gobi Desert of Asia, central and western Australia, southwestern United States, and in Pakistan, Argentina, and Africa south of the Equator.

The two major climates found in the **high latitudes** are "tundra" and "taiga." The word "tundra" meaning "marshy plain" is a Russian word and aptly describes the climatic conditions in the northern areas of Russia, Europe, and Canada. Winters are extremely cold and very long. Most of the year, the ground is frozen but becomes rather mushy during the very short summer months. Less snow falls in the area of the tundra than in the eastern part of the United States. Because of extreme cold, very few people live there and no crops can be raised. Nonetheless, many plants and animals are found there.

The "taiga" is the northern forest region and is located south of the tundra. The Russian word "taiga" means 'forest." The world's largest forestlands are found here along with vast mineral wealth and fur-bearing animals, and marshes and swamps. The climate is extreme, and few people live here because raising crops is almost impossible due to the extremely short growing season. The winter temperatures are colder and the summer temperatures are hotter than those in the tundra because the taiga climate region is farther from the waters of the Arctic Ocean. The taiga is found in the northern parts of Russia, Sweden, Norway, Finland, Canada, and Alaska. .

A climate unique to areas with high mountains is called a "**vertical climate.**" Temperatures, crops, vegetation, and human activities change with the elevation. An extreme example is Azerbaijan where the diversity of nine of the eleven climates is experienced. Azerbaijan is located at the crossroads of eastern Europe and western Asia.

Plate tectonics is the geological theory that explains the large movements of the solid portions of the earth's crust floating on the molten mantle. There are ten major tectonic plates with several smaller plates. The surface of the earth can be drastically affected at the boundaries of these plates.

There are three types of plate boundaries:

Convergent boundaries: Plates are moving toward one another. When this happens, the two plates either collide to push up against one another. This is called **continental collision.** When one plate slides under the other, this is called **subduction.** Continental collision can create high mountain ranges, such as the Andes and Himalayas. Subduction often results in volcanic activity along the boundary, as in the "**Ring of Fire**" along the northern coasts of the Pacific Ocean.

Divergent boundaries occur where plates are moving away from one another creating **rifts** in the surface. The **Mid-Atlantic Ridge** on the floor of the Atlantic Ocean and the **Great Rift Valley** in east Africa are examples of rifts at divergent plate boundaries.

Transform boundaries: Plates are moving in opposite directions along their boundary, grinding against one another. The tremendous pressures that build along these boundaries often lead to earthquake activity when this pressure is released. The **San Andreas Fault** along the West Coast of North America is an example of a transform boundary.

Erosion is the displacement of earth solids. Erosion is often a result of wind, water, or ice acting on surfaces with loose particles, such as sand, loose soils, or decomposing rock. Gravity can also cause erosion on loose surfaces. Factors such as slope, soil and rock composition, plant cover, and human activity all affect erosion. **Mechanical erosion** is natural. **Chemical erosion** is due to human activities.

Weathering is the natural decomposition of the earth's surface from contact with the atmosphere. It is not the same as erosion, but can be a factor in erosion. Heat, water, ice, and pressure are all factors that can lead to weathering. Chemicals in the atmosphere can also contribute to weathering.

Transportation is the movement of eroded material from one place to another by wind, water or ice. Examples of transportation include pebbles rolling down a stream bed and boulders carried by moving glaciers.

Deposition is when sediments or other geological materials build up. Sand dunes and moraines are formed by transportation and deposition.

Skill 4.1d Human Systems

Competition for control of areas of the earth's surface is a common trait of human interaction throughout history. This competition has resulted in both destructive conflict and productive cooperation. Societies and groups have sought control of regions of the earth's surface for a variety of reasons including religion, economics, politics, and administration. Numerous wars have been fought through the centuries for the control of territory for each of these reasons.

At the same time, groups and societies have peacefully worked together to establish boundaries around regions or territories in order to sustain the activities that support life and social organization.

Individuals and societies have divided the earth's surface through conflict for a number of reasons:

- The domination of peoples or societies (colonialism)
- The control of valuable resources (oil)
- The control of strategic routes (Panama Canal)

Conflicts can be spurred by religion, political ideology, national origin, language, and race. Conflicts can result from disagreement over how land, ocean, or natural resources will be developed, shared, and used. Conflicts have resulted from trade, migration, and settlement rights. Conflicts can occur between small groups of people, between cities, between nations, between religious groups, and between multi-national alliances.

Today, the world is primarily divided by political/administrative interests into **state sovereignties.** A particular region is recognized to be controlled by a particular government, including its territory, population, and natural resources. The only area of the earth's surface that today is not defined by state or national sovereignty is Antarctica.

Alliances are developed among nations based on political philosophy, economic concerns, cultural similarities, religious interests, and/or for military defense. Some of the most notable alliances today are:

- United Nations
- North Atlantic Treaty Organization
- Caribbean Community
- Common Market
- Council of Arab Economic Unity
- European Union

Large companies and **multi-national corporations** also compete for control of natural resources for manufacturing, development, and distribution.

The **Agricultural Revolution**, initiated by the invention of the plow, led to a thoroughgoing transformation of human society by making large-scale agricultural production possible and facilitating the development of agrarian societies. During the period when the plow was invented, the wheel, numbers, and writing were also invented. Coinciding with the shift from hunting wild game to the domestication of animals, this period was one of dramatic social and economic change.

Numerous changes in lifestyle and thinking accompanied the development of stable agricultural communities. Rather than gathering a wide variety of plants as hunter-gatherers, agricultural communities become dependent on a limited number of plants or crops that are harvested. Subsistence becomes vulnerable to the weather and dependent upon planting and harvesting times.

In the beginning of the transition to agriculture, the tools that were used for hunting and gathering were adequate to the tasks of agriculture. The initial challenge was in adapting to a new way of life. Once that challenge was met, attention turned to the development of more advanced tools and sources of energy. Six thousand years ago the first plow was invented in Mesopotamia. This plow was pulled by animals. Agriculture possibilities grew. Soon tools were developed that make such basic tasks as gathering seeds, planting, and cutting grain faster and easier.

Agriculture also required a great deal of physical labor and the development of a sense of discipline. Agricultural communities become stable in terms of location. Construction of dwellings became appropriate. These dwelling tended to be built relatively close together, creating villages or towns.

Settled communities that produce the necessities of life are self-supporting. Advances in agricultural technology and the ability to produce a surplus of produce create two opportunities:

- Opportunity to trade the surplus goods for other desired goods
- Vulnerability to others who steal to take those goods.

Protecting domesticated livestock and surplus and stored crops becomes an issue for the community. This, in turn, leads to the construction of walls and fortifications around the community.

Stable communities free people from the need to carry everything with them and move from hunting ground to hunting ground. This facilitates the invention of larger, more complex tools. As new tools are envisioned and developed, it begins to make sense to have some specialization within the society. Skills begin to have greater value, and people begin to do work on behalf of the community that utilizes their particular skills and abilities. Settled community life also gives rise to the notion of wealth. It is now possible to keep possessions.

It also becomes necessary to maintain social and political stability to ensure that planting and harvesting times are not interrupted by internal discord or a war with a neighboring community. It also becomes necessary to develop ways to store the crop and prevent its destruction by the elements and animals. And then it must be protected from thieves.

The ability to produce surplus crops also creates the opportunity to trade or barter with other communities in exchange for desired goods. Traders and trade routes begin to develop between villages and cities. The domestication of animals expands the range of trade and facilitates an exchange of ideas and knowledge.

Skill 4.1e Environment and Society

Humans have always turned to nature for resources, from wood for the first cooking fires, to iron ore for the first metal tools, to crude oil to refine into fuel for automobiles and airplanes. Some of these resources, such as oil and metal ores, have a large, but limited supply. This kind of resource is considered non-renewable; once it has all been used, more cannot be made.

Natural resources that are virtually unlimited in supply, or which can be grown, are considered renewable resources. Trees that supply wood for construction and paper are considered renewable resources if managed correctly. Solar and wind energy are renewable resources because their supply is practically infinite. Hydrogen is a potential renewable resource that is receiving increasing attention because it can be derived from water, which is virtually unlimited.

Since the dawn of agriculture, humans have modified their environment to suit their needs and to provide food and shelter. Agriculture, for instance, often involves loosening topsoil by plowing before planting. This in turn affects how water and wind act on the soil and can lead to erosion. In extreme cases, erosion can leave a plot of agricultural land unsuitable for use. Modern methods of farming rely less on plowing the soil before planting, but more on chemical fertilizers, pesticides, and herbicides. However, these chemicals can find their way into groundwater, affecting the environment.

Cities show how humans modify their environment to suit their needs. Cities have a major impact on the environment. Concentrated consumption of fuels by automobiles and home heating systems affect the quality of the air in and around cities. The lack of exposed ground means that rainwater runs off roads and rooftops into sewer systems instead of seeping into the ground, often making its way into nearby streams or rivers and carrying urban debris with it.

Most countries recognize the importance of limiting the impact human populations have on the environment and have laws in place toward this goal. Emissions of certain compounds by factories, power plants, automobiles, and other sources are regulated. Cities collect sewage water into plants where it is treated before returning to rivers and streams. Incentives have been put in place in some areas to encourage people to use cleaner, alternative fuel sources, and many governments are supporting research into new sources of fuel that will reduce the reliance on non-renewable resources.

Ecology is the study of how living organisms interact with the physical aspects of their surroundings (their environment) including soil, water, air, and other living things. **Biogeography** is the study of how the surface features of the earth – form, movement, and climate–affect living things.

Three levels of environmental understanding are critical. An **ecosystem** is a community consisting of a physical environment and the organisms that live within it. A **biome** is a large area of land with characteristic climate, soil, and a mixture of plants and animals. Biomes are made up of groups of ecosystems. Major biomes include deserts, chaparrals, savannas, tropical rain forests, temperate grasslands, temperate deciduous forests, taigas, and tundras. A **habitat** is the set of surroundings within which members of a species normally live. Elements of the habitat include soil, water, predators, and competitors.

Within habitats interactions between members of the species occur. These interactions occur between members of the same species and between members of different species. Interaction tends to be of three types: competition, predation, or symbiosis.

Competition occurs between members of the same species or between members of different species for resources required to continue life, to grow, or to reproduce. For example, competition for acorns can occur between squirrels or it can occur between squirrels and woodpeckers. One species can either push out or cause the demise of another species if it is better adapted to obtain the resource. When a new species is introduced into a habitat, the result can be a loss of the native species and/or significant change to the habitat. For example, the introduction of the Asian plant Kudzu into the American South has resulted in the destruction of several species because Kudzu grows and spreads very quickly and smothers everything in its path.

Predation occurs when organisms live by hunting and eating other organisms. The species best suited for hunting other species in the habitat will be the species that survives. Larger, predator species with better hunting skills reduce the amount of prey available for smaller and/or weaker species. This affects both the amount of available prey and the diversity of species that are able to survive in the habitat.

Symbiosis is a condition in which two organisms of different species are able to live in the same environment over an extended period of time without harming one another. In some cases, one species may benefit without harming the other. In other cases, both species benefit.

By nature, different organisms are best suited for existence in particular environments. When an organism is displaced to a different environment or when the environment changes for some reason, its ability to survive is determined by its ability to **adapt** to the new environment. Adaptation can take the form of structural change, physiological change, or behavioral modification.

Biodiversity refers to the variety of species and organisms, as well as the variety of habitats, available on the earth. Biodiversity provides the life-support system for the various habitats and species. The greater the degree of biodiversity, the more species and habitats will continue to survive.

Natural changes occur that can alter habitats (floods, volcanoes, storms, earthquakes). These changes can affect the species that exist within the habitat either by causing extinction or by changing the environment in a way that will no longer support the life systems. Climate changes can have similar effects. Inhabiting species, however, can also alter habitats particularly through migration. Human civilization, population growth, and efforts to control the environment can have many negative effects on various habitats. Humans change their environments to suit their particular needs and interests.

This can result in changes that result in the extinction of species or changes to the habitat itself. For example, deforestation damages the stability of mountain surfaces. One particularly devastating example is in the removal of the grasses of the Great Plains for agriculture. Tilling the ground and planting crops left the soil unprotected. Sustained drought dried the soil into dust. When wind storms occurred, the topsoil was stripped away and blown all the way to the Atlantic Ocean.

Skill 4.1f   The Uses of Geography

Physical geography is concerned with the locations of such earth features as climate, water, and land and how these relate to and affect each other and human activities; and what forces shaped and changed them. All three of these earth features affect the lives of all humans having a direct influence on what is made and produced, where it occurs, how it occurs, and what makes it possible. The combination of the different climate conditions and types of landforms and other surface features work together all around the earth to give the many varied cultures their unique characteristics and distinctions.

Cultural geography studies the location, characteristics, and influence of the physical environment on different cultures around the earth. Also included in these studies are comparisons and influences of the many varied cultures. Ease of travel and up-to-the-minute, state-of-the-art communication techniques ease the difficulties of understanding cultural differences making it easier to come in contact with them

Geographical studies are divided into:

- Regional: Elements and characteristics of a place or region

- Topical: One earth feature or one human activity occurring throughout the entire world

- Physical: Earth's physical features, what creates and changes them, their relationships to each other as well as to human activities

- Human: Human activity patterns and how they relate to the environment including political, cultural, historical, urban, and social geographical fields of study.

Special research methods used by geographers include mapping, interviewing, field studies, mathematics, statistics, and scientific instruments.

Maps have four main properties. They are 1) the size of the areas shown on the map; 2) the shapes of the areas; 3) consistent scales; and 4) straight line directions. A map can be drawn so that it is correct in one or more of these properties. No map can be correct in all of them.

Weather is the condition of the air which surrounds the day-to-day atmospheric conditions such as temperature, air pressure, wind, moisture or precipitation (which includes rain, snow, hail, or sleet).

Climate is average weather or daily weather conditions for a specific region or location over a long or extended period of time.

Human Systems in Geography

Canal-building, ski areas, slash and burn, fisheries, agriculture . . . the list goes on when we consider how humans relate to geography.

Cancun in Mexico becomes a tourist mecca. Vail in Colorado becomes a skier mecca. Climates work for these industries. Singapore and Abu Dhabai glitter with skyscrapers. Geography has provided ports, a desirable climate, oil for ultimate population growth.

In 1946, an earthquake struck the Aleutian Islands near Alaska and a tsunami swept Hilo, Hawaii, with 14 feet of water. The waves destroyed the waterfront and killed 159 people. Every house facing the Bay was demolished and struck the buildings across the street.

The Reno-Sparks area grows in population and needs water, but the high water levels in the reservoir are destroying the cui-ui fish of the Paiute tribe.

World human population is over six billion. One hundred years ago, population was less than two billion. Five-hundred years ago there were an estimated ten million Indians living in the Amazonian Rainforest. Today there are fewer than 200,000. Logging, mining, industrial development and large dams mean that more than an acre-and-a-half of rain forest is lost every second of every day. That rate means that every year an area of rainforest the size of Florida is gone. More than 20 percent of the world oxygen is produced in the Amazon rainforest. It has been only a century for humans to destroy a geographical system that has been in place for a million years. And rainforests, once destroyed, cannot be regenerated the way temperate forests can.

Because humans rely upon the environment to sustain life, social and environmental policy must be mutually supportable. Because humans draw upon the natural resources of the earth, and affect the environment in many ways, environmental and social policy must be mutually supportive.

Unprecedented demand upon natural resources requires that social and environmental policies become increasingly interdependent if the planet is to continue to support life and human civilization.

Environmental policy is concerned with the sustainability of the earth, the region under the administration of the governing group or individual or a local habitat. The concern of environmental policy is the preservation of region, habitat, or ecosystem.

Domain V: Economics

Skill 5.1a   Microeconomics I

Economics is the study of how a society allocates its scare resources to satisfy what are basically unlimited and competing wants. A fundamental fact of economics is that resources are scarce and that wants are infinite. The fact that scarce resources have to satisfy unlimited wants means that choices have to be made. If society uses its resources to produce good A, then it doesn't have those resources to produce good B. More of good A means less of good B. This trade-off is referred to as the opportunity cost or the value of the sacrificed alternative.

Economics is divided into two broad categories: **macroeconomics** and **microeconomics**.

Economic systems refer to the arrangements a society has devised to answer what are known as the **Three Questions**:

- **What** goods to produce
- **How** to produce the goods
- **Whom** the goods are being produced for

Different economic systems answer these questions in different ways. These are the different "isms" that define the method of resource and output allocation. A **market economy** answers these questions in terms of **demand** and **supply** and the **use of markets**.

Demand is based on consumer preferences and satisfaction and refers to the quantities of a good or service that buyers are willing and able to buy at different prices during a given period of time.

Supply is based on costs of production and refers to the quantities that sellers are willing and able to sell at different prices during a given period of time.

The determination of **market equilibrium price** is where the decisions of buyers coincide with the decisions of sellers.

Demand curves and supply curves have different shapes. We can define the term **elasticity** to be a measure of the responsiveness of quantity to changes in price. If quantity is very responsive to changes in price, then supply/demand is said to be elastic; if quantity is not very responsive to changes in price, then supply/demand is inelastic.

In a market economy, consumers vote for the products they want with their dollar spending. Goods acquiring enough dollar votes are profitable, signaling to the producers that society wants their scarce resources used in this way. This is how the "What" question is answered.

The producer looks for the most efficient or lowest cost method of production. The lower the firm's costs for any given level of revenue, the higher the firm's profits. This is the way in which the "How" question is answered in a market economy.

The "For Whom" question is answered in the marketplace by the determination of the equilibrium price. Price serves to ration the good to those who can and will transact at the market price of better. Those who can't or won't are excluded from the market.

This mechanism results in **market efficiency** or obtaining the most output consistent with the preferences of consumers. Society's scarce resources are being used the way society wants them to be used.

Comparative advantage refers to international trade. A nation should specialize in the production of the good it can produce at a relatively lower **opportunity cost** than the other nation and trade for goods that it can't produce as cheaply. Trade on this basis results in higher levels of output, income, and employment for the trading nations. This is the reasoning behind free trade agreements such as NAFTA.

Finally, even in a capitalist economy, there is a role for government. Government is required to provide the framework for the functioning of the economy. This requires a legal system, a monetary system, and a watch dog authority to protect consumers from bad or dangerous products and practices. We need a government to correct for the misallocation of resources when the market doesn't function properly as in the case of externalities, like pollution. Government functions to provide public goods, like national defense, and to correct for macro instability like inflation and unemployment. These are the more important roles that we define for government in our economy.

Free enterprise, individual entrepreneurship, competitive markets, and consumer sovereignty are all parts of a **market economy**.

In a **planned economy**, the means of production are publicly owned with little if any private ownership. Instead of the Three Questions being solved by markets, a planning authority makes the decisions in place of markets. The planning authority decides what will be produced and how.

Between the two extremes is **market socialism**. This is a mixed economic system that uses both markets and planning. Planning is usually used to direct resources at the upper levels of the economy, with markets being used to determine prices of consumer goods and wages.

Skill 5.1b Microeconomics II

Microeconomics is a study of the economy at the industry or firm level. Microeconomics is concerned with things like consumer behavior, output and input markets, and the distribution of income.

A firm's production decisions are based on its costs. Every product is produced using inputs or resources. These are called **factors of production.** The four factors used in the production of every good and service are **labor, land, capital, and entrepreneurship**.

The costs for fixed factors of production, such as land, plant, and equipment, are called **fixed costs**. The costs for variable factors, such as labor, are called **variable costs**. **Costs of production**, then, are the total of fixed and variable costs.

Each factor of production earns its **factor income** in the resource market. Labor earns **wages**. Capital earns **interest**. Land earns **rent**. The entrepreneur earns **profit**. The size of the factor income depends on the scarcity of the factor and the significance of its contribution to the production process. A market economy does not result in the equality of income. Each factor earns an income based on its contribution.

There are four kinds of market structures in the output market: perfect competition, monopoly, monopolistic competition, and oligopoly.

Perfect competition is most closely approximated by agriculture. The numerous firms sell a product identical to that sold by all other firms in the industry and have no control over the price. Buyers and sellers have full market information, and there are no barriers to entry. A **barrier to entry** is anything that makes it difficult for firms to enter or leave the industry. The opposite of a perfectly competitive firm is a monopoly.

Monopoly is a market structure in which there is only one seller who controls price. A monopolist becomes a monopolist and remains a monopolist because of barriers to entry, which are very high. These barriers to entry include a very high fixed cost structure, which keeps new firms from entering the industry. Monopoly is illegal in the U.S. economy.

Monopolistic competition is the situation seen in shopping centers. Numerous firms each sell products that are similar but not identical, such as brand name shoes or clothing. Barriers to entry are not as high as in an oligopoly which is why there are more firms.

Oligopoly is a market structure in which there are a few sellers of products that may be either homogeneous such as steel, or heterogeneous such as automobiles. There are high barriers to entry, which is why there are only a few firms in each industry.

Consumer behavior

Marginal propensity to consume means there is an increase in personal consumer spending with an increase in disposable income.

Utility is the measurement of happiness or satisfaction a person receives from consuming a good or service.

Skill 5.1c   Macroeconomics I

Macroeconomics is a study of the aggregates that comprise the economy on the national level: output, consumption, investment, government spending, and net exports.

Macroeconomics is concerned with a study of the economy's overall economic performance or what is called the **Gross Domestic Product (GDP)**. The GDP is a measure of the economy's output during a specified time period.

Tabulating the economy's output can be measured in two ways, both of which give the same result: the **expenditures approach** and the **incomes approach**. What is spent on national output by each sector of the economy is equal to what is earned producing national output by each of the factors of production.

The macroeconomy consists of four broad sectors: **consumers, businesses, government,** and the **foreign sector.**

In the **expenditures** approach, GDP is determined by the amount of spending in each sector. GDP is equal to the consumption expenditures (C) of consumers *plus* the investment expenditures (I) of businesses *plus* spending of all three levels of government (G) *plus* the net export spending (X-M) in the foreign sector.

$$GDP = C + I + G + (X-M)$$

What is spent **buying** the national output has to equal what is **earned** in producing the national output.

- Labor earns wages, which is called **Compensation of Employees**
- Land earns **Rental Income**
- Capital earns **Interest Income**

Since entrepreneurial ability can be in the form of individual effort or corporations, there are two different categories. Return to the individual entrepreneur is called **Proprietor's Income**. Return to the corporation is called **Corporate Profit**.

Corporations do three things with their profits: pay **corporate profits tax**, pay **dividends**, and keep the rest as **retained earnings**.

To complete the tabulation of GDP from the incomes approach, we have to adjust for two non-income charges, and both are subtracted:

- **Indirect Business Taxes**, such as property taxes and sales taxes.
- **Depreciation** (the amount of capital that is worn out producing the current term's output).

When the economy is functioning smoothly, **aggregate supply**--the amount of national output produced--is just equal to the **aggregate demand**--amount of national output purchased. Then we have an economy in a period of prosperity without economic instability.

But market economies experience the fluctuations of the business cycle, the ups and downs in the level of economic activity. There are four phases:

- **boom** - a period of prosperity
- **recession -** a period of declining GDP and rising unemployment
- **trough -** the low point of the recession
- **recovery -** a period of lessening unemployment and rising prices

There are no rules pertaining to the duration or severity of any of the phases.

The phases result in periods of **unemployment** and periods of **inflation**.

- **Inflation** results from too much spending in the economy. Buyers want to buy more than sellers can produce and bid up prices for the available output.
- **Unemployment** occurs when there is not enough spending in the economy. Sellers have produced more output than buyers are buying and the result is a surplus situation. Firms faced with surplus merchandise lower their production levels and layoff workers which leads to unemployment.

These are situations that require government policy actions.

Skill 5.1d Macroeconomics II

GDP, computed by either the expenditures approach or the incomes approach, is a measure of the overall performance of the national economy. From GDP government policymakers can:

- Determine what is happening in the economy and identify problem areas
- Measure economic growth
- Devise policies to help those problem areas

Macroeconomic instability problems of inflation and unemployment are mostly caused by inequality of aggregate demand and aggregate supply.

An economy that is growing too rapidly and has too high a level of spending has inflation, a period of rises in the price level. Inflation results in a dollar with less purchasing power and represents a situation where the appropriate governmental action is to slow down the economy. The government will implement policies that result in less spending in the economy to end inflation.

When there is not enough spending in the economy, producers who have surplus merchandise lower production levels and lay off workers causing unemployment. The appropriate action for government is to stimulate the economy and to take actions that result in higher levels of spending. The increase in demand leads to higher levels of employment.

Government can implement **contractionary** policies for inflation or **expansionary** policies for unemployment in two ways. **Fiscal policy** refers to changes in the level of government spending and/or taxes.

- Expansionary fiscal policy raises government spending and/or lowering taxes to increase spending in the economy, thus eliminating unemployment.
- Contractionary policies to stop inflation consist of a decrease in government spending and/or an increase in taxes, both of which lower the levels of spending in the economy.

Fiscal policy requires legislative action, and laws have to be enacted.

The other policy tool open to the government is **monetary policy**. Monetary policy in the United States is implemented by the **Federal Reserve System** (Fed) through changing the level of money in the banking system. Simply put, banks earn income by making loans. People and business borrow from banks and spend the borrowed funds. If the Fed changes the amount of funds that banks have available to loan out, they change the level of spending in the economy. There are three ways that the Fed can do this.

First of all, banks cannot loan out all of their deposits. They are required to hold a certain percentage as reserves. The percentage is called the **reserve ratio**. Raising the reserve ratio leaves banks with fewer reserves to loan out, and it is therefore an aspect of contractionary monetary policy (used during recessions). Lowering the reserve ratio increases lending ability and spending and is an aspect of expansionary monetary policy.

A second mechanism for implementing monetary policy is called the **Discount Rate**, which is the rate of interest charged by the Fed to banks that borrow from it. Lowering the Discount Rate encourages banks to borrow and make loans, thus leading to higher levels of spending. This is a form of expansionary monetary policy. Contractionary monetary policy would be indicated by an increase in the Discount Rate.

The third means of influencing the money supply is through **Open Market Operations**. This is when the Fed buys or sells bonds in the open market. When the Fed buys bonds from the public or banks, the Fed pays with dollars that are put into circulation. Thus, the Fed buying bonds represents a form of expansionary monetary policy as there are more dollars in the system for loans and spending. The Fed selling bonds is a form of contractionary monetary policy.

Since today's financial markets are international, banks can borrow and lend in foreign markets. They are not constrained by the domestic market. Financial capital goes where it earns the highest rate of return, regardless of national boundaries. This means that if the Fed is trying to implement contractionary monetary policy, banks and businesses can borrow in international markets and avoid the Fed's contractionary policies, at least in the short-run.

Domain VI: Behavioral Sciences

Skill 6.1a Sociology

Sociology is the study of human society through the individuals, groups, and institutions that make up human society. Sociology includes every feature of human social conditions. It deals with the predominant behaviors, attitudes, and types of relationships within a society as defined by a group of people with a similar cultural background living in a specific geographical area. Sociology is divided into five major areas of study:

- **Population studies**: General social patterns of groups of people living in a certain geographical area
- **Social behaviors**: Changes in attitudes, morale, leadership, conformity, and others
- **Social institutions**: Organized groups of people performing specific functions within a society such as churches, schools, hospitals, business organizations, and governments
- **Cultural influences**: Customs, knowledge, arts, religious beliefs, and language
- **Social change**: Wars, revolutions, inventions, fashions, and other events or activities

Sociologists use three major methods to test and verify theories:

- **Surveys**
- **Controlled experiments**
- **Field observations**

Sociology studies human society with its attitudes, behaviors, conditions, and relationships with others. It is closely related to several other disciplines:

- Anthropology, especially when applied to groups outside of one's region, nation, or hemisphere.
- Political Science with impact of political and governmental regulation of activities
- Geography - awareness of, influence of, and use of the physical environment
- Economics
- Psychology

Some important figures in the field of sociology:

Auguste Comte was the French philosopher who coined the term "sociology" and developed the theory called **positivism** which states that social behavior and events can be scientifically measured. Positivism denies metaphysical experience and relies on sensory information for evaluating human experience. Comte is generally regarded as the first Western sociologist.

Emile Durkheim is considered the father of sociology because he influenced universities to consider sociology as a discipline. He was influenced by Comte and positivism, and Durkheim essentially viewed the world as influenced by large factors such as group attitudes and cultural norms versus simply being influenced by individuals. Sociologists determine the "social facts." Durkheim is especially famous for his work on social cause of rates of suicide. He brought into this the word *anomie*, which means individuals affected by changes in society such as wide unemployment or groups feeling alienated from society at large.

Karl Marx and Friedrich Engels sociologically saw the world as a socio-economic struggle between classes. The main thesis in their book *The Communist Manifesto* is that work is a social activity and that the working class will ultimately have a revolution.

Herbert Spencer related the biology of Darwin's *Origin of Species* to sociology by viewing the development of society the same way. He coined the phrase: "the survival of the fittest." He saw connections between the physical and social parts of life. Despite his being a rival of Darwin, he is credited with Social Darwinism, in which competition drives society.

Max Weber saw the religions of the East and West as a cause for a different social directions--with Protestantism spurring capitalism. He said that he had observed that the state views itself as having legitimate causes for violence. The violence is demonstrated in military and police actions as well as citizens using violence to protect themselves or their property. His views were objective; he did not defend the reasons for the pursuit of violence.

Skill 6.1b Anthropology

Anthropology is the scientific study of human culture and humanity--the relationship between man and culture. Anthropologists study similarities and difference among different groups, how they relate to other cultures, and patterns of behavior. Their research is two-fold: cross-cultural and comparative. A major method of study is referred to as "participant observation." The anthropologist studies the people of a culture by living among them and participating with them in their daily lives. Other methods may be used, but this is the most characteristic method used.

There are four types of anthropology:

1. archaeology – study of material remains of humans
2. social-cultural - norms, values, standards
3. biological – genetic characteristics
4. linguistics – the historical development of language

Margaret Mead popularized the discipline of anthropology by her studies of sex in cultures in the South Pacific and Southeast Asia. Unusual for women of those times, Mead earned her Ph.D. from Columbia University in 1929. Her studies also involved breastfeeding and treatment of children in various cultures. One her well-known works was *Coming of Age in Samoa.*

Mary Leakey and Louis Leakey. Olduvai Gorge was a archaeological site where they found tools and fossils. She discovered Laetoli footprints and developed a classification system. He was a Kenyan who discovered prehistoric African human remains. After he was drafted into the Kenyan intelligence service when the Italians had invaded Ethiopia, Mary Leakey continued with the archaeological investigation at Olduvai Gorge.

Skill 6.1c   Psychology

Psychology is the scientific study of mental processes and behavior. Psychology is divided into scientific psychology and applied psychology.

Psychologists observe and record specific patterns. This observation enables psychologists to discern and predict certain behaviors. Scientific methods help verify their ideas. Psychologists help people fulfill their individual potential and strengthen understanding between individuals, groups, nations, and cultures. There is even consumer psychology that studies how people relate to various products and services.

http://www.psychology.org/links/
Encyclopedia of Psychology

Methods used in psychological research include:

- naturalistic observation
- survey method
- case study
- experimental method
- correlational design

> http://psych.hanover.edu/Research/exponnet.html
> **Psychological Research on the Net**

Psychological researchers choose the method based up what they are trying to learn.

For **naturalistic observation**, the researcher objectively watches people in their natural environment, making sure not to influence the outcome. In the **survey method**, researchers write a survey and distribute it to get answers and then tabulate those answers. **Case studies** tend to take a lot of time because they involved studying individuals or groups in depth. The **experimental method** involves designing the variables for an experimental group and a control group. **Correlational design** measures a positive or negative relationship between two variables. An example to measure would be the correlation between teachers' attitudes and students' attendance.

Aristotle, the Greek philosopher has often been credited with the beginnings of psychology. He was interested in the human mind. He believed that the mind was a feature of the body and that the psyche was a receiver of knowledge. In his view, the point of psychology was uncovering essence of the soul.

> http://www.indiana.edu/~intell/aristotle.shtml
> **Human Intelligence: Aristotle**

Rene Descartes was a French philosopher who described the strong influence of the body and mind on each other because of their being separate, and he suggested that the pineal gland in the brain was where this interaction took place. He developed the doctrine of **nativism**--that humans are born with certain knowledge that is not dependent on individual experience.

Thomas Hobbes, John Locke, David Hume, and **George Berkeley** were called **empiricists.** Rejecting Descartes' view of nativism, these four men believed that at birth a person's mind is empty and that people gain their knowledge through their senses and ideas from life experience.

Johannes P. Muller and Hermann L.F. von Hemholtz were two German scientists who pioneered the first organized studies of perception and sensation, showing the feasibility of the scientific study of the physical processes that support mental activity.

William James began the first psychology laboratory in the world. **William Wundt**, a German philosopher trained in physiology and medicine, published the first journal dealing with experimental psychology. Wundt and James put psychology in a field by itself, separate from philosophy. Their work, along with others, led to the method of research called **introspection**--training their subjects to observe and record feelings, experiences, and mental processes.

Sigmund Freud was an Austrian physician whose theory was that humans repress inner forces in the subconscious and that these repressed feelings caused personality

http://www.iep.utm.edu/f/freud.htm Internet Encyclopedia of Philosophy : Sigmund Freud

disorders. He developed **psychoanalysis**, to bring out the repressed thoughts and feelings. Sexual desire, in his view, is a primary human motivator.

Carl Jung was a theoretical psychologist who worked with Freud between 1907 and 1912. His exploration involved Eastern and Western philosophy, including astrology. Defining **introversion** and **extroversion** was a development of his work, along with the **collective unconscious** and **synchronicity**.

John B. Watson was an American psychologist who introduced **behaviorism** and believed in nurture over nature. He said: "Give me a dozen healthy infants, well-formed, and my own specified world to bring them up in and I'll guarantee to take any one at random and train him to become any type of specialist I might select–doctor, lawyer, artist, merchant-chief and, yes, even beggar-man and thief, regardless of his talents, penchants, tendencies, abilities, vocations, and race of his ancestors."

Ivan Pavlov and B.F. Skinner made significant contributions to this school of behaviorism, a reaction to the emphasis on introspection. The behaviorists believed that the environment was the important influence on one's behavior and looked for any correlation between environmental stimuli and observable behavior. Pavlov is most noted for his experiments proving **conditioned response**, in which he was able to link a bell to salivating in a dog. Skinner built on Pavlov's work to become a strong proponent of behaviorism, being most noted for his experimental device, the "Skinner Box."

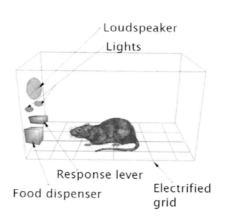

Loudspeaker
Lights
Response lever
Food dispenser
Electrified grid

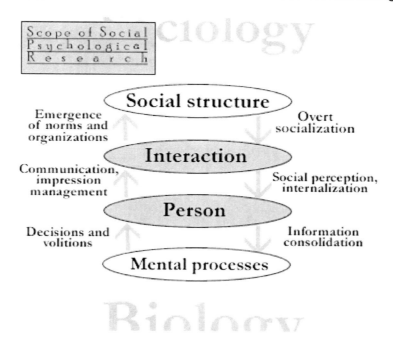

http://www.gestalttherapy.net/
Gestalt Therapy

Max Wertheimer developed **Gestalt psychology**. The word "**Gestalt**" means a pattern—a whole rather than separate incidents.

Modern psychology includes the teachings of the earlier schools as well as stimulus-response, cognitive, and humanistic psychology.

Social psychology studies how social conditions affect human beings.

Scope of Social Psychological Research

Social structure

Emergence of norms and organizations

Overt socialization

Interaction

Communication, impression management

Social perception, internalization

Person

Decisions and volitions

Information consolidation

Mental processes

Bibliography

Adams, James Truslow. (2006). The March of Democracy, Vol. 1. "The Rise of the Union." New York: Charles Scribner's Sons, Publisher.

Barbini, John & Warshaw, Steven. (2006). The World Past and Present. New York: Harcourt, Brace, Jovanovich, Publishers.

Berthon, Simon & Robinson, Andrew. (2006). The Shape of the World. Chicago: Rand McNally, Publisher.

Bice, David A. (2006). A Panorama of Florida II. 2nd ed. Marceline, Missouri: Walsworth Publishing Co., Inc.

Bram, Leon (Vice-President and Editorial Director). (2006). Funk and Wagnalls New Encyclopedia. United States of America.

Burns, Edward McNall & Ralph, Philip Lee. (2006). World Civilizations: Their History and Culture. (5th ed.) New York: W.W. Norton & Company, Inc., Publishers.

Dauben, Joseph W. (2006). The World Book Encyclopedia. Chicago: World Book Inc. A Scott Fetzer Company, Publisher.

De Blij, H.J. & Muller, Peter O. (2006). Geography Regions and Concepts. 6th ed. New York: John Wiley & Sons, Inc., Publisher.

Encyclopedia Americana. (2006). Danbury, Connecticut: Grolier Incorporated, Publisher.

Heigh, Christopher (Editor). (2006). The Cambridge Historical Encyclopedia of Great Britain and Ireland. Cambridge: Cambridge University Press, Publisher.

Hunkins, Francis P. & Armstrong, David G. (2006). World Geography People and Places. Columbus, Ohio: Charles E. Merrill Publishing Co. A Bell & Howell Company, Publishers.

Jarolimek, John; Anderson, J. Hubert & Durand, Loyal, Jr. (2006). World Neighbors. New York: Macmillan Publishing Company. London: Collier Macmillan, Publishers.

McConnell, Campbell R. (2006). Economics-Principles, Problems, and Policies. 10th ed. New York: McGraw-Hill Book Company, Publisher.

Millard, Dr. Anne & Vanags, Patricia. (2006). The Usborne Book of World History. London: Usborne Publishing Ltd., Publisher.

Novosad, Charles (Executive Editor). (2006). The Nystrom Desk Atlas. Chicago: Nystrom Division of Herff Jones, Inc., Publisher.

Patton, Clyde P.; Rengert, Arlene C.; Saveland, Robert N.; Cooper, Kenneth S. & Cam, Patricia T. (2006). A World View. Morristown, N.J.: Silver Burdette Companion, Publisher.

Schwartz, Melvin & O'Connor, John R. (2006). Exploring A Changing World. New York: Globe Book Company, Publisher.

The Annals of America: Selected Readings on Great Issues in American History 1620-1968. (2006). United States of America: William Benton, Publisher.

Tindall, George Brown & Shi, David E. (2006). America-A Narrative History. 4th ed. New York: W.W. Norton & Company, Publisher.

Todd, Lewis Paul & Curti, Merle. (2006). Rise of the American Nation. 3rd ed. New York: Harcourt, Brace, Jovanovich, Inc., Publishers.

Tyler, Jenny; Watts, Lisa; Bowyer, Carol; Trundle, Roma & Warrender, Annabelle (2006). The Usborne Book of World Geography. London: Usborne Publishing Ltd., Publisher.

Willson, David H. (2006). A History of England. Hinsdale, Illinois: The Dryder Press, Inc., Publisher.

Sample Test

On the following pages, you will find 125 multiple choice questions. The sample test is followed by the Answer Key, as well as the Answer Rationales that explain the correct answer to each question. The skill set that the question draws on is listed in parenthesis after each question. Note that while most questions will draw on a specific skill, some are broader, while others may require you to draw inferences from material in the text. Also note that, as on a real test, the questions are NOT presented in order with respect to the skills they cover.

1. **A historian would be interested in:** *(Average Rigor) (Skills 1.x & 2.x)*

   A. The manner in which scientific knowledge is advanced

   B. The effects of the French Revolution on world colonial policy

   C. The viewpoint of persons who have written previous "history"

   D. All of the above

2. **The Native Americans of the Eastern Woodlands lived on:** *(Average Rigor) (Skill 1.1a)*

   A. Buffalo and crops such as corn, beans, and sunflowers

   B. Chiefly farming of squash, beans, and corn

   C. A variety of game (deer, bear, moose) and crops (squash, pumpkins, corn)

   D. Wolves, foxes, polar bears, walruses, and fish

3. **3. Apartments built out of cliff faces; shared government by adult citizens; absence of aggression toward other groups. These factors characterize the Native American group known as:** *(Easy) (Skill 1.1a)*

   A. Pueblo

   B. Comanche

   C. Seminole

   D. Sioux

4. Bartholomeu Dias, in seeking a route around the tip of Africa, was forced to turn back. Nevertheless, the cape he discovered near the southern tip of Africa became known as: *(Easy) (Skill 1.1b)*

   A. Cape Horn

   B. Cabo Bojador

   C. Cape of Good Hope

   D. Cape Hatteras

5. Columbus first reached Western Hemisphere lands in what is now: *(Easy) (Skill 1.1b)*

   A. Florida

   B. Bermuda

   C. Puerto Rico

   D. Bahamas

6. The Middle Colonies of the Americas were: *(Easy) (Skill 1.1b)*

   A. Maryland, Virginia, North Carolina

   B. New York, New Jersey, Pennsylvania, Delaware

   C. Rhode Island, Connecticut, New York, New Jersey

   D. Vermont and New Hampshire

7. 7. France decided in 1777 to help the American colonies in their war against Britain. This decision was based on: *(Rigorous) (Skill 1.1c)*

   A. The naval victory of John Paul Jones over the British ship "Serapes"

   B. The survival of the terrible winter at Valley Forge

   C. The success of colonial guerilla fighters in the South

   D. The defeat of the British at Saratoga

8. The only colony not founded and settled for religious, political, or business reasons was: *(Rigorous) (Skill 1.1c)*

   A. Delaware

   B. Virginia

   C. Georgia

   D. New York

9. Which one of the following is <u>not</u> a reason why Europeans came to the New World? *(Rigorous) (Skill 1.1c)*

   A. To find resources in order to increase wealth

   B. To establish trade

   C. To increase a ruler's power and importance

   D. To spread Christianity

10. The first shots in what was to become the American Revolution were fired in: *(Easy) (Skill 1.1c)*

   A. Florida

   B. Massachusetts

   C. New York

   D. Virginia

11. A major quarrel between colonial Americans and the British concerned a series of British Acts of Parliament dealing with: *(Average Rigor) (Skill 1.1c)*

   A. Taxes

   B. Slavery

   C. Native Americans

   D. Shipbuilding

12. After ratification of the new Constitution, the most urgent of the many problems facing the new federal government was that of: *(Rigorous) (Skill 1.1d)*

   A. Maintaining a strong army and navy

   B. Establishing a strong foreign policy

   C. Raising money to pay salaries and war debts

   D. Setting up courts, passing federal laws, and providing for law enforcement officers

13. Which concept is not embodied as a right in the First Amendment to the U.S. Constitution? *(Average Rigor) (Skill 1.1d)*

A. Peaceful assembly

B. Unreasonable search and seizure

C. Freedom of speech

D. Petition for redress of grievances

14. The "Trail of Tears" relates to: *(Easy) (Skill 1.1e)*

A. The removal of the Cherokees from their native lands to Oklahoma Territory

B. The revolt and subsequent migration of the Massachusetts Pilgrims under pressure from the Iroquois

C. The journey of the Nez Perce under Chief Joseph before their capture by the U.S. Army

D. The 1973 standoff between federal marshals and Native Americans at Wounded Knee, S.D.

15.

15. It can be reasonably stated that the change in the United States from primarily an agricultural country into a industrial power was due to all of the following except: *(Rigorous) (Skill 1.1e)*

A. Tariffs on foreign imports

B. Millions of hardworking immigrants

C. An increase in technological developments

D. The change from steam to electricity for powering industrial machinery

16. The U.S. Constitution, adopted in 1789, provided for: *(Average Rigor)(Skill 1.1e)*

A. Direct election of the president by all citizens

B. Direct election of the president by citizens meeting a standard of wealth

C. Indirect election of the president by electors

D. Indirect election of the president by the U.S. Senate

17. Which of the following sets of inventors is correctly matched with the area in which they primarily worked? *(Average Rigor) (Skill 1.1e)*

   A. Thomas Edison and George Westinghouse: transportation

   B. Cyrus McCormick and George Washington Carver: household appliances

   C. Alexander Graham Bell and Samuel F. B. Morse: communications

   D. Isaac Singer and John Gorrie: agriculture

18. The area of the United States was effectively doubled through purchase of the Louisiana Territory under which president? *(Easy) (Skill 1.1e)*

   A. John Adams

   B. Thomas Jefferson

   C. James Madison

   D. James Monroe

19. Which one of the following was not a reason why the United States went to war with Great Britain in 1812? *(Rigorous) (Skill 1.1e)*

   A. Resentment by Spain over the sale, exploration, and settlement of the Louisiana Territory

   B. The westward movement of farmers because of the need for more land

   C. Canadian fur traders were agitating the northwestern Indians to fight American expansion

   D. Britain continued to seize American ships on the high seas and force American seamen to serve aboard British ships

20. The first territorial governor of Florida after Florida's purchase by the United States was: *(Easy)* *(Skill 1.1e)*

    A. Napoleon Bonaparte

    B. Robert Duval

    C. Andrew Jackson

    D. Davy Crockett

21. The Compromise of 1850 came about as a result of which state's entry into the Union? *(Easy)(Skill 1.1f)*

    A. Texas

    B. Missouri

    C. California

    D. Kansas

22. What was a major source of contention between American settlers in Texas and the Mexican government in the 1830s and 1840s? *(Rigorous)* *(Skill 1.1f)*

    A. The Americans wished to retain slavery which had been outlawed in Mexico

    B. The Americans had agreed to learn Spanish and become Roman Catholic, but failed to do so

    C. The Americans retained ties to the United States, and Santa Ana feared the power of the U.S.

    D. All of the above were contentious issues between American settlers and the Mexican government

23. Which of the following is most descriptive of the conflict between the U.S. government and the Seminoles between 1818 and 1858?
(Rigorous) (Skill 1.1f)

A. There was constant armed conflict between the Seminoles and the U.S. during these years

B. Historians discern three separate phases of hostilities (1818, 1835-42, 1855-58) known collectively as the Seminole Wars

C. On May 7, 1858, the Seminoles admitted defeat, signed a peace treaty with the U.S., and left for Oklahoma, except for fifty-one individuals

D. The former Seminole chief Osceola helped the U.S. defeat the Seminoles and effect their removal to Oklahoma

24. Slavery arose in the southern colonies partly as a perceived economical way to:
(Rigorous) (Skill 1.1f)

A. Increase the owner's wealth through human beings used as a source of exchange

B. Cultivate large plantations of cotton, tobacco, rice, indigo, and other crops

C. Provide Africans with humanitarian aid, such as health care, Christianity, and literacy

D. Keep ships' holds full of cargo on two out of three legs of the "triangular trade" voyage

25. Of the following, which contributed most to penetration of western areas by colonial Americans? *(Average Rigor) (Skill 1.1f)*

   A. Development of large ships capable of sailing upstream in rivers such as the Hudson, Susquehanna, and Delaware

   B. The invention of the steamboat

   C. Improved relations with Native Americans who invited colonial Americans to travel west to settle

   D. Improved roads, mail service, and communications

26. Which of the following groups were slave states? *(Easy) (Skill 1.1f)*

   A. Delaware, Maryland, Missouri

   B. California, Texas, Florida

   C. Kansas, Missouri, Kentucky

   D. Virginia, West Virginia, Indiana

27. A consequence of the Gold Rush that led Americans to California in 1848 and 1849 was that: *(Average Rigor) (Skill 1.1f)*

   A. California spent the minimum amount of time as a territory and was admitted as a slave state

   B. California was denied admission on its first application since most Americans felt that the settlers were too "uncivilized" to deserve statehood

   C. California was purchased from Mexico for the express purpose of gaining immediate statehood

   D. California did not go through the normal territorial stage but applied directly for statehood as a free state

28. Which American Secretary of War later became President of the Confederate States? *(Easy) (Skill 1.1g)*

   A. Henry Clay

   B. William Seward

   C. Franklin Pierce

   D. Jefferson Davis

29. Who was the first commander for the North in the Civil War? *(Easy) (Skill 1.1g)*

   A. Gen. Ulysses S. Grant

   B. Gen. Robert E. Lee

   C. Gen. Irwin McDowell

   D. Gen. George Meade

30. Abraham Lincoln won reelection in 1864 chiefly through: *(Average Rigor) (Skill 1.1g)*

   A. His overwhelming force of personality and appeal to all segments of the electorate

   B. His reputation as the Great Emancipator

   C. People's sympathy for him because of his difficulties

   D. His shrewd political manipulation, clever use of patronage jobs, and wide-appeal selection of cabinet members

31. How many states reentered the Union before 1868? *(Easy) (Skill 1.1g)*

State	Date of Readmission
Alabama	1868
Arkansas	1868
Florida	1868
Georgia	1870
Louisiana	1868
Mississippi	1870
North Carolina	1868
South Carolina	1868
Tennessee	1866
Texas	1870
Virginia	1870

A. 0 states

B. 1 state

C. 2 states

D. 3 states

32. The Radical Republicans who pushed the harsh Reconstruction measures through Congress after Lincoln's death lost public and moderate Republican support when they went too far: *(Rigorous) (Skill 1.1g)*

A. In their efforts to impeach the President

B. By dividing ten southern states into military-controlled districts

C. By making the ten southern states give freed African Americans the right to vote

D. Sending carpetbaggers into the South to build up support for Congressional

33. In the 1920s, the United States almost completely stopped all immigration. One of the reasons was:
(Rigorous) (Skill 1.1i)

   A. Plentiful cheap, unskilled labor was no longer needed by industrialists

   B. War debts from World War I made it difficult to render financial assistance

   C. European nations were reluctant to allow people to leave since there was a need to rebuild populations and economic stability

   D. The United States did not become a member of the League of Nations

34. The Interstate Commerce Commission (ICC) was established in reaction to abuses and corruption in what industry?
(Average Rigor) (Skill 1.1i)

   A. Textile

   B. Railroad

   C. Steel

   D. Banking

35. The Teapot Dome scandal related to:
(Average Rigor) (Skill 1.1i)

   A. The improper taxing of tea surpluses in Boston

   B. The improper awarding of building contracts in Washington, DC

   C. The improper sale of policy decisions by various Harding administration officials

   D. The improper sale of oil reserves in Wyoming

36. Which of the following was NOT a factor in the United States' entry into World War I?
(Rigorous) (Skill 1.1i)

   A. The closeness of the presidential election of 1916

   B. The German threat to sink all allied ships, including merchant ships

   C. The desire to preserve democracy as practiced in Britain and France as compared to the totalitarianism of Germany

   D. The sinking of the Lusitania and the Sussex

37. 37. What 1924 Act of Congress severely restricted immigration in the United States?
(Average Rigor) (Skill 1.1i)

   A. Taft-Hartley Act

   B. Smoot-Hawley Act

   C. Tordney-McCumber Act

   D. Johnson-Reed Act

38. Of all the major causes of both World War I and II, the most significant one is considered to be:
(Rigorous) (Skill 1.1i)

   A. Extreme nationalism

   B. Military buildup and aggression

   C. Political unrest

   D. Agreements and alliances

39. Which of the following contributed to the severity of the Great Depression in California?
(Rigorous)(Skill 1.1i)

   A. An influx of Chinese immigrants

   B. The Dust Bowl drove people out of the cities

   C. An influx of Mexican immigrants

   D. An influx of "Okies"

40. In the first aggression of World War II outside the Orient, identify the aggressor nation and the nation which was invaded: *(Average Rigor) (Skill 1.1j)*

    A. Germany; Sudetenland

    B. Italy; Abyssinia

    C. Germany; Poland

    D. Italy; Yugoslavia

41. 41. In issuing an ultimatum for Soviet ships not to enter Cuban waters in October, 1962, President John F. Kennedy, as part of his decision, used the provisions of the: *(Average Rigor) (Skill 1.1k)*

    A. Monroe Doctrine

    B. Declaration of the Rights of Man

    C. Geneva Convention

    D. Truman Doctrine

42. President Truman suspended Gen. Douglas MacArthur from command of Allied forces in Korea because of: *(Rigorous) (Skill 1.1k)*

    A. MacArthur's inability to make any progress against North Koreans

    B. MacArthur's criticism of Truman claiming that the president would not allow him to pursue aggressive tactics against communists

    C. The harsh treatment MacArthur exhibited toward the Japanese after World War II

    D. The ability of the U.S. Navy to continue the conflict without the presence of MacArthur

43. Which of the following most closely characterizes the Supreme Court's decision in *Brown v. Board of Education*? *(Rigorous)* *(Skill 1.1k)*

   A. Chief Justice Warren had to cast the deciding vote in a sharply divided the Supreme Court

   B. The decision was rendered along sectional lines, with northerners voting for integration and southerners voting for continued segregation

   C. The decision was 7-2 with dissenting justices not even preparing a written dissent

   D. Chief Justice Warren was able to persuade the Supreme Court to render a unanimous decision

44. The native metaphysical outlook of Japan, usually characterized as a religion, is: *(Easy) (Skill 2)*

   A. Tao

   B. Shinto

   C. Hindu

   D. Sunni

45. Indo-European languages are native languages to each of the following EXCEPT: *(Average Rigor) (Skill 2)*

   A. Germany

   B. India

   C. Italy

   D. Finland

46. Which of the following developments is most closely associated with the Neolithic Age? *(Average Rigor) (Skill 2.1a)*

   A. Human use of fire

   B. First use of stone chipping instruments

   C. Domestication of plants

   D. Development of metallurgical alloys

47. The end to hunting, gathering, and fishing of prehistoric people was due to: *(Average Rigor) (Skill 2.1a)*

    A. Domestication of animals

    B. Building crude huts and houses

    C. Development of agriculture

    D. Organized government in villages

48. The principle of zero in mathematics is the discovery of the ancient civilization found in: *(Easy)(Skill 2.1b)*

    A. Egypt

    B. Persia

    C. India

    D. Babylon

49. 49. The Tigris-Euphrates Valley was the site of which two primary ancient civilizations? *(Easy) (Skill 2.1b)*

    A. Babylonian and Assyrian

    B. Sumerian and Egyptian

    C. Hyksos and Hurrian

    D. Persian and Phoenician

50. The first ancient civilization to introduce and practice monotheism was the: *(Easy)(Skill 2.1b)*

    A. Sumerians

    B. Minoans

    C. Phoenicians

    D. Hebrews

51. Which one of the following is <u>not</u> an important legacy of the Byzantine Empire? *(Rigorous) (Skill 2.1b)*

   A. It protected Western Europe from various attacks from the East by such groups as the Persians, Ottoman Turks, and Barbarians

   B. It played a part in preserving the literature, philosophy, and language of ancient Greece

   C. Its military organization was the foundation for modern armies

   D. It kept the legal traditions of Roman government, collecting and organizing many ancient Roman laws

52. 52. For the historian studying ancient Egypt, which of the following would be least useful? *(Rigorous) (Skill 2.1c)*

   A. The record of an ancient Greek historian on Greek-Egyptian interaction

   B. Letters from an Egyptian ruler to his/her regional governors

   C. Inscriptions of the Fourteenth Egyptian Dynasty

   D. Letters from a nineteenth-century Egyptologist to his wife

53. The _____ were fought between the Roman Empire and Carthage. *(Easy) (Skill 2.1c)*

   A. Civil Wars

   B. Punic Wars

   C. Caesarian Wars

   D. Persian Wars

54. Which one of the following did not contribute to the early medieval European civilization? *(Rigorous) (Skill 2.1d)*

   A. The heritage from the classical cultures

   B. The Christian religion

   C. The influence of the German Barbarians

   D. The spread of ideas through trade and commerce

55. Of the legacies of the Roman Empire listed below, the most influential, effective and lasting is: *(Rigorous) (Skill 2.1d)*

   A. The language of Latin

   B. Roman law, justice, and political system

   C. Engineering and building

   D. The writings of its poets and historians

56. 56. What Holy Roman Emperor was forced to do public penance because of his conflict with Pope Gregory VII over lay investiture of the clergy? *(Average Rigor) (Skill 2.1d)*

   A. Charlemagne

   B. Henry IV

   C. Charles V

   D. Henry VIII

57. Monophysitism (the belief that Jesus was completely divine with no admixture of humanity) was declared a heresy by _____? *(Average Rigor)(Skill 2.1d)*

   A. Council of Nicaea

   B. Diet of Worms

   C. Council of Trent

   D. Council of Chalcedon

58. Which of the following areas would NOT be a primary area of hog production?
(Rigorous) (Skill 2.1d)

A. Midland England

B. The Mekong delta of Vietnam

C. Central Syria

D. Northeast Iowa

59. Which of the following is NOT one of the Pillars of Faith of Islam?
(Average Rigor) (Skill 2.1d)

A. Alms-giving (zakah)

B. Pilgrimage (hajj)

C. Membership in a school of law(al-madhahib)

D. Fasting (sawm)

60. 60. Chinese civilization is generally credited with the original development of which of the following sets of technologies:
(Average Rigor) (Skill 2.1e)

A. Movable type and mass production of goods

B. Wool processing and domestication of the horse

C. Paper and gunpowder manufacture

D. Leather processing and modern timekeeping

61. Colonial expansion by Western European powers in the 18th and 19th centuries was due primarily to:
(Rigorous) (Skill 2.1e)

A. The Industrial Revolution

B. Marked improvements in transportation

C. Complete independence of all the Americas and loss of European domination and influence

D. Building and opening the Suez Canal

62. The ideas and innovations of the period of the Renaissance were spread throughout Europe mainly because of:
(Rigorous) (Skill 2.1e)

   A. Extensive exploration

   B. Craft workers and their guilds

   C. The invention of the printing press

   D. Increased travel and trade

63. Luther issued strong objection to all but which of the following practices of the 15th Century Roman Catholic Church?
(Average Rigor) (Skill 2.1e)

   A. The sacrament of Baptism

   B. Absolution of sins through the intermediation of a priest and through ceremony

   C. The sale of indulgences, whereby the buyer may purchase purgation of sins

   D. Imposed church control over the individual conscience

64. 64. The results of the Renaissance, Enlightenment, and Commercial and Industrial Revolutions were more unfortunate for the people of:
(Rigorous) (Skill 2.1e)

   A. Asia

   B. Latin America

   C. Africa

   D. Middle East

65. Great Britain became the center of technological and industrial development during the nineteenth century chiefly on the basis of:
(Rigorous) (Skill 2.1f)

   A. Central location relative to the population centers of Europe

   B. Colonial conquests and military victories over European powers

   C. Reliance on exterior sources of financing

   D. Resources of coal and production of steel

66. The years 1793-94 in France, characterized by numerous trials and executions of supposed enemies of the Revolutionary Convention, were known as the: *(Average Rigor) (Skill 2.1f)*

    A. Reign of Terror

    B. Dark Ages

    C. French Inquisition

    D. Glorious Revolution

67. In 1990, Alberto Fujimori was the first Asian to be elected president of: *(Easy) (Skill 2.1h)*

    A. Canada

    B. Mexico

    C. South Africa

    D. Peru

68. 68. Which of the following most closely characterizes the geopolitical events of the USSR in 1991-92: *(Rigorous) (Skill 2.1h)*

    A. The USSR established greater military and economic control over the fifteen Soviet republics

    B. The Baltic states (Estonia, Latvia, Lithuania) declared independence, while the remainder of the USSR remained intact.

    C. Fourteen of fifteen Soviet republics declared some degree of autonomy; the USSR was officially dissolved; and the Supreme Soviet rescinded the Soviet Treaty of 1922

    D. All fifteen Soviet republics simultaneously declared immediate and full independence from the USSR with no provisions for a transitional form of government

69. A political scientist might use all of the following except:
(Rigorous) (Skill 3.1a)

   A. An investigation of government documents

   B. A geological time-line

   C. Voting patterns

   D. Polling data

70. The early ancient civilizations developed systems of government:
(Rigorous) (Skill 3.1a)

   A. To provide for defense against attack

   B. To regulate trade

   C. To regulate and direct the economic activities of the people as they worked together in groups

   D. To decide on the boundaries of the different fields during planting seasons

71. 71.Political science is primarily concerned with _____. (Average Rigor) (Skill 3.1a)

   A. Elections

   B. Economic Systems

   C. Boundaries

   D. Public Policy

72. A political philosophy favoring or supporting rapid social changes in order to correct social and economic inequalities is called: (Rigorous) (Skill 3.1a)

   A. Nationalism

   B. Liberalism

   C. Conservatism

   D. Federalism

73. Consider the following passage from the Mayflower Compact: "...covenant, & combine ourselves together into a Civil body politick;" This demonstrates what theory of social organization? *(Average Rigor) (Skill 3.1a)*

   A. Darwinian

   B. Naturalistic

   C. Nonconsensual

   D. Constitutional

74. In the United States, if a person is accused of a crime and cannot afford a lawyer: *(Average Rigor) (Skill 3.1b)*

   A. The person cannot be tried

   B. A court will appoint a lawyer, but the person must pay the lawyer back when able to do so

   C. The person must be tried without legal representation

   D. A court will appoint a lawyer for the person free of charge

75. 75.Which of the following are usually considered the responsibilities of citizenship under the American system of government? *(Average Rigor) (Skill 3.1b)*

   A. Serving in public office, voluntary government service, military duty

   B. Paying taxes, jury duty, upholding the Constitution

   C. Maintaining a job, giving to charity, turning in fugitives

   D. Quartering of soldiers, bearing arms, government service

76. Why is the system of government in the United States referred to as a federal system? *(Rigorous) (Skill 3.1b)*

   A. There are different levels of government

   B. There is one central authority in which all governmental power is vested

   C. The national government cannot operate except with the consent of the governed

   D. Elections are held at stated periodic times, rather than as called by the head of the government

77. 77. In the presidential election of 1888, Grover Cleveland lost to Benjamin Harrison, although Cleveland received more popular votes. How is this possible? *(Average Rigor) (Skill 3.1b)*

   A. The votes of certain states (New York, Indiana) were thrown out because of voting irregularities

   B. Harrison received more electoral votes that Cleveland

   C. None of the party candidates received a majority of votes, and the House of Representatives elected Harrison according to Constitutional procedures

   D. Because of accusations of election law violations, Cleveland withdrew his name and Harrison became President

78. A person who receives more votes than anyone else in an election is said to have a _____ of the votes cast; a person who has over 50 percent of the votes in an election is said to have a _____ of the votes cast. *(Average Rigor) (Skill 3.1b)*

A. Plurality; majority

B. Majority; minority

C. Plurality; minority

D. Majority; plurality

79. 79. How are major party candidates chosen to run for President in the United States? *(Average Rigor) (Skill 3.1b)*

A. Caucuses of major party officeholders meet to select a state's choice for the party, and the candidate selected by the most states becomes the nominee

B. Potential presidential nominees seek pledges from each state party's chair and co-chair, and the candidate with the most pledges becomes the nominee

C. Nationwide primaries are held by each party, to select delegates to a national nominating convention

D. Each state party decides how to select delegates to a nominating convention; these selection processes may be caucuses, primaries, or any other method chosen by the state party

80. Which of the following are NOT local governments in the United States? *(Easy)* *(Skill 3.1b)*

   A. Cities

   B. Townships

   C. School boards

   D. All of these are forms of local government

81. The major expenditures of state governments in the United States go toward: *(Average Rigor) (Skill 3.1b)*

   A. Parks, education, and highways

   B. Law enforcement, libraries, and highways

   C. Education, highways, and law enforcement

   D. Recreation, business regulation, and education

82. 82.In the Constitutional system of checks and balances, one of the "checking" powers of the President is: *(Average Rigor) (Skill 3.1b)*

   A. Executive privilege

   B. Approval of judges nominated by the Senate

   C. Veto of Congressional legislation

   D. Approval of judged nominated by the House of Representatives

83. A historian might compare the governmental systems of the Roman Empire and the twentieth century United States with regard to which of the following commonalties? *(Rigorous) (Skill 3.1b)*

   A. Totalitarianism

   B. Technological development

   C. Constitutional similarities

   D. Federalism

84. How does the government of France differ from that of the United States? *(Rigorous) (Skill 3.1c)*

   A. France is a direct democracy while the United States is a representative democracy

   B. France has a unitary form of national government while the United States has a federal form of government

   C. France is a representative democracy while the United States is a direct democracy

   D. France does not elect a president while the United States elects a president

85. Capitalism and communism are alike in that they are both: *(Average Rigor) (Skill 3.1c)*

   A. Organic systems

   B. Political systems

   C. Centrally-planned systems

   D. Economic systems

86. Peace studies might include elements of all of the following disciplines except: *(Easy) (Skill 3.1d)*

   A. Geography

   B. History

   C. Economics

   D. All of these might contribute to peace studies

87. A geographer wishes to study the effects of a flood on subsequent settlement patterns. Which might he or she find most useful? *(Rigorous) (Skill 4.1)*

   A. A film clip of the floodwaters

   B. An aerial photograph of the river's source

   C. Census data taken after the flood

   D. A soil map of the A and B horizons beneath the flood area

88. If geography is the study of how human beings live in relationship to the earth on which they live, why do geographers include physical geography within the discipline? *(Rigorous)* *(Skill 4.1c/4.1e)*

   A. The physical environment serves as the location for the activities of human beings

   B. No other branch of the natural or social sciences studies the same topics

   C. The physical environment is more important than the activities carried out by human beings

   D. It is important to be able to subdue natural processes for the advancement of humankind

89. A coral island, or series of islands, which consists of a reef which surrounds a lagoon describes a(n): *(Easy)* *(Skill 4.1b)*

   A. Needle

   B. Key

   C. Atoll

   D. Mauna

90. Which of the following is an island nation? *(Easy)* *(Skill 4.1b)*

   A. Luxembourg

   B. Finland

   C. Monaco

   D. Nauru

91. The Mediterranean-type climate is characterized by: *(Average Rigor) (Skill 4.1c)*

   A. Hot, dry summers and mild, relatively wet winters

   B. Cool, relatively wet summers and cold winters

   C. Mild summers and winters, with moisture throughout the year

   D. Hot, wet summers and cool, dry winters

92. The climate of Southern Florida is the

   _____

   type. *(Average Rigor) (Skill 4.1c)*

   A. Humid subtropical

   B. Marine West Coast

   C. Humid continental

   D. Tropical wet-dry

93. Which location may be found in Canada? *(Rigorous) (Skill 4.1c)*

   A. 27 N 93 W

   B. 41 N 93 E

   C. 50 N 111 W

   D. 18 N 120 W

94. The highest point in North America is: *(Easy) (Skill 4.1c)*

   A. Mt. St. Helens

   B. Denali or Mr. McKinley

   C. Mt. Everest

   D. Pikes Peak

95. A physical geographer would be concerned with which of the following groups of terms? *(Average Rigor) (Skill 4.1c)*

   A. Landform, biome, precipitation

   B. Scarcity, goods, services

   C. Nation, state, administrative subdivision

   D. Cause and effect, innovation, exploration

96. The principal of "popular sovereignty," allowing the people to make their own decisions concerning slavery was stated by (Rigorous) (Skill 1.1g)

   A. Henry Clay

   B. Daniel Webster

   C. John C. Calhoun

   D. Stephen A. Douglas

97. We can credit modern geography with which of the following? (Average Rigor) (Skill 4.1f)

   A. Building construction practices designed to withstand earthquakes

   B. Advances in computer cartography

   C. Better methods of linguistic analysis

   D. Making it easier to memorize countries and their capitals

98. An economist might engage in which of the following activities? (Rigorous) (Skill 5)

   A. An observation of the historical effects of a nation's banking practices

   B. The application of a statistical test to a series of data

   C. Introduction of an experimental factor into a specified population to measure the effect of the factor

   D. An economist might engage in all of these

99. Economics is best described as: *(Average Rigor) (Skill 5.1)*

   A. The study of how money is used in different societies

   B. The study of how different political systems produce goods and services

   C. The study of how human beings use limited resources to supply their necessities and wants

   D. The study of how human beings have developed trading practices through the years

100. An economist investigates the spending patterns of low-income individuals. Which of the following would yield the most pertinent information? *(Rigorous) (Skill 5.1)*

   A. Prime lending rates of neighborhood banks

   B. The federal discount rate

   C. City-wide wholesale distribution figures

   D. Census data and retail sales figures

101. As your income rises, you tend to spend more money on entertainment. This is an expression of the: *(Rigorous) (Skill 5.1a)*

   A. Marginal propensity to consume

   B. Allocative efficiency

   C. Compensating differential

   D. Marginal propensity to save

102. A student buys a candy bar at lunch. The decision to buy a second candy bar relates to the concept of: *(Rigorous) (Skill 5.1b)*

A. Equilibrium pricing

B. Surplus

C. Utility

D. Substitutability

103. In a barter economy, which of the following would not be an economic factor? *(Rigorous) (Skill 5.1b)*

A. Time

B. Goods

C. Money

D. Services

104. Of the following, the best example of an oligopoly in the United States is: *(Average Rigor) (Skill 5.1b)*

A. Automobile industry

B. Electric power provision

C. Telephone service

D. Clothing manufacturer

105. An agreement in which a company allows a business to use its name and sell its products, usually for a fee, is called a: *(Average Rigor) (Skill 5.1b)*

A. Sole proprietorship

B. Partnership

C. Corporation

D. Franchise

106. What is a major difference between monopolistic competition and perfect competition? *(Rigorous) (Skill 5.1b)*

    A. Perfect competition has many consumers and suppliers while monopolistic competition does not

    B. Perfect competition provides identical products while monopolistic competition provides similar, but not identical, products

    C. Entry to perfect competition is difficult while entry to monopolistic competition is relatively easy

    D. Monopolistic competition has many consumers and suppliers while perfect competition does not

107. If the price of Good G increases, what is likely to happen with regard to comparable Good H? *(Rigorous) (Skill 5.1c)*

    A. The demand for Good G will stay the same

    B. The demand for Good G will increase

    C. The demand for Good H will increase

    D. The demand for Good H will decrease

108. The macro-economy consists of all but which of the following sectors? *(Rigorous) (Skill 5.1c)*

    A. Consumer

    B. Business

    C. Foreign

    D. Private

109. A command economy is considered the opposite of an open economy. Therefore, in a command economy: *(Rigorous)* *(Skill 5.1d)*

A. The open market determines how much of a good is produced and distributed

B. The government determines how much of a good is produced and distributed

C. Individuals produce and consume a specified good as commanded by their needs

D. The open market determines the demand for a good, and then the government produces and distributes the good

110. Which best describes the economic system of the United States? *(Average Rigor) (Skill 5.1d)*

A. Most decisions are the result of open markets with little or no government modification or regulation

B. Most decisions are made by the government, but there is some input by open market forces

C. Most decisions are made by open market factors with important regulatory functions and other market modifications the result of government activity

D. There is joint decision making by government and private forces with final decisions resting with the government

111. The advancement of understanding in dealing with human beings has led to a number of interdisciplinary areas. Which of the following interdisciplinary studies would most likely NOT be considered under the social sciences? *(Rigorous) (Skill 6)*

    A. Molecular biophysics

    B. Peace studies

    C. African-American studies

    D. Cartographic information systems

112. Which of the following is most reasonably studied under the social sciences? *(Average Rigor) (Skill 6.1)*

    A. Political science

    B. Geometry

    C. Physics

    D. Grammar

113. Which of the following is not generally considered to be a discipline within the social sciences? *(Average Rigor) (Skill 6.1)*

    A. Geometry

    B. Anthropology

    C. Geography

    D. Sociology

114. Which of the following best describes current thinking on the major purpose of social science? *(Rigorous) (Skill 6.1a)*

    A. Social science is designed primarily for students to acquire facts

    B. Social science should not be taught earlier than the middle school years

    C. A primary purpose of social sciences is the development of good citizens

    D. Social science should be taught as an elective

115. A social scientist studies the behavior of four persons in a carpool. This is an example of: *(Average Rigor) (Skill 6.1a)*

   A. Developmental psychology

   B. Experimental psychology

   C. Social psychology

   D. Macroeconomics

116. As a sociologist, you would be most likely to observe: *(Rigorous) (Skill 6.1a)*

   A. The effects of an earthquake on farmland

   B. The behavior of rats in sensory-deprivation experiments

   C. The change over time in Babylonian obelisk styles

   D. The behavior of human beings in television focus groups

117. Margaret Mead may be credited with major advances in the study of: *(Average Rigor) (Skill 6.1b)*

   A. The marginal propensity to consume

   B. The thinking of the Anti-Federalists

   C. The anxiety levels of non-human primates

   D. Interpersonal relationships in non-technical societies

118. "Participant observation" is a method of study most closely associated with and used in: *(Rigorous) (Skill 6.1b)*

   A. Anthropology

   B. Archaeology

   C. Sociology

   D. Political Science

119. The study of social behavior of minority groups would be in the area of: *(Average Rigor) (Skill 6.1c)*

A. Psychohistory

B. Psychology

C. Sociology

D. Cultural Geography

120. A teacher and a group of students take a field trip to an Indian mound to examine artifacts. This activity most closely fits under which branch of the social sciences? *(Average Rigor) (Skill 6.1b)*

A. Anthropology

B. Sociology

C. Psychology

D. Political Science

121. Which of the following demonstrates evidence of the interaction between physical and cultural anthropology? *(Rigorous) (Skill 6.1b)*

A. Tall Nilotic herdsmen are often expert warriors

B. Until recent years, the diet of most Asian peoples caused them to be shorter in stature than most other peoples

C. Native South American peoples adopted potato production after invasion by Europeans

D. Polynesians exhibit different skin coloration than Melanesians

122. Psychology is a social science because: *(Average Rigor) (Skill 6.1c)*

    A. It focuses on the biological development of individuals

    B. It focuses on the behavior of individual persons and small groups of persons

    C. It bridges the gap between the natural and the social sciences

    D. It studies the behavioral habits of lower animals.

123. A social scientist observes how individual persons react to the presence or absence of noise. This scientist is most likely a: *(Average Rigor) (Skill 6.1c)*

    A. Geographer

    B. Political Scientist

    C. Economist

    D. Psychologist

124. Cognitive, developmental, and behavioral are three types of: *(Easy) (Skill 6.1c)*

    A. Economists

    B. Political Scientists

    C. Psychologists

    D. Historians

125. Of the following lists, which includes persons who have made major advances in the understanding of psychology? *(Average Rigor) (Skill 6.1c)*

    A. Herodotus, Thucydides, Ptolemy

    B. Adam Smith, Milton Friedman, John Kenneth Galbraith

    C. Edward Hall, E.L. Thorndike, B.F. Skinner

    D. Thomas Jefferson, Karl Marx, Henry Kissinger

Answer Key

1.	D	34.	B	67.	D	100.	D
2.	C	35.	D	68.	C	101.	A
3	A	36.	A	69.	B	102.	C
4.	C	37.	D	70.	C	103.	C
5.	D	38.	A	71.	D	104.	A
6.	B	39.	D	72.	B	105.	D
7.	D	40.	B	73.	D	106.	B
8.	C	41.	A	74.	D	107.	C
9.	B	42.	B	75.	B	108.	D
10.	B	43.	D	76.	A	109.	B
11.	A	44.	B	77.	B	110.	C
12.	C	45.	D	78.	A	111.	A
13.	B	46.	C	79.	D	112.	A
14.	A	47.	C	80.	D	113.	A
15.	A	48.	C	81.	C	114.	C
16.	C	49.	A	82.	C	115.	C
17.	C	50.	D	83.	D	116.	D
18.	B	51.	C	84.	B	117.	D
19.	A	52.	D	85.	D	118.	A
20.	C	53.	B	86.	D	119.	C
21.	C	54.	D	87.	C	120.	A
22.	D	55.	B	88.	A	121.	B
23.	B	56.	B	89.	C	122.	B
24.	B	57.	D	90.	D	123.	D
25.	D	58.	C	91.	A	124.	C
26.	A	59.	C	92.	A	125.	C
27.	D	60.	C	93.	C		
28.	D	61.	B	94.	B		
29.	C	62.	C	95.	A		
30.	D	63.	A	96.	B		
31.	B	64.	C	97.	B		
32.	A	65.	D	98.	D		
33.	A	66.	A	99.	C		

Rigor Table

	Easy 20 percent	Average Rigor 40 percent	Rigorous 40 percent
Question #	3,4,5,6,10,14,18, 20, 21,26,28,29,31,44,48 49,50,53,67,80,86,89, 90,94,124	1,2,11,13,16,17,25,27,30, 34,35,37,40,41,45,46,47, 56,57,59,60,63,66,71,73, 74,75,77,78,79,81,82,85, 91,92,95,97,99,104,105, 110,112,113,115,117,119, 120,122,123,125	7,8,9,12,15,19,22,23,24, 32,33,36,38,39,42,43,51, 52,54,55,58,61,62,64,65, 68,69,70,72,76,83,84,87, 88,93,96,98,100,101,102, 103,106,107,108,109,111, 114,116,118,121

Rationales with Sample Questions

1.   **A historian would be interested in:**
     (Average Rigor) (Skills 1.x & 2.x)

   A. The manner in which scientific knowledge is advanced

   B. The effects of the French Revolution on world colonial policy

   C. The viewpoint of persons who have written previous "history"

   D. All of the above

Answer: D

D. All of the above

Historians are interested in broad developments through history (A), as well as how individual events affected the time in which they happened (B). Knowing the viewpoint of earlier historians can also help explain the common thinking among historical cultures and groups (C), so all of these answers are correct (D).

2.   **The Native Americans of the Eastern Woodlands lived on:**
     (Average Rigor) (Skill 1.1a)

   A. Buffalo and crops such as corn, beans, and sunflowers

   B. Chiefly farming of squash, beans, and corn

   C. A variety of game (deer, bear, moose) and crops (squash, pumpkins, corn)

   D. Wolves, foxes, polar bears, walruses, and fish

Answer: C

C. A variety of game (deer, bear, moose) and crops (squash, pumpkins, corn)

(A) Buffalo live in the plains habitat found in Western and Midwestern North America. (B) & (C) While the Native Americans did farm the "Three Sisters" of corn, squash and beans, the woods of the East also meant that a variety of game (deer, bear, moose) were widely available for them to hunt. (D) However, wolves, foxes, walruses, polar bears, and fish are only found together within the Arctic Circle, not the eastern woodlands.

3.   Apartments built out of cliff faces; shared government by adult citizens; absence of aggression toward other groups. These factors characterize the Native American group known as:
(Easy) (Skill 1.1a)

A. Pueblo

B. Comanche

C. Seminole

D. Sioux

Answer: A

A. Pueblos

(B) The Comanches were a nomadic Native American group which emerged around 1700 AD in the North American Plains and were decidedly aggressive towards their neighbors. (C) The Seminoles are a Native American group which originally emerged in Florida in the mid-18th century and was made up of refugees from other Native tribes and escaped slaves. (D) The Sioux were a Native American people who originally lived in the Dakotas, Nebraska, and Minnesota and clashed extensively with white settlers.

4. **Bartholomeu Dias, in seeking a route around the tip of Africa, was forced to turn back. Nevertheless, the cape he discovered near the southern tip of Africa became known as:**
(Easy) (Skill 1.1b)

    A. Cape Horn

    B. Cabo Bojador

    C. Cape of Good Hope

    D. Cape Hatteras

Answer: C

C. Cape of Good Hope

(A) Cape Horn was discovered by Sir Francis Drake as he sailed around the globe in 1578, and it is located at the southern tip of Chile. (B) Cajo Bojador on the Western coast of northern Africa was first successfully navigated by a European, Portuguese Gil Eanes, in 1434. (D) Cape Hatteras is located on the U.S. Atlantic coast at North Carolina.

5. **Columbus first reached Western Hemisphere lands in what is now:**
(Easy) (Skill 1.1b)

    A. Florida

    B. Bermuda

    C. Puerto Rico

    D. Bahamas

Answer: D

D. Bahamas

Christopher Columbus (1451-1506) would visit the Bahamas in 1492 and Puerto Rico in 1493, but he would never land on either Bermuda or Florida.

6.   **The Middle Colonies of the Americas were:**
     (Easy) (Skill 1.1b)

     A. Maryland, Virginia, North Carolina

     B. New York, New Jersey, Pennsylvania, Delaware

     C. Rhode Island, Connecticut, New York, New Jersey

     D. Vermont and New Hampshire

Answer: B

B. New York, New Jersey, Pennsylvania, Delaware

(A) Maryland, Virginia and North Carolina were southern colonies, (C & part of D) Rhode Island, Connecticut and New Hampshire were New England colonies, and (part of D) Vermont was not one of the 13 original colonies.

7.   **France decided in 1777 to help the American colonies in their war against Britain. This decision was based on:** *(Rigorous) (Skill 1.1c)*

     A. The naval victory of John Paul Jones over the British ship "Serapis"

     B. The survival of the terrible winter at Valley Forge

     C. The success of colonial guerilla fighters in the South

     D. The defeat of the British at Saratoga

Answer: D

D. The defeat of the British at Saratoga

The defeat of the British at Saratoga was the overwhelming factor in the Franco-American alliance of 1777 that helped the American colonies defeat the British. Some historians believe that without the Franco-American alliance, the American colonies would not have been able to defeat the British, and America would have remained a British colony.

8. **The only colony not founded and settled for religious, political, or business reasons was:** *(Rigorous) (Skill 1.1c)*

    A. Delaware

    B. Virginia

    C. Georgia

    D. New York

Answer: C

C. Georgia

The Swedish and the Dutch established Delaware and New York as Middle Colonies. They were established with the intention of growth by economic prosperity from farming across the countryside. The English, with the intention of generating a strong farming economy settled Virginia, a Southern colony. Georgia was the only one of these colonies not settled for religious, political or business reasons as it was started as a place for debtors from English prisons.

9. **Which one of the following is <u>not</u> a reason why Europeans came to the New World?** *(Rigorous) (Skill 1.1c)*

    A. To find resources in order to increase wealth

    B. To establish trade

    C. To increase a ruler's power and importance

    D. To spread Christianity

Answer: B

B. To establish trade

The Europeans came to the New World for a number of reasons; often they came to find new natural resources to extract for manufacturing. The Portuguese, Spanish and English were sent over to increase the monarch's power and spread influences such as religion (Christianity) and culture. Therefore, the only reason given that Europeans did *not* come to the New World was to establish trade.

10. **The first shots in what was to become the American Revolution were fired in:** *(Easy) (Skill 1.1c)*

   A. Florida

   B. Massachusetts

   C. New York

   D. Virginia

Answer: B

B. Massachusetts

(A) Florida, while at the time a British possession, was not directly involved in the Revolutionary War. (B) The American Revolution began with the battles of Lexington and Concord in 1775. (C) There would be no fighting in New York until 1776 and none in Virginia until 1781.

11. **A major quarrel between colonial Americans and the British concerned a series of British Acts of Parliament dealing with:** *(Average Rigor) (Skill 1.1c)*

   A. Taxes

   B. Slavery

   C. Native Americans

   D. Shipbuilding

Answer: A

A. Taxes

Acts of Parliament imposing taxes on the colonists always provoked resentment. Because the colonies had no direct representation in Parliament, they felt it unjust that that body should impose taxes on them with so little knowledge of their very different situation in America and no real concern for the consequences of such taxes. (B) While slavery continued to exist in the colonies long after it had been completely abolished in Britain, it never was a source of serious debate between Britain and the colonies. By the time Britain outlawed slavery in its colonies in 1833, the American Revolution had already taken place and the United States was free of British control. (C) There was no series of British Acts of Parliament passed concerning Native Americans. (D) Colonial shipbuilding was an industry which received little interference from the British.

12.   After ratification of the new Constitution, the most urgent of the many problems facing the new federal government was that of: *(Rigorous) (Skill 1.1d)*

   A. Maintaining a strong army and navy

   B. Establishing a strong foreign policy

   C. Raising money to pay salaries and war debts

   D. Setting up courts, passing federal laws, and providing for law enforcement officers

Answer: C

C. Raising money to pay salaries and war debts

Maintaining strong military forces, establishment of a strong foreign policy, and setting up a justice system were important problems facing the United States under the newly ratified Constitution. However, the most important and pressing issue was how to raise money to pay salaries and war debts from the Revolutionary War. Alexander Hamilton (1755-1804) then Secretary of the Treasury proposed increased tariffs and taxes on products such as liquor. This money would be used to pay off war debts and to pay for internal programs. Hamilton also proposed the idea of a National Bank.

13.   Which concept is not embodied as a right in the First Amendment to the U.S. Constitution? *(Average Rigor) (Skill 1.1d)*

   A. Peaceful assembly

   B. Unreasonable search and seizure

   C. Freedom of speech

   D. Petition for redress of grievances

Answer: B

B. Unreasonable search and seizure

The first amendment to the Constitution reads, "Congress shall make no law respecting [...] abridging the (C) freedom of speech, or of the press; or the right of the people (A) peaceably to assemble, and to (D) petition the government for a redress of grievances." The protection against (B) unreasonable search and seizure is a constitutional right found in the fourth amendment, not the first.

14. The "Trail of Tears" relates to: *(Easy) (Skill 1.1e)*

   A. The removal of the Cherokees from their native lands to Oklahoma Territory

   B. The revolt and subsequent migration of the Massachusetts Pilgrims under pressure from the Iroquois

   C. The journey of the Nez Perce under Chief Joseph before their capture by the U.S. Army

   D. The 1973 standoff between federal marshals and Native Americans at Wounded Knee, S.D.

Answer: A

A. The removal of the Cherokees from their native lands to Oklahoma Territory (1838-39)

(B) There never was a revolt and migration of the Massachusetts Pilgrims under pressure from the Iroquois. (C) The 1877 journey of the Nez Perce under Chief Joseph was a strategically impressive attempt to retreat from an oncoming US Army into Canada. (D) The 1973 Wounded Knee incident was the occupation of the town of Wounded Knee, South Dakota, by the American Indian Movement to call attention to issues of Native American civil rights.

15. It can be reasonably stated that the change in the United States from primarily an agricultural country into an industrial power was due to all of the following except: *(Rigorous) (Skill 1.1e)*

   A. Tariffs on foreign imports

   B. Millions of hardworking immigrants

   C. An increase in technological developments

   D. The change from steam to electricity for powering industrial machinery

Answer: A

A. Tariffs on foreign imports

The change in the United States from primarily an agricultural country into an industrial power was a combination of millions of hard-working immigrants, an increase in technological developments, and the change from steam to electricity for powering industrial machinery. The only reason given that really had little effect was the tariffs on foreign imports.

16.	The U.S. Constitution, adopted in 1789, provided for: *(Average Rigor)(Skill 1.1e)*

A. Direct election of the president by all citizens

B. Direct election of the president by citizens meeting a standard of wealth

C. Indirect election of the president by electors

D. Indirect election of the president by the U.S. Senate

Answer: C

C. Indirect election of the president by electors

The United States Constitution has always arranged for the indirect election of the president by electors. The question, by mentioning the original date of adoption, might mislead someone to choose B. While standards of citizenship have been changed by amendment, the president has never been directly elected, nor does the Senate have anything to do with presidential elections. The House of Representatives, not the Senate, settles cases where neither candidates wins in the Electoral College.

17.	Which of the following sets of inventors is correctly matched with the area in which they primarily worked? *(Average Rigor) (Skill 1.1e)*

A. Thomas Edison and George Westinghouse: transportation

B. Cyrus McCormick and George Washington Carver: household appliances

C. Alexander Graham Bell and Samuel F. B. Morse: communications

D. Isaac Singer and John Gorrie: agriculture

Answer: C

C. Alexander Graham Bell and Samuel F. B. Morse: communications

Bell, inventor of the telephone, and Morse, inventor of the telegraph and Morse code, were both working in the area of communications. While Westinghouse did invent various technologies crucial to the railroads and thus transportation, Edison did not; both are strongly linked to electrical inventions. McCormick and Carver specialized in agricultural inventions, while Singer, an inventor of the sewing machine, and Gorrie, the inventor of air conditioning and refrigeration, were best known for their household appliances.

18. **The area of the United States was effectively doubled through purchase of the Louisiana Territory under which president?** *(Easy)* *(Skill 1.1e)*

    A. John Adams

    B. Thomas Jefferson

    C. James Madison

    D. James Monroe

Answer: B

B. Thomas Jefferson

(B) The Louisiana Purchase, an acquisition of territory from France in 1803, occurred under Thomas Jefferson. (A) John Adams (1735-1826) was president from 1797-1801, before the purchase, and (C) James Madison, (1751-1836) after the Purchase (1809-1817). (D) James Monroe (1758-1831) was actually a signatory on the Purchase but did not become president until 1817.

19. **Which one of the following was not a reason why the United States went to war with Great Britain in 1812?** *(Rigorous) (Skill 1.1e)*

    A.   Resentment by Spain over the sale, exploration, and settlement of the Louisiana Territory

    B.   The westward movement of farmers because of the need for more land

    C.   Canadian fur traders were agitating the northwestern Indians to fight American expansion

    D.   Britain continued to seize American ships on the high seas and force American seamen to serve aboard British ships

Answer: A

A. Resentment by Spain over the sale, exploration, and settlement of the Louisiana Territory

The United States went to war with Great Britain in 1812 for a number of reasons including the expansion of settlers westward and the need for more land, the agitation of Indians by Canadian fur traders in eastern Canada, and the continued seizures of American ships by the British on the high seas. Therefore, the only statement given that was not a reason for the War of 1812 was the resentment by Spain over the sale, exploration and settlement of the Louisiana Territory. In fact, the Spanish continually held more hostility towards the British than towards the United States. The War of 1812 is often considered to be the second American war for independence.

20. The first territorial governor of Florida after Florida's purchase by the United States was: *(Easy) (Skill 1.1e)*

A. Napoleon Bonaparte

B. Robert Duval

C. Andrew Jackson

D. Davy Crockett

Answer: C

C. Andrew Jackson

Napoleon Bonaparte (A) was the Emperor of France and never ruled Florida. Robert Duvall (B) is an American actor and not a politician. Davy Crockett (D) was a frontiersman who died at the Alamo, in Texas.

21. The Compromise of 1850 came about as a result of which state's entry into the Union? *(Easy) (Skill 1.1f)*

A. Texas

B. Missouri

C. California

D. Kansas

Answer: C

C. California

Texas (A) entered the Union in 1845. Missouri (B) was the subject of the Missouri Compromise of 1824, which would be the first such compromise between slave and free states. California (C) entered the union after the Compromise of 1850 was drafted to avoid the issue of secession by the slave states. Kansas (D) became a violent battleground between pro-slavery and anti-slavery forces when it was organized as a territory in 1854, before achieving statehood in 1861 as a free state.

22. **What was a major source of contention between American settlers in Texas and the Mexican government in the 1830s and 1840s?** *(Rigorous) (Skill 1.1f)*

    A. The Americans wished to retain slavery which had been outlawed in Mexico

    B. The Americans had agreed to learn Spanish and become Roman Catholic, but failed to do so

    C. The Americans retained ties to the United States, and Santa Anna feared the power of the U.S.

    D. All of the above were contentious issues between American settlers and the Mexican government

Answer: D

D: All of the above were contentious issues between American settlers and the Mexican government

The American settlers simply were not willing to assimilate into Mexican society but maintained their prior commitments to slave holding, the English language, Protestantism, and the United States government.

23.   **Which of the following is most descriptive of the conflict between the U.S. government and the Seminoles between 1818 and 1858? (Rigorous) (Skill 1.1f)**

A. There was constant armed conflict between the Seminoles and the U.S. during these years

B. Historians discern three separate phases of hostilities (1818, 1835-42, 1855-58) known collectively as the Seminole Wars

C. On May 7, 1858, the Seminoles admitted defeat, signed a peace treaty with the U.S., and left for Oklahoma, except for fifty-one individuals

D. The former Seminole chief Osceola helped the U.S. defeat the Seminoles and effect their removal to Oklahoma

Answer: B

B. Historians discern three separate phases of hostilities (1818, 1835-42, 1855- 58) known collectively as the Seminole Wars

(A) Intermittent conflicts between the U.S. government and the Seminole Native Americans can be classified into (B) three separate phases of hostilities.

24. **Slavery arose in the southern colonies partly as a perceived economical way to:** *(Rigorous) (Skill 1.1f)*

    A. Increase the owner's wealth through human beings used as a source of exchange

    B. Cultivate large plantations of cotton, tobacco, rice, indigo, and other crops

    C. Provide Africans with humanitarian aid, such as health care, Christianity, and literacy

    D. Keep ships' holds full of cargo on two out of three legs of the "triangular trade" voyage

Answer: B

B. Cultivate large plantations of cotton, tobacco, rice, indigo and other crops

The southern states, with their smaller populations, were heavily dependent on slave labor as a means of being able to fulfill their role and remain competitive in the greater U.S. economy. (A) When slaves arrived in the South, the vast majority would become permanent fixtures on plantations, intended for work, not as a source of exchange. (C) While some slave owners instructed their slaves in Christianity, provided health care, and some level of education, such attention was not their primary reason for owning slaves – a cheap and ready labor force was. (D) Whether or not ships' holds were full on two or three legs of the triangular journey was not the concern of southerner plantation owners as the final purchasers of slaves. Such details would have concerned the slave traders.

25. **Of the following, which contributed most to penetration of western areas by colonial Americans?** *(Average Rigor) (Skill 1.1f)*

   A. Development of large ships capable of sailing upstream in rivers such as the Hudson, Susquehanna, and Delaware

   B. The invention of the steamboat

   C. Improved relations with Native Americans who invited colonial Americans to travel west to settle

   D. Improved roads, mail service, and communications

Answer: D

D. Improved roads, mail service and communications

(A) As the Susquehanna, Delaware, and Hudson are limited to the northeast, they would not have helped the colonists penetrate any further West. (B) Since these were the waterways that they had immediate access to, the development of the steamboat was similarly unhelpful in this regard. (C) In general, colonist-Native American relations worsened as colonists moved West, so colonists were unlikely to have been invited yet further west! (D) Improved roads, mail service, and communications made traveling west easier and more attractive as they meant not being completely cut off from news and family in the east.

26. **Which of the following groups were slave states?** *(Easy) (Skill 1.1f)*

A. Delaware, Maryland, Missouri

B. California, Texas, Florida

C. Kansas, Missouri, Kentucky

D. Virginia, West Virginia, Indiana

Answer: A

A. Delaware, Maryland, Missouri

(A) Delaware, Maryland, and Missouri were all slave states at the time of the Civil War. (B) Florida and Texas were slave states, while California was a free state. (C) Kansas, Missouri, and Kentucky were all originally slave territories, and Missouri and Kentucky were admitted to the Union as such. However, Kansas' petition to join the union in 1858 was blocked in order to preserve the balance between slave and free states. Kansas was admitted as a free state in 1861. (D) Virginia and West Virginia were both slave states, but Indiana was a free state.

27.   **A consequence of the Gold Rush that led Americans to California in 1848 and 1849 was that:** *(Average Rigor) (Skill 1.1f)*

   A. California spent the minimum amount of time as a territory and was admitted as a slave state

   B. California was denied admission on its first application since most Americans felt that the settlers were too "uncivilized" to deserve statehood

   C. California was purchased from Mexico for the express purpose of gaining immediate statehood

   D. California did not go through the normal territorial stage, but applied directly for statehood as a free state

Answer: D

D. California did not go through the normal territorial stage, but applied directly for statehood as a free state

California, suddenly undergoing a massive increase in population and wealth and desiring orderly government, found it had little recourse but to claim status as a free state and appeal directly for statehood. Congress had moved too slowly on the question of making California United States Territory. California was never a territory, but only a military district. California was not denied admission to the Union but was an essential part of the Compromise of 1850. Immediate statehood was definitely not an express policy of the U.S. in acquiring California, but the Gold Rush changed attitudes quickly.

28. **Which American Secretary of War later became President of the Confederate States?** *(Easy) (Skill 1.1g)*

    A. Henry Clay

    B. William Seward

    C. Franklin Pierce

    D. Jefferson Davis

Answer: D

D. Jefferson Davis

Jefferson Davis was the Secretary of War in question. Franklin Pierce was the 14th President of the United States. Neither Henry Clay nor William Seward was ever Secretary of War.

29. **Who was the first commander for the North in the Civil War?** *(Easy) (Skill 1.1g)*

    A. Gen. Ulysses S. Grant

    B. Gen. Robert E. Lee

    C. Gen. Irwin McDowell

    D. Gen. George Meade

Answer: C

C. General Irwin McDowell

(A) Gen. Ulysses S. Grant was the final commander of the Union army during the Civil War. (B) Gen. Robert E. Lee was the commander of the Confederate army. (D) Gen. George Meade was the Union commander at the Battle of Gettysburg in 1863.

30. **Abraham Lincoln won reelection in 1864 chiefly through:** *(Average Rigor) (Skill 1.1g)*

   A. His overwhelming force of personality and appeal to all segments of the electorate

   B. His reputation as the Great Emancipator

   C. The fact that people felt sorry for him because of his difficulties

   D. His shrewd political manipulation, clever use of patronage jobs, and wide-appeal selection of cabinet members

Answer: D

D. His shrewd political manipulation, clever use of patronage jobs, and wide-appeal selection of cabinet members

President Lincoln in his own lifetime was a hugely divisive figure, even in the North. He did not appeal to all segments of the electorate, his reputation as the Great Emancipator really developed after the war, and few felt sorry for him for his personal and political difficulties. Rather, Lincoln constantly maneuvered to maintain the advantage, using all the powers of the Presidency to win reelection despite his own unpopularity.

31.   **How many states reentered the Union before 1868?** *(Easy) (Skill 1.1g)*

State	Date of Readmission
Alabama	1868
Arkansas	1868
Florida	1868
Georgia	1870
Louisiana	1868
Mississippi	1870
North Carolina	1868
South Carolina	1868
Tennessee	1866
Texas	1870
Virginia	1870

A. 0 states

B. 1 state

C. 2 states

D. 3 states

Answer: B

B. 1 state

Only Tennessee was readmitted before 1868, as the above table indicates.

32. **The Radical Republicans who pushed the harsh Reconstruction measures through Congress after Lincoln's death lost public and moderate Republican support when they went too far:** *(Rigorous)* *(Skill 1.1g)*

   A. In their efforts to impeach the President

   B. By dividing ten southern states into military-controlled districts

   C. By making the ten southern states give freed African Americans the right to vote

   D. Sending carpetbaggers into the South to build up support for Congressional legislation

Answer: A

A. In their efforts to impeach the President

The public support and the moderate Republicans were actually being drawn towards the more radical end of the Republican spectrum following Lincoln's death during Reconstruction. Many felt as though Andrew Johnson's policies towards the South were too soft and were running the risk of rebuilding the old system of white power and slavery. Even moderate Republicans in the North felt as though it was essential to rebuild the South but with the understanding that they must abide by the Fourteenth and Fifteenth Amendments assuring blacks freedom and the right to vote. The Radical Republicans were so frustrated that the President would make concessions to the old Southerners that they attempted to impeach him. This turned back the support that they had received from the public and from moderates.

33.   **In the 1920s, the United States almost completely stopped all immigration. One of the reasons was:** *(Rigorous) (Skill 1.1i)*

        A. Plentiful cheap, unskilled labor was no longer needed by industrialists

        B. War debts from World War I made it difficult to render financial assistance

        C. European nations were reluctant to allow people to leave since there was a need to rebuild populations and economic stability

        D. The United States did not become a member of the League of Nations

Answer: A

A. Plentiful cheap, unskilled labor was no longer needed by industrialists

The primary reason that the United States almost completely stopped all immigration during the 1920s was because their once much-needed, cheap, unskilled labor jobs, made available by the once booming industrial economy, were no longer needed. This has much to do with the increased use of machines to do the work once done by cheap, unskilled laborers.

34.   **The Interstate Commerce Commission (ICC) was established in reaction to abuses and corruption in what industry?** *(Average Rigor) (Skill 1.1i)*

        A. Textile

        B. Railroad

        C. Steel

        D. Banking

Answer: B

B. Railroad

The ICC was established to fight abuses in the railroad industry.

35. **The Teapot Dome scandal related to:** *(Average Rigor)* *(Skill 1.1i)*

A. The improper taxing of tea surpluses in Boston

B. The improper awarding of building contracts in Washington, DC

C. The improper sale of policy decisions by various Harding administration officials

D. The improper sale of oil reserves in Wyoming

Answer: D

D. The improper sale of oil reserves in Wyoming

This scandal refers to the improper sale of federal oil reserves in Teapot Dome, Wyoming, an infamous event in the Harding Administration (1921-25). (C) would be tempting, especially since the Secretary of the Interior personally benefited from the sale, but no significant policy decisions were involved. No building of a dome nor tea to put in the Teapot were involved in the making of this scandal.

36. **Which of the following was NOT a factor in the United States' entry into World War I?** *(Rigorous)* *(Skill 1.1i)*

A. The closeness of the presidential election of 1916

B. The German threat to sink all allied ships, including merchant ships

C. The desire to preserve democracy as practiced in Britain and France as compared to the totalitarianism of Germany

D. The sinking of the Lusitania and the Sussex

Answer: A

A. The closeness of the presidential election of 1916

Since there was no presidential election of 1916, this could not have been a factor the United States' entry into the war; the last election had been in 1914. All the other answers were indeed factors.

37. **What 1924 Act of Congress severely restricted immigration in the United States?** *(Average Rigor) (Skill 1.1i)*

    A. Taft-Hartley Act

    B. Smoot-Hawley Act

    C. Tordney-McCumber Act

    D. Johnson-Reed Act

Answer: D

D. Johnson-Reed Act

(A) The Taft-Harley Act (1947) prohibited unfair labor practices by labor unions. (B) The Smoot-Hawley Act (1930) raised U.S. tariffs on imported goods to negative effect on the U.S. economy and world trade as (C) the Fordney-McCumber Act (1922) had done before it.

38.   **Of all the major causes of both World War I and II, the most significant one is considered to be:** *(Rigorous) (Skill 1.1i)*

A. Extreme nationalism

B. Military buildup and aggression

C. Political unrest

D. Agreements and alliances

Answer: A

A. Extreme nationalism

Although military buildup and aggression, political unrest, and agreements and alliances were all characteristic of the world climate before and during World War I and World War II, the most significant cause of both wars was extreme nationalism. Nationalism is the idea that the interests and needs of a particular nation are of the utmost and primary importance above all else. Some nationalist movements could be liberation movements while others were oppressive regimes, much depends on their degree of nationalism. The nationalism that sparked WWI included a rejection of German, Austro-Hungarian, and Ottoman imperialism by Serbs, Slavs and others culminating in the assassination of Archduke Ferdinand by a Serb nationalist in 1914. Following WWI and the Treaty of Versailles, many Germans and others in the Central Alliance Nations, malcontent at the concessions and reparations of the treaty, started a new form of nationalism. Adolf Hitler and the Nazi regime led this extreme nationalism. Hitler's ideas, an example of extreme, oppressive nationalism combined with political, social and economic scapegoating, were the primary cause of WWII.

39. **Which of the following contributed to the severity of the Great Depression in California?** *(Rigorous)* *(Skill 1.1i)*

    A. An influx of Chinese immigrants

    B. The Dust Bowl drove people out of the cities

    C. An influx of Mexican immigrants

    D. An influx of "Okies"

Answer: D

D. An influx of "Okies"

The answer is an influx of "Okies" (D). The Dust Bowl of the Great Plains destroyed agriculture in the area. People living in the plains areas lost their livelihood, and many lost their homes and possessions in the great dust storms that resulted from a period of extended drought. People from all of the states affected by the Dust Bowl made their way to California in search of a better life. Because the majority of the people were from Oklahoma, they were all referred to as "Okies." These migrants brought with them their distinctive plains culture. The great influx of people seeking jobs exacerbated the effects of the Great Depression in California.

40. **In the first aggression of World War II outside the Orient, identify the aggressor nation and the nation which was invaded:** *(Average Rigor) (Skill 1.1j)*

   A. Germany; Sudetenland

   B. Italy; Abyssinia

   C. Germany; Poland

   D. Italy; Yugoslavia

Answer: B

B. Italy; Abyssinia

(A) The Sudetenland (part of Czechoslovakia) was ceded to Nazi Germany in 1938 by the Munich Agreement of France, Britain, Italy, and Germany. The pretense for the annexation was the mistreatment of resident Germans by the Czechs. (B) Italy's invasion and annexation of Abyssinia in 1935-36 was condemned by the League of Nations, but it was left unchallenged until the East African Campaign of World War II in 1941. Nazi Germany invaded Poland in 1939 and would occupy it until 1945. (D) After attempts to convince the Yugoslavians to join the Axis powers, Germany and Italy invaded Yugoslavia in 1941 and established the Independent State of Croatia.

41. **In issuing an ultimatum for Soviet ships not to enter Cuban waters in October 1962, President John F. Kennedy, as part of his decision, used the provisions of the:** *(Average Rigor) (Skill 1.1k)*

A. Monroe Doctrine

B. Declaration of the Rights of Man

C. Geneva Convention

D. Truman Doctrine

Answer: A

A. Monroe Doctrine

(A) The Monroe Doctrine, initially formulated by Presidents James Monroe (1758-1831) and John Quincy Adams (1767-1848) and later enhanced by President Theodore Roosevelt (1858-1915), opposed European colonization or interference in the Americas and perceived any such attempts as a threat to U.S. security. It also promised U.S. neutrality in conflicts between European powers and/or their already established colonies. (B) The Declaration of the Rights of Man, widely adapted in future declarations about international human rights, was formulated in France during the French Revolution and adopted by the National Constituent Assembly in 1789 as the premise of any future French constitution. (C) The Geneva Conventions (1864, 1929 and 1949, with later additions and amendments) established humanitarian and ethical standards for conduct during times of war and has been widely accepted as international law. (D) The Truman Doctrine (1947), formulated by President Harry Truman (1884-1972), provided for the support of Greece and Turkey as a means of protecting them from Soviet influence. It thereby began the Cold War (1947-1991), a period in which the US sought to contain the Soviet Union by limiting its influence in other countries.

42.   **President Truman suspended Gen. Douglas MacArthur from command of Allied forces in Korea because of:** *(Rigorous) (Skill 1.1k)*

A. MacArthur's inability to make any progress against North Koreans

B. MacArthur's criticism of Truman claiming that the president would not allow him to pursue aggressive tactics against communists

C. The harsh treatment MacArthur exhibited toward the Japanese after World War II

D. The ability of the U.S. Navy to continue the conflict without the presence of MacArthur

Answer: B

B. MacArthur's criticism of Truman, claiming that the president would not allow him to pursue aggressive tactics against communists

Truman suspended MacArthur because of clear insubordination: MacArthur had publicly criticized the president, his Commander in Chief, and had openly undermined his policy of negotiating a settlement with the communists. MacArthur was a general of proven effectiveness; so, (A) cannot be correct. MacArthur was actually rather lenient to the Japanese after World War II, and he was a general, not an admiral of the Navy.

43. Which of the following most closely characterizes the Supreme Court's decision in *Brown v. Board of Education*? *(Rigorous) (Skill 1.1k)*

A. Chief Justice Warren had to cast the deciding vote in a sharply divided the Supreme Court

B. The decision was rendered along sectional lines with northerners voting for integration and southerners voting for continued segregation

C. The decision was 7-2 with dissenting justices not even preparing a written dissent

D. Chief Justice Warren was able to persuade the Supreme Court to render a unanimous decision

Answer: D

D. Chief Justice Warren was able to persuade the Court to render a unanimous decision

The Supreme Court decided 9-0 against segregated educational facilities.

44. The native metaphysical outlook of Japan, usually characterized as a religion, is: *(Easy) (Skill 2)*

A. Tao

B. Shinto

C. Hindu

D. Sunni

Answer: B

B. Shinto

(A) Tao is the Chinese philosophical work which inspired Taoism, the religious tradition sourced in China. (B) Shinto is the system of rituals and beliefs honoring the deities and spirits believed to be native to the landscape and inhabitants of Japan. (C) Hindu is the primary religion of India, with a pantheon of deities and a caste system. (D) Sunni is a branch of Islam, along with Shiite.

45. **Indo-European languages are native languages to each of the following EXCEPT:** *(Average Rigor)* *(Skill 2)*

    A. Germany

    B. India

    C. Italy

    D. Finland

Answer: D

D. Finland

German, the native language of (A) Germany, Hindi, the official language of (B) India, and Italian, spoken in (C) Italy, are three of the hundreds of languages that are part of the Indo-European family which also includes French, Greek, and Russian. Finnish, the language of (D) Finland, is part of the Uralic family of languages, which also includes Estonian. It developed independently of the Indo-European family.

46. **Which of the following developments is most closely associated with the Neolithic Age?** *(Average Rigor)* *(Skill 2.1a)*

    A. Human use of fire

    B. First use of stone chipping instruments

    C. Domestication of plants

    D. Development of metallurgical alloys

Answer: C

C. Domestication of plants

The Neolithic, or "New Stone" Age as its name implies, is characterized by the use of stone implements, but the first use of stone chipping instruments appears in the Paleolithic period. Human use of fire may go back still farther and certainly predates the Neolithic era. The Neolithic period is distinguished by the domestication of plants. The development of metallurgical alloys marks the conclusion of the Neolithic Age.

47. **The end to hunting, gathering, and fishing of prehistoric people was due to:** *(Average Rigor) (Skill 2.1a)*

A. Domestication of animals

B. Building crude huts and houses

C. Development of agriculture

D. Organized government in villages

Answer: C

C. Development of agriculture

Although the domestication of animals, the building of huts and houses and the first organized governments were all very important steps made by early civilizations, it was the development of agriculture that ended the once dominant practices of hunting, gathering, and fishing among prehistoric people. The development of agriculture provided a more efficient use of time and for the first time a surplus of food. This greatly improved the quality of life and contributed to early population growth.

48. **The principle of zero in mathematics is the discovery of the ancient civilization found in:** *(Easy) (Skill 2.1b)*

A. Egypt

B. Persia

C. India

D. Babylon

Answer: C

C. India

Although the Egyptians practiced algebra and geometry, the Persians developed an alphabet, and the Babylonians developed Hammurabi's Code, which would come to be considered among the most important contributions of the Mesopotamian civilization, it was the Indians that created the idea of zero in mathematics, changing drastically our ideas about numbers.

49. **The Tigris-Euphrates Valley was the site of which two primary ancient civilizations?** *(Easy) (Skill 2.1b)*

   A. Babylonian and Assyrian

   B. Sumerian and Egyptian

   C. Hyksos and Hurrian

   D. Persian and Phoenician

Answer: A

A. Babylonian and Assyrian

(B) While the Sumerians also lived in the southern Tigris-Euphrates valley, Egyptian civilization grew up in the Nile delta (3500BC-30 BC). (C) The Hyksos were an Asiatic people who controlled the Nile Delta during the 15th and 16th Dynasties (1674BC-1548BC). The Hurrians (2500BC-1000BC) came from the Khabur River Valley in northern Mesopotamia where they spread out to establish various small kingdoms in the region. (D) The Persians (648BC- early 19th century AD) had a succession of empires based in the area known as modern day Iran. The Phoenicians were a seafaring people who dominated the Mediterranean during the first century BC.

50. **The first ancient civilization to introduce and practice monotheism was the:** *(Easy) (Skill 2.1b)*

    A. Sumerians

    B. Minoans

    C. Phoenicians

    D. Hebrews

Answer: D

D. Hebrews

The (A) Sumerians and (C) Phoenicians both practiced religions in which many gods and goddesses were worshipped. Often these Gods/Goddesses were based on a feature of nature such as a sun, moon, weather, rocks, water, etc. The (B) Minoan culture shared many religious practices with the Ancient Egyptians. It seems that the king was somewhat of a god figure and the queen, a goddess. Much of the Minoan art point to worship of multiple gods. Therefore, only the (D) Hebrews introduced and fully practiced monotheism, or the belief in one god.

51. **Which one of the following is not an important legacy of the Byzantine Empire?** *(Rigorous) (Skill 2.1b)*

A. It protected Western Europe from various attacks from the East by such groups as the Persians, Ottoman Turks, and Barbarians

B. It played a part in preserving the literature, philosophy, and language of ancient Greece

C. Its military organization was the foundation for modern armies

D. It kept the legal traditions of Roman government, collecting and organizing many ancient Roman laws

Answer: C

C. Its military organization was the foundation for modern armies

The Byzantine Empire (1353-1453) was the successor to the Roman Empire in the East and protected Western Europe from invaders such as the Persians and Ottomans. The Byzantine Empire was a Christian incorporation of Greek philosophy, language, and literature along with Roman government and law. Therefore, although regarded as having a strong infantry, cavalry, and Engineering corps along with excellent morale amongst its soldiers, the Byzantine Empire is not particularly considered a foundation for modern armies.

52. **For the historian studying ancient Egypt, which of the following would be least useful?** *(Rigorous) (Skill 2.1c)*

   A. The record of an ancient Greek historian on Greek-Egyptian interaction

   B. Letters from an Egyptian ruler to his/her regional governors

   C. Inscriptions of the Fourteenth Egyptian Dynasty

   D. Letters from a nineteenth-century Egyptologist to his wife

Answer: D

D. Letters from a nineteenth-century Egyptologist to his wife

Historians use primary sources from the actual time they are studying whenever possible. (A) Ancient Greek records of interaction with Egypt, (B) letters from an Egyptian ruler to regional governors, and (C) inscriptions from the Fourteenth Egyptian Dynasty are all primary sources created at or near the actual time being studied. (D) Letters from a nineteenth century Egyptologist would not be considered a primary source, as they were created thousands of years after the fact and may not actually be about the subject being studied.

53. **The_____were fought between the Roman Empire and Carthage.** *(Easy) (Skill 2.1c)*

   A. Civil Wars

   B. Punic Wars

   C. Caesarian Wars

   D. Persian Wars

Answer: B

B. Punic Wars

The Punic Wars (264-146 BC) were fought between Rome and Carthage. All the other answers are not proper titles of wars.

54. **Which one of the following did not contribute to the early medieval European civilization?** *(Rigorous)* *(Skill 2.1d)*

   A. The heritage from the classical cultures

   B. The Christian religion

   C. The influence of the German Barbarians

   D. The spread of ideas through trade and commerce

Answer: D

D. The spread of ideas through trade and commerce

The heritage of the classical cultures such as Greece, the Christian religion which became dominant, and the influence of the Germanic Barbarians (Visigoths, Saxons, Ostrogoths, Vandals and Franks) were all contributions to early medieval Europe and its plunge into feudalism. During this period, lives were often difficult and lived out on one single manor, with very little travel or spread of ideas through trade or commerce. Civilization seems to have halted progress during these years.

55. **Of the legacies of the Roman Empire listed below, the most influential, effective, and lasting is:** *(Rigorous)* *(Skill 2.1d)*

   A. The language of Latin

   B. Roman law, justice, and political system

   C. Engineering and building

   D. The writings of its poets and historians

Answer: B

B. Roman law, justice, and political system

Of the lasting legacies of the Roman Empire, it is its law, justice, and political system (B) that has been the most effective and influential on our Western world today. English, Spanish, Italian, French, and others are all based on Latin (A), although that Roman language has itself has died out. The Roman engineering and building (C) and their writings and poetry (D) have also been influential but not nearly to the degree that their governmental and justice systems have been.

56. What Holy Roman Emperor was forced to do public penance because of his conflict with Pope Gregory VII over lay investiture of the clergy? *(Average Rigor) (Skill 2.1d)*

   A. Charlemagne

   B. Henry IV

   C. Charles V

   D. Henry VIII

Answer: B

B. Henry IV

Henry IV (1050-1106) clashed with Pope Gregory VII by insisting upon the right of a ruler to appoint members of the clergy to their offices, but he repented in 1077. Charlemagne & Charles V were also Holy Roman Emperors but in the 9th and 16th centuries, respectively. Henry VIII, King of England, broke with the Roman Church over his right to divorce and remarry in 1534.

57. **Monophysitism (the belief that Jesus was completely divine with no admixture of humanity) was declared a heresy by _____?** *(Average Rigor)* *(Skill 2.1d)*

   A. Council of Nicaea

   B. Diet of Worms

   C. Council of Trent

   D. Council of Chalcedon

Answer: D

D. Council of Chalcedon

(A) In response to the Arian heresy asserting that Christ was a created being like other created beings, the Council of Nicaea (325 AD) established the divinity of Jesus Christ by declaring him to be of the same substance as God the Father, an article of faith then enshrined in the Nicene Creed. (B) At the Diet of Worms (1521 AD), the Holy Roman Empire tried and condemned Martin Luther and his writings. (C) The Council of Trent (1545 AD-1563 AD), an ecumenical council of the Roman Catholic Church, clarified many aspects of Catholic doctrine and liturgical life in an attempt to counter the Protestant Reformation. (D) The Council of Chalcedon (451 AD) confirmed the humanity of Christ by affirming that the Virgin Mary was indeed his human mother and therefore worthy of the Greek title Theotokos ("God-bearer").

58. **Which of the following areas would NOT be a primary area of hog production?** *(Rigorous) (Skill 2.1d)*

   A. Midland England

   B. The Mekong delta of Vietnam

   C. Central Syria

   D. Northeast Iowa

Answer: C

C. Central Syria

Pork is a common ingredient in the American, English, and Vietnamese cuisine, so one would reasonably expect to find hog production in (A) Midland England, (B) The Mekong Delta of Vietnam, and (D) Northeast Iowa. The population of Syria is predominantly Islamic, and Islam prohibits the eating of pork. Therefore, one would be unlikely to find extensive hog production in (C) Central Syria.

59. **Which of the following is NOT one of the Pillars of Faith of Islam?** *(Average Rigor) (Skill 2.1d)*

   A. Alms-giving (zakah)

   B. Pilgrimage (hajj)

   C. Membership in a school of law (al-madhahib)

   D. Fasting (sawm)

Answer: C

C. Membership in a school of law (al-madhahib)

The Five Pillars of Islam are the faith profession that there is no God but Allah and that Muhammad is his prophet. Prayer (salah), pilgrimage to Mecca (hajj), almsgiving (zakah), and fasting during the holy month of Ramadan (sawm) are all Pillars of Faith.

60. **Chinese civilization is generally credited with the original development of which of the following sets of technologies: (Average Rigor) (Skill 2.1e)**

   A. Movable type and mass production of goods

   B. Wool processing and domestication of the horse

   C. Paper and gunpowder manufacture

   D. Leather processing and modern timekeeping

Answer: C

C. Paper and gunpowder manufacture

(A) While China's Bi Sheng (d. 1052) is credited with the earliest forms of moveable type (1041-48), mass production was spearheaded by America's Henry Ford (1863-1947) in his campaign to create the first truly affordable automobile, the Model T Ford. (B) While wool has been processed in many ways in many cultures, production on a scale beyond cottage industries was not possible without the many advances made in England during the Industrial revolution (18th century). Various theories exist about the domestication of the horse with estimates ranging from 4600 BCE to 2000 BC in Eurasia. Recent DNA evidence suggests that the horse may actually have been domesticated in different cultures at independent points. (C) The earliest mention of gunpowder appears in ninth-century Chinese documents. The earliest examples of paper made of wood pulp come from China and have been dated as early as the second century BCE. (D) Leather processing and timekeeping have likewise seen different developments in different places at different times.

61. **Colonial expansion by Western European powers in the 18th and 19th centuries was due primarily to:** *(Rigorous) (Skill 2.1e)*

    A. Building and opening the Suez Canal

    B. The Industrial Revolution

    C. Marked improvements in transportation

    D. Complete independence of all the Americas and loss of European domination and influence

Answer: B

B. The Industrial Revolution

Colonial expansion by Western European powers in the late 18th and 19th centuries was due primarily to the Industrial Revolution in Great Britain that spread across Europe and needed new natural resources and therefore, new locations from which to extract the raw materials needed to feed the new industries.

62. **The ideas and innovations of the period of the Renaissance were spread throughout Europe mainly because of:** *(Rigorous) (Skill 2.1e)*

    A. Extensive exploration

    B. Craft workers and their guilds

    C. The invention of the printing press

    D. Increased travel and trade

Answer: C

C. The invention of the printing press

The ideas and innovations of the Renaissance were spread throughout Europe for a number of reasons. While exploration, increased travel, and spread of craft may have aided the spread of the Renaissance to small degrees, nothing was as important to the spread of ideas as Gutenberg's invention of the printing press in Germany.

63. **Luther issued strong objection to all but which of the following practices of the fifteenth-century Roman Catholic Church?** *(Average Rigor) (Skill 2.1e)*

   A. The sacrament of Baptism

   B. Absolution of sins through the intermediation of a priest and through ceremony

   C. The sale of indulgences, whereby the buyer may purchase purgation of sins

   D. Imposed church control over the individual conscience

Answer: A

A. The sacrament of Baptism

Absolution of sins by priests, the sale of indulgences, and imposed church control over individual consciences were all practices which Martin Luther (1483-1546) and subsequent Protestants objected to on the basis that they required the Church to act as an intermediary between God and the individual believer. The sacrament of Baptism, however, continues to be practiced in some form in most Protestant denominations as the rite of initiation into the Christian community.

64. **The results of the Renaissance, Enlightenment, and Commercial and Industrial Revolutions were more unfortunate for the people of:** *(Rigorous) (Skill 2.1e)*

   A. Asia

   B. Latin America

   C. Africa

   D. Middle East

Answer: C

C. Africa

The results of the Renaissance, Enlightenment, Commercial and Industrial Revolutions were quite beneficial for many people in much of the world. New ideas of humanism, religious tolerance, and secularism were spreading. Increased trade and manufacturing were surging economies in much of the world. The people of Africa, however, suffered during these times as they became largely left out of the developments. Also, the people of Africa were stolen, traded, and sold into slavery to provide a cheap labor force for the growing industries of Europe and the New World.

65. **Great Britain became the center of technological and industrial development during the nineteenth century chiefly on the basis of: (Rigorous) (Skill 2.1f)**

   A. Central location relative to the population centers of Europe

   B. Colonial conquests and military victories over European powers

   C. Reliance on exterior sources of financing

   D. Resources of coal and production of steel

Answer: D

D. Resources of coal and production of steel

Great Britain possessed a unique set of advantages in the 18th and 19th century making it the perfect candidate for the technological advances of the industrial revolutions. (A) Relative isolation from the population centers in Europe meant little to Great Britain, which benefited from its own relatively unified and large domestic market and enabled it avoid the tariffs and inefficiencies of trading on the diverse (and complicated) continent. (B) Colonial conquests and military victories over European powers were fueled by Great Britain's industrial advances in transportation and weaponry, rather than being causes of them. (C) Reliance of exterior sources of funding – while Great Britain would enjoy an increasing influx of goods and capital from its colonies, the efficiency of its own domestic market consistently generated an impressive amount of capital for investment in the new technologies and industries of the age. (D) Great Britain's rich natural resources of coal and ore enabled steel production and, set alongside new factories in a Britain's landscape, allowed the production of goods quickly and efficiently.

66. **The years 1793-94 in France, characterized by numerous trials and executions of supposed enemies of the Revolutionary Convention, were known as the:** *(Average Rigor) (Skill 2.1f)*

    A. Reign of Terror

    B. Dark Ages

    C. French Inquisition

    D. Glorious Revolution

Answer: A

A. Reign of Terror

(A) The period of the French Revolution known as the Reign of Terror (1793-94) is estimated to have led to the deaths of up to 40,000 people: aristocrats, clergy, political activists, and any one else denounced as an enemy of the Revolutionary Convention, many falsely so. (B) The Dark Ages is the term commonly used for the Early Middle Ages in Europe, from the fall of Rome in 476 to 1000. (C) The French Inquisition was the Roman Catholic Church's attempts to codify into ecclesiastical and secular law the prosecution of heretics, most notably at the time, the Albigensians, in the 13th century. (D) The Glorious Revolution (1688-1689) is the title given to the overthrow of the last Catholic British monarch, James II, in favor of his Protestant daughter, Mary, and her husband, the Dutch Prince William of Orange.

67.   In 1990, Alberto Fujimori was the first Asian to be elected president of: *(Easy) (Skill 2.1h)*

A. Canada

B. Mexico

C. South Africa

D. Peru

Answer: D

D. Peru

(A) Japan has a constitutional monarchy, symbolically led by the Queen (or King). (B) Mexico does elect a president, but it would be unlikely for anyone of other than Hispanic origins to be elected. (C) With a modern history including racial tensions between blacks and whites, it is highly unlikely that South Africa would elect an Asian as president. (D) Alberto Fujimori, a dual citizen of Peru and Japan, was the first Asian to lead a Latin American country.

68. **Which of the following most closely characterizes the geopolitical events of the USSR in 1991-92:** *(Rigorous) (Skill 2.1h)*

    A. The USSR established greater military and economic control over the fifteen Soviet republics

    B. The Baltic States (Estonia, Latvia, and Lithuania) declared independence, while the remainder of the USSR remained intact.

    C. Fourteen of fifteen Soviet republics declared some degree of autonomy; the USSR was officially dissolved; and the Supreme Soviet rescinded the Soviet Treaty of 1922

    D. All fifteen Soviet republics simultaneously declared immediate and full independence from the USSR with no provisions for a transitional form of government

Answer: C

C. Fourteen of fifteen Soviet republics declared some degree of autonomy; the USSR was officially dissolved; and the Supreme Soviet rescinded the Soviet Treaty of 1922

The unraveling of the USSR in 1991-92 and the establishment of independent republics in its wake was a complex, if relatively peaceful, end to its existence. After a succession of declarations of autonomy by constituent states forced the dissolution of the central government, the Baltic States of Latvia, Lithuania, and Estonia immediately declared their independence. Other republics took longer to reconfigure their relationships to one another. There was no serious attempt by the central government to resist these changes militarily or economically.

69. **A political scientist might use all of the following except:** *(Rigorous)* *(Skill 3.1a)*

   A. An investigation of government documents

   B. A geological time-line

   C. Voting patterns

   D. Polling data

Answer: B

B. A geological time-line

Political science is primarily concerned with the political and governmental activities of societies. (A) Government documents can provide information about the organization and activities of a government. (C) Voting patterns reveal the political behavior of individuals and groups. (D) Polling data can provide insight into the predominant political views of a group of people. (B) A geological timeline describes the changes in the physical features of the earth over time, and would not be useful to a political scientist.

70. **The early ancient civilizations developed systems of government:** *(Rigorous)* *(Skill 3.1a)*

   A. To provide for defense against attack

   B. To regulate trade

   C. To regulate and direct the economic activities of the people as they worked together in groups

   D. To decide on the boundaries of the different fields during planting seasons

Answer: C

C. To regulate and direct the economic activities of the people as they worked together in groups

Although ancient civilizations were concerned with defense, trade regulation and the maintenance of boundaries in their fields, they could not have done any of them without first regulating and directing the economic activities of the people as they worked in groups. This provided for a stable economic base from which they could trade and actually had something worth providing defense for.

71. **Political science is primarily concerned with _____.**
    (Average Rigor) (Skill 3.1a)

    A. Elections

    B. Economic Systems

    C. Boundaries

    D. Public Policy

Answer: D

D. Public policy

Political science studies the actions and policies of the government of a society. (D) Public policy is the official stance of a government on an issue, and it is a primary source for studying a society's dominant political beliefs. (A) Elections are also an interest of political scientists, but are not a primary field of study. (B) Economic systems are of interest to an economist, and (C) boundaries are of interest to a geographer

72. **A political philosophy favoring or supporting rapid social changes in order to correct social and economic inequalities is called:**
    (Rigorous) (Skill 3.1a)

    A. Nationalism

    B. Liberalism

    C. Conservatism

    D. Federalism

Answer:

B. Liberalism

A political philosophy favoring rapid social changes in order to correct social and economic inequalities are called Liberalism. Liberalism was a theory that could be said to have started with the great French philosophers Montesquieu (1689-1755) and Rousseau (1712-1778). It is important to understand the difference between political, economic, and social liberalism, as they are different and how they sometimes contrast one another in the modern world.

73. **Consider the following passage from the Mayflower Compact: "...covenant, & combine ourselves together into a Civil body politick;" This demonstrates what theory of social organization?** *(Average Rigor) (Skill 3.1a)*

A. Darwinian

B. Naturalistic

C. Nonconsensual

D. Constitutional

Answer: D

D. Constitutional

(D) Constitutional social organization requires at its heart clearly-stated and mutually agreed-upon constitutional principles, which all involved parties promise to uphold. (B) A naturalistic theory of social organization is one freely chosen by its participants and not yet bound by a clear set of constitutional principles. A (A) Darwinian theory would reflect the "survival of the fittest" element of Darwin's theory of the evolution of natural life, as applied to the relationship of different groups within a society. (C) Nonconsensual theories compel participation in a system of social organization and thus would never be characterized by the word "covenant", which means an agreement entered into freely by both parties.

74. In the United States, if a person is accused of a crime and cannot afford a lawyer: *(Average Rigor) (Skill 3.1b)*

   A. The person cannot be tried

   B. A court will appoint a lawyer, but the person must pay the lawyer back when able to do so

   C. The person must be tried without legal representation

   D. A court will appoint a lawyer for the person free of charge

Answer: D

D. A court will appoint a lawyer for the person free of charge

The Sixth Amendment to the Constitution grants the right to a speedy and public jury trial in a criminal prosecution, as well as the right to "the assistance of counsel for his defense." This has been interpreted as the right to receive legal assistance at no charge if a defendant cannot afford one. (D) A court will appoint a lawyer for the person free of charge, is the correct answer.

75.   **Which of the following are usually considered responsibilities of citizenship under the American system of government?** *(Average Rigor) (Skill 3.1b)*

A.   Serving in public office, voluntary government service, military duty

B.   Paying taxes, jury duty, upholding the Constitution

C.   Maintaining a job, giving to charity, turning in fugitives

D.   Quartering of soldiers, bearing arms, government service

Answer: B

B. Paying taxes, jury duty, upholding the Constitution

Only paying taxes, jury duty and upholding the Constitution are responsibilities of citizens as a result of rights and commitments outlined in the Constitution. For example, the right of citizens to a jury trial in the Sixth and Seventh Amendments and the right of the federal government to collect taxes in Article 1, Section 8. (A) Serving in public office, voluntary government service, military duty, (C) maintaining a job, giving to charity, and turning in fugitives are all highly admirable actions undertaken by many exemplary citizens, but they are considered purely voluntary actions, even when officially recognized and compensated. The United States has none of the compulsory military or civil service requirements of many other countries. (D) The quartering of soldiers is an act, which, according to the Third Amendment of the Bill of Rights, requires a citizen's consent. Bearing arms is a right guaranteed under the Second Amendment of the Bill of Rights.

76. **Why is the system of government in the United States referred to as a federal system?** *(Rigorous) (Skill 3.1b)*

    A. There are different levels of government

    B. There is one central authority in which all governmental power is vested

    C. The national government cannot operate except with the consent of the governed

    D. Elections are held at stated periodic times, rather than as called by the head of the government

Answer: A

A. There are different levels of government

(A) The United States is composed of fifty states each responsible for its own affairs but united under a federal government. (B) A centralized system is the opposite of a federal system. (C) That national government cannot operate except with the consent of the governed is a founding principle of American politics. It is not a political system. A centralized democracy could still be consensual but would not be federal. (D) This is a description of electoral procedure, not a political system.

77. **In the presidential election of 1888, Grover Cleveland lost to Benjamin Harrison, although Cleveland received more popular votes. How is this possible?** *(Average Rigor) (Skill 3.1b)*

   A. The votes of certain states (New York, Indiana) were thrown out because of voting irregularities

   B. Harrison received more electoral votes that Cleveland

   C. None of the party candidates received a majority of votes, and the House of Representatives elected Harrison according to Constitutional procedures

   D. Because of accusations of election law violations, Cleveland withdrew his name and Harrison became president

Answer: B

B. Harrison received more electoral votes that Cleveland

Presidential elections, according to the United States Constitution, are decided in the Electoral College. This college mirrors the composition of the House of Representatives. The popular vote for each presidential candidate determines which slate of electors in each state is selected. Thus, while Cleveland won enough support in certain states to win a majority of the national popular vote, he did not win enough states to carry the Electoral College. If neither candidate had won the necessary majority, the House of Representatives would have made the final decision, but this did not occur in 1888. The other two answers are not envisioned by the Constitution and did not occur.

78.   A person who receives more votes than anyone else in an election is said to have a _____ of the votes cast; a person who has over 50 percent of the votes in an election is said to have a _____ of the votes cast. *(Average Rigor) (Skill 3.1b)*

A. Plurality; majority

B. Majority; minority

C. Plurality; minority

D. Majority; plurality

Answer: A

A. Plurality; majority

A majority means more than half of the whole. A plurality means the largest portion, when no one achieves a majority. A minority of the votes would be less than half of the votes.

79.   **How are major party candidates chosen to run for president in the United States?**

A. Caucuses of major party officeholders meet to select a state's choice for the party, and the candidate selected by the most states becomes the nominee

B. Potential presidential nominees seek pledges from each state party's chair and co-chair, and the candidate with the most pledges becomes the nominee

C. Nationwide primaries are held by each party, to select delegates to a national nominating convention

D. Each state party decides how to select delegates to a nominating convention; these selection processes may be caucuses, primaries, or any other method chosen by the state party

Answer: D

D. Each state party decides how to select delegates to a nominating convention; these selection processes may be caucuses, primaries, or any other method chosen by the state party

A nominating convention selects each party nominee, and the delegates from each state are chosen as the state party sees fit. Caucuses are only one possible method. Pledges or nationwide primaries have never been a way of determining the nominee.

80. **Which of the following are NOT local governments in the United States?** *(Easy) (Skill 3.1b)*

    A. Cities

    B. Townships

    C. School boards

    D. All of these are forms of local government

Answer: D

D. All of these are forms of local government

A local government is a body with the authority to make policy and enforce decisions on behalf of a local community. Cities and townships are by definition local, not statewide or federal, governments. A more central authority might make school policy in other countries, but, in the United States, school boards are local authorities. [However, according to the 2002 Census, several states run certain school districts themselves without a local school board]

81. **The major expenditures of state governments in the United States go toward:** *(Average Rigor) (Skill 3.1b)*

    A. Parks, education, and highways

    B. Law enforcement, libraries, and highways

    C. Education, highways, and law enforcement

    D. Recreation, business regulation, and education

Answer: C

C. Education, highways, and law enforcement

Education and highways are among the largest expenditures of state governments. Law enforcement is also significant, if much smaller than these other expenditures. Parks and recreation, business regulation, and libraries are all minor items by comparison.

82. **In the Constitutional system of checks and balances, one of the "checking" powers of the President is:** *(Average Rigor) (Skill 3.1b)*

   A. Executive privilege

   B. Approval of judges nominated by the Senate

   C. Veto of Congressional legislation

   D. Approval of judged nominated by the House of Representatives

Answer: C

C. Veto of Congressional legislation

The power to (C) veto congressional legislation is granted to the U.S. President in Article I of the Constitution, which states that all legislation passed by both houses of Congress must be given to the President for approval. This is a primary check on the power of Congress by the President. Congress may override a presidential veto by a two-thirds majority vote of both houses, however. (A) Executive privilege refers to the privilege of the President to keep certain documents private. Answers (B) and (D) are incorrect, as Congress does not nominate judges. This is a presidential power.

83.   A historian might compare the governmental systems of the Roman
      Empire and the twentieth century United States with regard to which
      of the following commonalties? *(Rigorous) (Skill 3.1c)*

      A. Totalitarianism

      B. Technological development

      C. Constitutional similarities

      D. Federalism

Answer: D

D. Federalism

(A) Totalitarianism is a form of government where citizens are completely
subservient to the state. While this was sometimes the case during the reign of
the Roman Empire, it was not common in 20th-century America. (B)
Technological development does not necessarily address similarities in
governmental systems. (C) The Roman constitution applied to the Republic of
Rome - not directly to the empire as a whole. (D) Federalism is a type of
governmental system where several separate states join under a common
government. This describes both the United States and the Roman Empire and
so (D) is the best answer.

84. **How does the government of France differ from that of the United States?** *(Rigorous) (Skill 3.1c)*

    A. France is a direct democracy while the United States is a representative democracy

    B. France has a unitary form of national government while the United States has a federal form of government

    C. France is a representative democracy while the United States is a direct democracy

    D. France does not elect a president while the United States elects a president

Answer: B

B. France has a unitary form of national government while the United States has a federal form of government

The United States has a federal form of government since its 50 states are responsible for their own affairs and do not have their governments appointed or supervised by a central government. France has a unitary form of national government, where the central government is responsible for regional as well as national affairs. Neither the U.S. nor France is a direct democracy, and both have an elected president.

85. **Capitalism and Communism are alike in that they are both:** *(Average Rigor) (Skill 3.1c)*

    A. Organic systems

    B. Political systems

    C. Centrally-planned systems

    D. Economic systems

Answer: D

D. Economic systems

While economic and (B) political systems are often closely connected, capitalism and Communism are primarily (D) economic systems. Capitalism is a system of economics that allows the open market to determine the relative value of goods and services. Communism is an economic system where the market is planned by a central state. While Communism is a (C) centrally-planned system, this is not true of capitalism. (A) Organic systems are studied in biology, a natural science.

86. **Peace studies might include elements of all of the following disciplines except:** *(Easy) (Skill 3.1d)*

    A. Geography

    B. History

    C. Economics

    D. All of these might contribute to peace studies

Answer: D

D. All of these might contribute to peace studies

(A) Geography might examine the current and historical borders between two regions or nations. (B) History would contribute information on the origins of conflict and peace between peoples. Because scarcity of goods and differences in the relative wealth of nations are often factors in conflict and cooperation, (C) economics can be included in peace studies.

87. **A geographer wishes to study the effects of a flood on subsequent settlement patterns. Which might he or she find most useful?** *(Rigorous) (Skill 4.1)*

   A. A film clip of the floodwaters

   B. An aerial photograph of the river's source

   C. Census data taken after the flood

   D. A soil map of the A and B horizons beneath the flood area

Answer: C

C. Census data taken after the flood

(A) A film clip of the flood waters may be of most interest to a historian, (B) an aerial photograph of the river's source and (D) soil maps tell little about the behavior of the individuals affected by the flood. (C) Census surveys record the population for certain areas on a regular basis, allowing a geographer to tell if more or less people are living in an area over time. These would be of most use to a geographer undertaking this study.

88. **If geography is the study of how human beings live in relationship to the earth on which they live, why do geographers include physical geography within the discipline?** *(Rigorous) (Skill 4.1c/4.1e)*

A. The physical environment serves as the location for the activities of human beings

B. No other branch of the natural or social sciences studies the same topics

C. The physical environment is more important than the activities carried out by human beings

D. It is important to be able to subdue natural processes for the advancement of humankind

Answer: A

A. The physical environment serves as the location for the activities of human beings

Cultures will develop different practices depending on the predominant geographical features of the area in which they live. For instance, cultures that live along a river will have a different kind of relationship to the surrounding land than those who live in the mountains. Answer (A) best describes why physical geography is included in the social science of geography. Answer (B) is false, as physical geography is also studied under other natural sciences (such as geology). Answers (C) and (D) are matters of opinion and do not pertain to the definition of geography as a social science.

89. **A coral island, or series of islands, which consists of a reef which surrounds a lagoon describes a(n):** *(Easy) (Skill 4.1b)*

   A. Needle

   B. Key

   C. Atoll

   D. Mauna

Answer: C

C. Atoll

An atoll (C) is a formation that occurs when a coral reef builds up around the top of a submerged volcanic peak, forming a ring or horseshoe of islands with a seawater lagoon in the center.

90. **Which of the following is an island nation?** *(Easy) (Skill 4.1b)*

   A. Luxembourg

   B. Finland

   C. Monaco

   D. Nauru

Answer: D

D. Nauru

(D) Nauru is located in Micronesia in the South Pacific and is the world's smallest island nation. (A) Luxembourg is a small principality in Europe, bordered by Belgium, France, and Germany. (B) Finland is a Scandinavian country on the Baltic Sea bordered by Norway, Sweden, and Russia. (C) Monaco is a small principality on the coast of the Mediterranean Sea that is bordered by France.

91. **The Mediterranean-type climate is characterized by:** *(Average Rigor)* *(Skill 4.1c)*

    A. Hot, dry summers and mild, relatively wet winters

    B. Cool, relatively wet summers and cold winters

    C. Mild summers and winters, with moisture throughout the year

    D. Hot, wet summers and cool, dry winters

Answer: A

A. Hot, dry summers and mild, relatively wet winters

Westerly winds and nearby bodies of water create stable weather patterns along the west coasts of several continents and the coast of the Mediterranean Sea, (after which this type of climate is named). Temperatures rarely fall below the freezing point and have a mean between 70 and 80 degrees Fahrenheit in the summer. Stable conditions make for little rain during the summer months.

92. **The climate of Southern Florida is the _____ type.** *(Average Rigor) (Skill 4.1c)*

    A. Humid subtropical

    B. Marine West Coast

    C. Humid continental

    D. Tropical wet-dry

Answer: A

A. Humid subtropical

The (B) marine west coast climate is found on the western coasts of continents. Florida is on the eastern side of North America. The (C) humid continental climate is found over large land masses, such as Europe and the American Midwest, not along coasts such as where Florida is situated. The (D) tropical wet-dry climate occurs in the tropics within about 15 degrees of the equator. Florida is sub-tropical. Florida is in a (A) humid subtropical climate, which extends along the East Coast of the United States to about Maryland, and along the Gulf Coast to northeastern Texas.

93. **Which location may be found in Canada?** *(Rigorous) (Skill 4.1c)*

    A. 27 N 93 W

    B. 41 N 93 E

    C. 50 N 111 W

    D. 18 N 120 W

Answer: C

C. 50 N 111 W

(A) 27 North latitude, 93 West longitude is located in the Gulf of Mexico. (B) 41 N 93 E is located in northwest China. (D) 18 N 120 W is in the Pacific Ocean, off the coast of Mexico. (C) 50 N 120 W is located near the town of Medicine Hat in the Canadian province of Alberta.

94. **The highest point in North America is:** *(Easy) (Skill 4.1c)*

    A. Mt. St. Helens

    B. Denali or Mt. McKinley

    C. Mt. Everest

    D. Pikes Peak

Answer: B

B. Denali

(B) Denali, also known as Mt. McKinley, has an elevation of 20,320 feet, and is in the Alaska Range of North America. It is the highest point on the continent. (A) Mt. St. Helen, an active volcano located in the state of Washington, is 8,364 feet in elevation since its eruption in 1980. (D) Pike's Peak, located in Colorado, is 14,100 feet in elevation. (C) Mt. Everest, in the Himalayan Mountains between China and Tibet, is the highest point on the earth at 29,035 feet, but is not located in North America.

95. **A physical geographer would be concerned with which of the following groups of terms?** *(Average Rigor) (Skill 4.1c)*

   A. Landform, biome, precipitation

   B. Scarcity, goods, services

   C. Nation, state, administrative subdivision

   D. Cause and effect, innovation, exploration

Answer: A

A. Landform, biome, precipitation

(A) Landform, biome, and precipitation are all terms used in the study of geography. A landform is a physical feature of the earth, such as a hill or valley. A biome is a large community of plants or animals, such as a forest. Precipitation is the moisture that falls to earth as rain or snow. (B) Scarcity, goods, and services are terms encountered in economics. (C) Nation, state, and administrative subdivision are terms used in political science. (D) Cause and effect, innovation, and exploration are terms in developmental psychology.

96. The principle of "popular sovereignty", allowing people in any Territory to make their own decision concerning slavery was stated by:
(Rigorous) (Skill 1.1g)

A. Henry Clay

B. Daniel Webster

C. John C. Calhoun

D. Stephen A. Douglas

Answer:

D. Stephen A. Douglas

(A) Henry Clay (1777-1852) and (B) Daniel Webster (1782-1852) were prominent Whigs whose main concern was keeping the United States one nation. They opposed Andrew Jackson and his Democratic party around the 1830s in favor of promoting what Clay called "the American System". (C) John C. Calhoun (1782-1850) served as Vice-President under John Quincy Adams and Andrew Jackson, and then as a state senator from South Carolina. He was very pro-slavery and a champion of states' rights. The principle of "popular sovereignty", in which people in each territory could make their own decisions concerning slavery, was the doctrine of (D) Stephen A. Douglas (1813-1861). Douglas was looking for a middle ground between the abolitionists of the North and the pro-slavery Democrats of the South. However, as the polarization of pro- and anti-slavery sentiments grew, he lost the presidential election to Republican Abraham Lincoln, who later abolished slavery.

97. **We can credit modern geography with which of the following? (Average Rigor) (Skill 4.1f)**

   A. Building construction practices designed to withstand earthquakes

   B. Advances in computer cartography

   C. Better methods of linguistic analysis

   D. Making it easier to memorize countries and their capitals

Answer: B

B. Advances in computer cartography

(B) Cartography is concerned with the study and creation of maps and geographical information and falls under the social science of geography.

98. **An economist might engage in which of the following activities? (Rigorous) (Skill 5)**

   A. An observation of the historical effects of a nation's banking practices

   B. The application of a statistical test to a series of data

   C. Introduction of an experimental factor into a specified population to measure the effect of the factor

   D. An economist might engage in all of these

Answer: D

D.   An economist might engage in all of these

Economists use statistical analysis of economic data, controlled experimentation, and historical research in their field of social science.

99. **Economics is best described as:** *(Average Rigor) (Skill 5.1)*

A. The study of how money is used in different societies

B. The study of how different political systems produce goods and services

C. The study of how human beings use limited resources to supply their necessities and wants

D. The study of how human beings have developed trading practices through the years

Answer: C

C. The study of how human beings use limited resources to supply their necessities and wants

(A) How money is used in different societies might be of interest to a sociologist or anthropologist. (B) The study of how different political systems produce goods and services is a topic of study that could be included under the field of political science. (D) The study of historical trading practices could fall under the study of history. (C) is the best general description of the social science of economics as a whole.

100. **An economist investigates the spending patterns of low-income individuals. Which of the following would yield the most pertinent information? (Rigorous) (Skill 5.1)**

    A. Prime lending rates of neighborhood banks

    B. The federal discount rate

    C. City-wide wholesale distribution figures

    D. Census data and retail sales figures

Answer: D

D. Census data and retail sales figures

(A) Local lending rates and (B) the federal discount rate might provide information on borrowing habits, but not necessarily spending habits, and it gives no information on income levels. (C) Citywide wholesale distribution figures would provide information on the business activity of a city, but tell nothing about consumer activities. (D) Census data records the income levels of households within a certain area, and retail sales figures for that area would give an economist data on spending which can be compared to income levels.

101. **As your income rises, you tend to spend more money on entertainment. This is an expression of the:** *(Rigorous) (Skill 5.1a)*

    A. Marginal propensity to consume

    B. Allocative efficiency

    C. Compensating differential

    D. Marginal propensity to save

Answer: A

A. Marginal propensity to consume

The (A) marginal propensity to consume is a measurement of how much consumption changes compared to how much disposable income changes. Entertainment expenses are an example of disposable income. Dividing your change in entertainment spending by your total change in disposable income will give you your marginal propensity to consume.

102. **A student buys a candy bar at lunch. The decision to buy a second candy bar relates to the concept of:** *(Rigorous) (Skill 5.1b)*

   A. Equilibrium pricing

   B. Surplus

   C. Utility

   D. Substitutability

Answer: C

C. Utility

As used in the social science of economics, (C) utility is the measurement of happiness or satisfaction a person receives from consuming a good or service. The decision of the student to increase his satisfaction by buying a second candy bar relates to this concept because he is spending money to increase his happiness.

103. **In a barter economy, which of the following would not be an economic factor?** *(Rigorous) (Skill 5.1b)*

   A. Time

   B. Goods

   C. Money

   D. Services

Answer: C

C. Money

A barter economy is one where (B) goods and (D) services are exchanged for one another and not for money. Just as in an economy with currency, (A) time is a factor in determining the value of goods and services. Since no money changes hands in a barter economy, the correct answer is (C) money.

104. Of the following, the best example of an oligopoly in the US is: *(Average Rigor) (Skill 5.1b)*

    A. Automobile industry

    B. Electric power provision

    C. Telephone service

    D. Clothing manufacturer

Answer: A

A. Automobile industry

An oligopoly exists when a small group of companies controls an industry. In the United States at present, there are hundreds of (B) electric power providers, (C) telephone service providers, and (D) clothing manufacturers. There are currently still just three major automobile manufacturers, however, making the (A) automobile industry an oligopoly.

105. An agreement in which a company allows a business to use its name and sell its products, usually for a fee, is called a: *(Average Rigor) (Skill 5.1b)*

    A. Sole proprietorship

    B. Partnership

    C. Corporation

    D. Franchise

Answer: D

D. Franchise

A (A) sole proprietorship is where a person operates a company with his own resources. All income from this kind of business is considered income to the proprietor. A (B) partnership is an agreement between two or more people to operate a business and divide the proceeds in a specified way. A (C) corporation is a formal business arrangement where a company is considered a separate entity for tax purposes. In a (D) franchise, individuals can purchase the rights to use a company's name, designs, logos, etc. in exchange for a fee. Examples of franchise companies are McDonald's and Krispy Kreme.

106. What is a major difference between monopolistic competition and perfect competition? *(Rigorous) (Skill 5.1b)*

A. Perfect competition has many consumers and suppliers while monopolistic competition does not

B. Perfect competition provides identical products while monopolistic competition provides similar, but not identical, products

C. Entry to perfect competition is difficult while entry to monopolistic competition is relatively easy

D. Monopolistic competition has many consumers and suppliers while perfect competition does not

Answer: B

B. Perfect competition provides identical products while monopolistic competition provides similar, but not identical, products

A perfect market is a hypothetical market used in economics to discuss the underlying effects of supply and demand. To control for differences between products, it is assumed in perfect competition that all products are identical, with no differences, and the prices for these products will rise and fall based on a small number of factors. Monopolistic competition takes place in a market where each producer can act monopolistically and raise or lower the cost of its product or change its product to make different from similar products. This is the primary difference between these two models; (B) perfect competition provides identical products, while monopolistic competition provides similar, but not identical, products.

107. **If the price of Good G increases, what is likely to happen with regard to comparable Good H?** *(Rigorous)* *(Skill 5.1c)*

   A. The demand for Good G will stay the same

   B. The demand for Good G will increase

   C. The demand for Good H will increase

   D. The demand for Good H will decrease

Answer: C

C. The demand for Good H will increase

If Good G and Good H are viewed by consumers as equal in value but the cost of Good G increases, it follows that consumers will now choose Good H at a higher rate, increasing the demand.

108. **The macro-economy consists of all but which of the following sectors?** *(Rigorous)* *(Skill 5.1c)*

   A. Consumer

   B. Business

   C. Foreign

   D. Private

Answer: D

D. Private

The private sector (D) refers to that area of politics and society not controlled by the public (i.e. the government). While it may include businesses and individual consumers, it is not considered part of the macro-economy.

109. **A command economy is considered the opposite of an open economy. Therefore, in a command economy:** *(Rigorous) (Skill 5.1d)*

   A. The open market determines how much of a good is produced and distributed

   B. The government determines how much of a good is produced and distributed

   C. Individuals produce and consume a specified good as commanded by their needs

   D. The open market determines the demand for a good, and then the government produces and distributes the good

Answer: B

B. The government determines how much of a good is produced and distributed

A command economy is where (B) the government determines how much of a good is produced and distributed, as was the case in the Soviet Union and is still the case in Cuba and North Korea. A command economy is the opposite of a market economy where (A) the open market determines how much of a good is produced and distributed.

110. **Which best describes the economic system of the United States?** *(Average Rigor) (Skill 5.1d)*

   A. Most decisions are the result of open markets with little or no government modification or regulation

   B. Most decisions are made by the government but there is some input by open market forces

   C. Most decisions are made by open market factors with important regulatory functions and other market modifications the result of government activity

   D. There is joint decision making by government and private forces with final decisions resting with the government

Answer: C

C. Most decisions are made by open market factors with important regulatory functions and other market modifications the result of government activity

The United States does not have a planned economy, as described in answers (B) and (D). Neither is the U.S. market completely free of regulation (A). Products are regulated for safety, and many services are regulated by certification requirements, for example. The best description of the US economic system is therefore (C).

111. **The advancement of understanding in dealing with human beings has led to a number of interdisciplinary areas. Which of the following interdisciplinary studies would NOT be considered under the social sciences?** *(Rigorous) (Skill 6)*

    A. Molecular biophysics

    B. Peace studies

    C. African-American studies

    D. Cartographic information systems

Answer: A

A. Molecular biophysics

(A) Molecular biophysics is an interdisciplinary field combining the fields of biology, chemistry and physics. These are all natural sciences and not social sciences

112. **Which of the following is most reasonably studied under the social sciences?** *(Average Rigor) (Skill 6.1)*

    A. Political science

    B. Geometry

    C. Physics

    D. Grammar

Answer: A

A. Political science

Social sciences deal with the social interactions of people. (B) Geometry is a branch of mathematics. (C) Physics is a natural science that studies the physical world. Although it may be studied as part of linguistics, (D) grammar is not recognized as a scientific field of study in itself. Only (A) political science is considered a general field of the social sciences.

113. **Which of the following is not generally considered a discipline within the social sciences?** *(Average Rigor) (Skill 6.1)*

 A. Geometry

 B. Anthropology

 C. Geography

 D. Sociology

Answer: A

A. Geometry

(B) Anthropology studies the culture of groups of people. (C) Geography examines the relationship between societies and the physical place on earth where they live. (D) Sociology studies the predominant attitudes, beliefs, and behaviors of a society. All three of these fields are related to the social interactions of humans, and so are considered social sciences. (A) Geometry is a field of mathematics and does not relate to the social interactions of people, so it is not considered a social science.

114. **Which of the following best describes current thinking on the major purpose of social science?** *(Rigorous) (Skill 6.1a)*

 A. Social science is designed primarily for students to acquire facts

 B. Social science should not be taught earlier than the middle school years

 C. A primary purpose of social sciences is the development of good citizens

 D. Social science should be taught as an elective

Answer: C

C. A primary purpose of social sciences is the development of good citizens

By making students aware of the importance of their place in society, how their society and others are governed, how societies develop and advance, and how cultural behaviors arise, the social sciences are currently thought to be of primary importance in (C) developing good citizens.

115. **A social scientist studies the behavior of four persons in a carpool. This is an example of:** *(Average Rigor) (Skill 6.1a)*

   A. Developmental psychology

   B. Experimental psychology

   C. Social psychology

   D. Macroeconomics

Answer: C

C. Social psychology

(A) Developmental psychology studies the mental development of humans as they mature. (B) Experimental psychology uses formal experimentation with control groups to examine human behavior. (C) Social psychology is a branch of the field that investigates people's behavior as they interact within society, and it is the type of project described in the question. (D) Macroeconomics is a field within economics and would not apply to this project.

116. **As a sociologist, you would be most likely to observe:** *(Rigorous) (Skill 6.1a)*

   A. The effects of an earthquake on farmland

   B. The behavior of rats in sensory-deprivation experiments

   C. The change over time in Babylonian obelisk styles

   D. The behavior of human beings in television focus groups

Answer: D

D. The behavior of human beings in television focus groups

Predominant beliefs and attitudes within human society are studied in the field of sociology. (A) The effects of an earthquake on farmland might be studied by a geographer. (B) The behavior of rats in an experiment falls under the field of behavioral psychology. (C) Changes in Babylonian obelisk styles might interest a historian. None of these answers fit easily within the definition of sociology. (D) A focus group, where people are asked to discuss their reactions to a certain product or topic, would be the most likely method for a sociologist of observing and discovering attitudes among a selected group.

117. **Margaret Mead may be credited with major advances in the study of:** *(Average Rigor) (Skill 6.1b)*

  A. The marginal propensity to consume

  B. The thinking of the Anti-Federalists

  C. The anxiety levels of non-human primates

  D. Interpersonal relationships in non-technical societies

Answer: D

D. Interpersonal relationships in non-technical societies

Margaret Mead (1901-1978) was a pioneer in the field of anthropology, living among the people of Samoa while observing and writing about their culture in the book Coming of Age in Samoa in 1928. (A) The marginal propensity to consume is an economic subject. (B) The thinking of the Anti-Federalists is a topic in American history. (C) The anxiety levels of non-human primates are a subject studied in behavioral psychology.

118. **"Participant observation" is a method of study most closely associated with and used in:** *(Rigorous) (Skill 6.1b)*

  A. Anthropology

  B. Archaeology

  C. Sociology

  D. Political science

Answer: A

A. Anthropology

"Participant observation" is a method of study most closely associated with and used in (A) anthropology or the study of current human cultures. (B) Archaeologists typically the study of the remains of people, animals or other physical things. (C) Sociology is the study of human society and usually consists of surveys, controlled experiments, and field studies. (D) Political science is the study of political life including justice, freedom, power and equality in a variety of methods.

119. **The study of the social behavior of minority groups would be in the area of:** *(Average Rigor) (Skill 6.1c)*

    A. Anthropology

    B. Psychology

    C. Sociology

    D. Cultural Geography

Answer: C

C. Sociology

The study of social behavior in minority groups would be primarily in the area of Sociology, as it is the discipline most concerned with social interaction and being. However, it could be argued that Anthropology, Psychology, and Cultural Geography could have some interest in the study as well.

120. **A teacher and a group of students take a field trip to an Indian mound to examine artifacts. This activity most closely fits under which branch of the social sciences?** *(Average Rigor) (Skill 6.1b)*

    A. Anthropology

    B. Sociology

    C. Psychology

    D. Political Science

Answer: A

A. Anthropology

(A) Anthropology is the study of human culture and the way in which people of different cultures live. The artifacts created by people of a certain culture can provide information about the behaviors and beliefs of that culture, making anthropology the best fitting field of study for this field trip. (B) Sociology, (C) psychology, and (D) political science are more likely to study behaviors and institutions directly than through individual artifacts created by a specific culture.

121. **Which of the following demonstrates evidence of the interaction between physical and cultural anthropology?** *(Rigorous) (Skill 6.1b)*

A. Tall Nilotic herdsmen are often expert warriors

B. Until recent years, the diet of most Asian peoples caused them to be shorter in stature than most other peoples

C. Native South American peoples adopted potato production after invasion by Europeans

D. Polynesians exhibit different skin coloration than Melanesians

Answer: B

B. Until recent years, the diet of most Asian peoples caused them to be shorter in stature than most other peoples

Cultural anthropology is the study of culture. Physical anthropology studies human evolution and other biologically related aspects of human culture. Answers (A) and (D) describe physical attributes of members of different cultures, but they make no connection between these attributes and the behaviors of these cultures. Answer (C) describes a cultural behavior of Native Americans but makes no connection to any physical attributes of the people of this culture. Answer (B) draws a connection between a cultural behavior (diet) and a physical attribute (height), and it is the best example demonstrating the interaction between cultural and physical anthropology.

122. **Psychology is a social science because:** *(Average Rigor) (Skill 6.1c)*

   A. It focuses on the biological development of individuals

   B. It focuses on the behavior of individual persons and small groups of persons

   C. It bridges the gap between the natural and the social sciences

   D. It studies the behavioral habits of lower animals

Answer: B

B. It focuses on the behavior of individual persons and small groups of persons

While it is true that (C) psychology draws from natural sciences, it is (B) the study of the behavior of individual persons and small groups that defines psychology as a social science. (A) The biological development of human beings and (D) the behavioral habits of lower animals are studied in the developmental and behavioral branches of psychology.

123. **A social scientist observes how individual persons react to the presence or absence of noise. This scientist is most likely a:** *(Average Rigor) (Skill 6.1c)*

   A. Geographer

   B. Political Scientist

   C. Economist

   D. Psychologist

Answer: D

D. Psychologist

(D) Psychologists scientifically study the behavior and mental processes of individuals. Studying how individuals react to changes in their environment falls under this social science. (A) Geographers, (B) political scientists, and (C) economists are more likely to study the reactions of groups rather than individual reactions.

124. **Cognitive, developmental, and behavioral are three types of:** *(Easy)* *(Skill 6.1c)*

    A. Economist

    B. Political Scientist

    C. Psychologist

    D. Historian

Answer: C

C. Psychologists

(C) Psychologists study mental processes (cognitive psychology,) the mental development of children (developmental psychology,) and observe human and animal behavior in controlled circumstances (behavioral psychology).

125. **Of the following lists, which includes persons who have made major advances in the understanding of psychology?** *(Average Rigor) (Skill 6.1c)*

    A. Herodotus, Thucydides, Ptolemy

    B. Adam Smith, Milton Friedman, John Kenneth Galbraith

    C. Edward Hall, E.L. Thorndike, B.F. Skinner

    D. Thomas Jefferson, Karl Marx, Henry Kissinger

Answer: C

C. Edward Hall, E.L. Thorndike, B.F. Skinner

Edward Hall wrote in the 1960's about the effects of overcrowding on humans, especially in large cities. E.L. Thorndike (1874-1949) was an early developer of an experimental approach to studying learning in animals and of educational psychology. B.F. Skinner (1904-1990) was a pioneer in behavioral psychology. (A) Herodotus, Thucydides, and Ptolemy were early historians. (B) Smith, Friedman, and Galbraith made significant contributions to the field of economics. (D) Jefferson, Marx, and Kissinger are figures in political science.

XAMonline, INC. 21 Orient Ave. Melrose, MA 02176

Toll Free number 800-509-4128

TO ORDER Fax 781-662-9268 OR www.XAMonline.com

WEST SERIES

PO#   Store/School:

Address 1:

Address 2 (Ship to other):

City, State Zip

Credit card number_____-_____-_____-_____ expiration_____

EMAIL _____

PHONE   **FAX**

ISBN	TITLE	Qty	Retail	Total
978-1-58197-638-0	WEST-B Basic Skills		$27.95	
978-1-58197-609-0	WEST-E Biology 0235		$59.95	
978-1-58197-693-9	WEST-E Chemistry 0245		$59.95	
978-1-58197-566-6	WEST-E Designated World Language: French Sample Test 0173		$15.00	
978-1-58197-557-4	WEST-E Designated World Language: Spanish 0191		$59.95	
978-1-58197-614-4	WEST-E Elementary Education 0014		$28.95	
978-1-58197-636-6	WEST-E English Language Arts 0041		$59.95	
978-1-58197-634-2	WEST-E General Science 0435		$59.95	
978-1-58197-637-3	WEST-E Health & Fitness 0856		$59.95	
978-1-58197-635-9	WEST-E Library Media 0310		$59.95	
978-1-58197-674-8	WEST-E Mathematics 0061		$59.95	
978-1-58197-556-7	WEST-E Middle Level Humanities 0049, 0089		$59.95	
978-1-58197-568-0	WEST-E Physics 0265		$59.95	
978-1-58197-563-5	WEST-E Reading/Literacy 0300		$59.95	
978-1-58197-552-9	WEST-E Social Studies 0081		$59.95	
978-1-58197-639-7	WEST-E Special Education 0353		$73.50	
978-1-58197-633-5	WEST-E Visual Arts Sample Test 0133		$15.00	
	SUBTOTAL		**Ship**	$8.25
	FOR PRODUCT PRICES VISIT WWW.XAMONLINE.COM		**TOTAL**	

CPSIA information can be obtained at www.ICGtesting.com
Printed in the USA
LVOW031356030712

288728LV00001B/115/P